北京高等学校青年英才计划资助（项目编号：YETP0783）
中央高校基本科研业务费专项奖金（2015ZCQ-WY-01）

中国典籍英译赏析系列

中国典籍英译析读

史宝辉 丛书主编

李芝 朱红梅 卢晓敏 许景城 编著

知识产权出版社

全国百佳图书出版单位

图书在版编目（CIP）数据

中国典籍英译析读/李芝等编著．—北京：知识产权出版社，2017.3（2024.3 重印）
（中国典籍英译赏析系列/史宝辉主编）
ISBN 978 - 7 - 5130 - 4472 - 1

Ⅰ.①中…　Ⅱ.①李…　Ⅲ.①古籍—中国—英语—翻译　Ⅳ.①H315.9

中国版本图书馆 CIP 数据核字（2016）第 224031 号

内容提要

该书分为散文篇、小说篇和诗歌篇三个部分，并依据专题内容对原著和译作进行了精心的选取。散文篇内容涵盖了儒家经典、道家经典和《史记》节选；小说篇选取了唐代、明代和清代小说的经典章节；诗歌篇则撷取了《诗经》《楚辞》及唐诗、宋词和元曲中的典范作品。全书内容涉及面广、结构完整，力求在有限的篇幅范围内，较为全面地展现中国典籍英译的精粹，帮助高校英语学习者了解和掌握中国传统文化典籍的知识及其翻译状况与策略。在译者和译文的选择上，我们力求在版权许可的范畴内，选取知名译者的经典译文，用高质量的英文来阐释我国古代典籍，同时兼顾时代特征和译者主体的不同风格。本书适用于高校非英语专业本科生和研究生，也可供英语专业本科生、翻译硕士生和其他英语爱好者借鉴所用。

责任编辑：陈晶晶　　　　　**责任出版：刘译文**

中国典籍英译析读

李　芝　朱红梅　卢晓敏　许景城　编著

出版发行：**知识产权出版社** 有限责任公司　　网　　址：http：//www.ipph.cn
社　　址：北京市海淀区西外太平庄 55 号　　　邮　　编：100081
责编电话：010 - 82000860 转 8391　　　　　　责编邮箱：shiny-chjj@163.com
发行电话：010 - 82000860 转 8101/8102　　　发行传真：010 - 82000893/82005070/82000270
印　　刷：北京建宏印刷有限公司　　　　　　经　　销：各大网上书店、新华书店及相关专业书店
开　　本：720mm×960mm　1/16　　　　　　印　　张：15.5
版　　次：2017 年 3 月第 1 版　　　　　　　　印　　次：2024 年 3 月第 3 次印刷
字　　数：240 千字　　　　　　　　　　　　　定　　价：49.00 元
ISBN 978 - 7 -5130 -4472 -1

序　言

教育部《完善中华优秀传统文化教育指导纲要》明确指出，大学阶段应深入学习中国古代思想文化的重要典籍，理解中华优秀传统文化的精髓，强化学生的文化主体意识和文化创新意识。同时，随着国际学术交流与合作的日渐频繁，高校学生也越来越多地参与国际交流，成为中外文化交流的桥梁和使者。在这样的时代背景下，使用流利的英语介绍具有几千年悠久历史的中国文化，为往圣继绝学，让世界人民充分了解和认识中华民族，是新时代大学生肩负的使命和责任。

基于以上考虑，我们编写了《中国典籍英译析读》。全书分为散文篇、小说篇和诗歌篇三个部分，按照专题内容安排原著和译作的选取。全书内容涉及面广，结构完整，力求在有限的篇幅范围内，较为全面地展现中国典籍英译的精粹，帮助高校学生了解和掌握中国传统文化典籍知识及其翻译策略。在译者和译文的选择上，我们选取了经典译者的经典译文，同时兼顾时代特征和译者主体的不同风格。本书所选的译者既有开中国典籍英译滥觞的海外汉学名家，也有多年来致力丁我国传统文化对外传播的中国学者。他们对典籍的解读各有千秋，具有独特的阐释视角和语言特色，富有极高的学习和研究价值。对于当代译者，我们尽力联系，取得版权许可；对于未能联系上的译者，本书已为其署名，并承诺按照国家规定支付稿酬。

　　中国典籍以言简意赅、含义丰富著称，这也是其不朽魅力所在。典籍英译的难处在于，在原文含意尚且莫衷一是的情况下，提供一种译文只能提供一种解读，而无法完全传递原文无定规、开放式的多重意义。译者要做深入研究之后，才能选取恰当的理解来进行翻译。何况古汉语的简洁玄妙，更难以用英文完美地表达出来。因此，在阅读典籍英译的文本时，结合原文、注释和译文进行批判性分析才是较为理想的学习状态。

　　在结构上，每一章节的编写均包括导读、作家和作品概述、中文原文及注释、英文译作及注释、英译评述和练习，附录中还有各位译者的简介，并提供了参考书目便于学习者做进一步研读。为了帮助学习者更好地掌握典籍含义，本书中的古文原作配有注释和白话译文，英文译作配有词句讲解和文化点注释。本书的每一章配备了相应的练习以培养学生的语言输出表达能力，进一步提高学生对中国典籍英译的兴趣和实践翻译能力。

　　本书的主要读者对象为高校非英语专业本科生和研究生，也可供英语专业本科生、翻译硕士生和其他英语爱好者使用。本教材的出版得到了北京市高等学校"青年英才计划"项目（YETP0783）、中央高校基本科研业务费专项资金（2015ZCQ－WY－01）和教育部大学英语教学改革示范点项目的资助，北京林业大学郭陶、武田田、黄佩娟、刘真、欧阳宏亮、吴增欣老师参与了本书的课件制作和校对工作，特此致谢。典籍英译博大精深，鉴于编者水平有限，在编写过程中难免存在疏漏、不足之处，敬请各位读者批评指正。

编　者

2016 年 1 月于北京

目录

下篇　诗歌

第一章

儒家经典

导　读

儒家是我国传统文化中至关重要的思想体系，由春秋时期思想家孔子开创，以"仁义礼智信"为核心，强调对社会伦理和长幼尊卑秩序的遵从。孔子的思想在后世不断得到阐释和发展，确立了以"四书"（《论语》《孟子》《大学》《中庸》）和"五经"（《诗经》《尚书》《礼记》《易经》《春秋》）为核心的典籍系列。其中"四书"是南宋理学家朱熹编辑定稿，蕴含了儒家思想的核心内容，是儒学认识论和方法论的集中体现，是中国传统知识分子的必读书目，在汉族思想史上产生过深远的影响，至今依然有其深刻的教育意义和启迪价值，堪称中华文化的典范著作。本章节选了"四书"的经典片断英译，从中英双语角度体会儒家思想的精妙之处。

第一节　《论语》选译

《论语》是儒家的经典著作之一，由孔子❶（前551—前479）的弟子及其再传弟子编撰而成。它以语录体和对话文体为主，记录了孔子及其弟子的言行，集中体现了孔子的政治主张、伦理思想、道德观念及教育原则等。

作为儒家的"至圣先师"，孔子是儒家弟子效仿的楷模。他既是开创儒学

---

❶ 孔子，名丘，字仲尼，春秋时期鲁国陬邑（今山东曲阜市南辛镇）人。

的思想家，又是"知其不可而为之"的政治家，更是率先创办私学、论述教育理念的教育家。《论语》生动记录了孔子循循善诱的教诲之言，或简单应答，点到即止；或启发论辩，侃侃而谈；富于变化，娓娓动人。许多表达已成为中国人为人处世的至理箴言。

《论语》成书于战国初期。因秦始皇焚书坑儒，《论语》历尽劫难，到西汉时期仅有口头传授以及从曲阜孔子故宅夹壁中所得的残稿，是若干断片的篇章集合体。几经编撰，现在的《论语》版本是二十篇，本节选取的是第一篇《学而》片断。《论语》中各篇一般都是以该篇第一章的前两三个字作为该篇的篇名。《学而》一篇包括十六章，内容涉及治学、修身等诸多方面。其中的重点是"吾日三省吾身""节用而爱人，使民以时""礼之用，和为贵"以及仁、孝、信等道德理念。

论语·学而❶

01. 子曰："学而时习之，不亦说[1]乎？有朋自远方来，不亦乐乎？人不知而不愠[2]，不亦君子乎？"

02. 有子[3]曰："其为人也孝弟[4]，而好犯上者，鲜[5]矣；不好犯上，而好作乱者，未之有也。君子务本，本立而道生。孝弟也者，其为仁之本与！"

03. 子曰："巧言令色[6]，鲜矣仁！"

04. 曾子[7]曰："吾日三省[8]吾身：为人谋而不忠乎？与朋友交而不信乎？传不习乎[9]？"

05. 子曰："道千乘之国[10]，敬事而信，节用而爱人，使民以时。"

---

❶ 朱熹. 四书章句集注［M］. 北京：中华书局，2011：49-54.（根据英译本对原文略有改动，分小节加了序号）

06. 子曰："弟子入则孝，出则弟，谨而信，泛爱众而亲仁。行有余力，则以学文。"

07. 子夏[11]曰："贤贤易色[12]；事父母能竭其力，事君能致其身，与朋友交言而有信。虽曰未学，吾必谓之学矣。"

08. 子曰："君子不重则不威，学则不固。主忠信。无友不如己者。过，则勿惮改。"

09. 曾子曰："慎终追远，民德归厚矣。"

10. 子禽[13]问于子贡[14]曰："夫子至于是邦也，必闻其政，求之与？抑与之与？"子贡曰："夫子温、良、恭、俭、让以得之。夫子之求之也，其诸异乎人之求之与？"

11. 子曰："父在，观其志；父没，观其行；三年无改于父之道，可谓孝矣。"

12. 有子曰："礼之用，和为贵。先王之道斯为美，小大由之。有所不行，知和而和，不以礼节之，亦不可行也。"

13. 有子曰："信近于义，言可复也；恭近于礼，远耻辱也。因不失其亲，亦可宗也。"

14. 子曰："君子食无求饱，居无求安，敏于事而慎于言，就有道而正焉，可谓好学也已。"

15. 子贡曰："贫而无谄，富而无骄，何如？"子曰："可也。未若贫而乐，富而好礼者也。"子贡曰："《诗》云：'如切如磋，如琢如磨'[15]，其斯之谓与？"子曰："赐也，始可与言《诗》已矣！告诸往而知来者。"

16. 子曰："不患人之不己知，患不知人也。"

中文注释

[1] 说（yuè）：通"悦"，喜悦。

[2] 愠（yùn）：恼怒。

[3] 有子：有若（前518—约前5世纪中期），字子有，孔子重要弟子，在思想上与孔子非常接近。

[4] 孝弟（tì）：即"孝悌"，善事父母曰孝，善事兄长曰弟。

[5] 鲜（xiǎn）：少。下文中"鲜"字皆为此意。

[6] 巧言令色：花言巧语，虚伪讨好。令：好，善。

[7] 曾子：曾子（前505—前435），名参（shēn），字子舆，春秋末期著名思想家、教育家。16岁时拜孔子为师，勤奋好学，颇得孔子真传。据说《孝经》就是他撰写的。

[8] 三省（xǐng）：省，察看，检查。"三省"有几种解释，一是进行三次检查；二是从三个方面检查；三是进行多次检查。此书取第二种意思翻译。

[9] 传不习乎：有没有践行老师传授的知识？

[10] 道千乘（shèng）之国：道，有版本作"导"，作动词用，"治理"的意思。乘，辆，古代军队的基层单位。每乘拥有四匹马拉的兵车一辆，车上甲士三人，车下步卒七十二人，后勤人员二十五人，共计一百人。千乘之国，指拥有一千辆兵车的国家，即诸侯国。

[11] 子夏：姓卜，名商，字子夏，孔子的学生。孔子去世后，他在魏国宣传孔子的思想主张。

[12] 贤贤易色：尊重贤者而轻视女色。第一个"贤"字用作动词；易，轻看。

[13] 子禽：姓陈，名亢，字子禽，或为孔子的学生。

[14] 子贡：姓端木，名赐，字子贡，卫国人，是孔子的学生。子贡善辩，孔子认为他可以做大国的宰相。据《史记》记载，子贡在卫国做了商人，家有财产千金。

[15] "如切如磋，如琢如磨"：此二句出自《诗经·卫风·淇澳》的"瞻彼淇澳，绿竹猗猗；有匪君子，如切如磋，如琢如磨……"，是赞美品德高尚的人温润如玉的形象。《诗经》是孔子极为看重的典籍，是儒家六经之首。切、磋、琢、磨指的是对象牙、兽骨、玉、石等材料的精细加工，否则不能成器。子贡举一反三，认为君子也要经过富贵贫贱的考验才能成器，此想法得到了孔子的赞许。

┌─────────────┐
│ 白话译文❶ │
└─────────────┘

01. 孔子说："学习知识又时常温习和练习，不是一件很愉快的事儿吗？有志同道合的人从远方来，不是很令人高兴的吗？人家不了解你，你也不怨恨恼怒，不正是君子的风范吗？"

02. 有子说："一个人孝顺父母，顺从兄长，却喜欢冒犯上级，这样的人是很少见的。不喜欢触犯上级，而喜欢造反的人是没有的。君子专心致力于根本之道，根本建立了，治国做人的原则也就有了。孝顺父母、顺从兄长，这就是仁的根本啊！"

03. 孔子说："花言巧语，装出和颜悦色的样子，这种人的仁心就很少了。"

04. 曾子说："我每天就三个问题进行自我反省：为别人办事是不是尽心竭力了？同朋友交往是不是做到了诚实可信？师长传授给我的学业是不是践行了？"

05. 孔子说："治理一个拥有一千辆兵车的国家，就要严谨认真地办埋国家大事而又恪守信用，诚实无欺，节约财政开支而又爱护官吏臣僚，役使百姓而又不误农时。"

06. 孔子说："弟子们在父母跟前，要孝顺父母；出门在外，要顺从师长，言行要谨慎可信，要广泛地去爱众人，亲近那些有仁德的人。这样亲身实践之后，还有余力的话，就再去学习文化知识。"

07. 子夏说："一个人能够看重贤德而轻视女色；侍奉父母能够竭尽全力；服侍君主能够献出自己的生命；同朋友交往，说话诚实、恪守信用。这样的人，即使他自己说没有学习过，我一定说他已经学习过了。"

08. 孔子说："君子，不庄重就没有威严，学习可以使人不闭塞；要以忠

---

❶ 白话译文参考：樊森．《论语·学而第一》译文［EB/OL］．（2011-06-01）［2015-08-09］．http://lunyu.baike.com/article-29298.html#3，编者根据英语译文有所修改。

信为主，不要与品德不如自己的人交朋友；有了过错，就不要怕改正。"

09. 曾子说："如果能恭谨地对待父母的去世，追念久远的祖先，老百姓自然会日趋忠厚老实了。"

10. 子禽问子贡说："老师到了一个国家，总是要了解这个国家的政事。（这种礼遇）是他自己求得的呢，还是人家国君主动给他的呢？"子贡说："老师温和、善良、谦恭、简约、礼让，所以才得到这样的礼遇，（这种礼遇也可以说是求得的），但他求的方法，或许与别人的求法不同吧？"

11. 孔子说："当他父亲在世的时候，要观察他对父亲的态度；在他父亲死后，要考察他的行为；若是他继承了父亲的为人之道而长期不加改变，这样的人可以说是尽到孝了。"

12. 有子说："礼的应用，以和谐为贵。古代君主的治国方法，可宝贵的地方就在这里。但不论大事小事只顾按和谐的办法去做，有的时候就行不通。（这是因为）为和谐而和谐，不以礼来节制和谐，也是不可行的。"

13. 有子说："讲信用要符合于义，（符合于义的）言辞才能得以实行；恭敬要符合于礼，这样才能远离耻辱；所依靠的都是可靠的人，也就值得尊敬了。"

14. 孔子说："君子，饮食不求饱足，居住不求舒适，对工作勤劳敏捷，说话小心谨慎，到有道德的人那里去匡正自己，这样可以说是好学了。"

15. 子贡说："贫穷而能不谄媚，富有而能不骄傲自大，怎么样？"孔子说："这也算可以了。但是还不如虽贫穷却很快乐，虽富裕而又好礼之人。"子贡说："《诗经》上说，'要像对待骨、角、象牙、玉石一样，切磋它，琢磨它'，就是讲的这个意思吧？"孔子说："赐呀，我可以与你谈论《诗经》了。你已能从我已经讲过的话中领会到我还没有说出的意思了。"

16. 孔子说："不怕别人不了解自己，只怕自己不了解别人。"

Confucian Analects[1]

Translated by James Legge
Book I. Hsio R.

01. The Master said, "Is it not pleasant to learn with a constant perseverance (坚韧) and application? Is it not delightful to have friends coming from distant quarters? Is he not a man of complete virtue, who feels no discomposure (不安) though men may take no note of him?"

02. The philosopher Yû[2] said, "They are few who, being filial (孝敬的) and fraternal (兄弟友爱的), are fond of offending against their superiors. There have been none, who, not liking to offend against their superiors, have been fond of stirring up confusion. The superior man bends his attention to what is radical (根本的). That being established, all practical courses naturally grow up. Filial piety and fraternal submission! —are they not the root of all benevolent (仁慈的) actions?"

03. The Master said, "Fine words and an insinuating (曲意逢迎的) appearance are seldom associated with true virtue."

04. The philosopher Tsang said, "I daily examine myself on three points: — whether, in transacting business for others, I may have been not faithful; —

---

[1] James Legge. The Chinese Classics, Volume I [M]. Taipei：SMC Publishing INC. 1991：137-145. （为了便于对照阅读，编者对原文和译文加了章节序号，按原文的语句调整了译文的句序）

[2] The Philosopher Yû：有子。早期典籍英译里的中国人名音译多采用威妥玛拼音方式，与当代汉语拼音有所不同，如下文中的曾子音译为 The philosopher Tsang，子夏为 Tsze - hsia，等等。威妥玛（Thomas Francis Wade, 1818—1895），英国外交官、著名汉学家，曾在中国生活四十余年，因发明用罗马字母标注汉语发音系统——威妥玛注音——而著称，此方法在欧美广为使用，但该方法现已逐渐被汉语拼音取代。

whether, in intercourse with friends, I may have been not sincere; —whether I may have not mastered and practiced the instructions of my teacher. "

05. The Master said, "To rule a country of a thousand chariots (战车), there must be reverent (虔敬的) attention to business, and sincerity; economy (节省) in expenditure, and love for men; and the employment of the people at the proper seasons. "

06. The Master said, "A youth, when at home, should be filial, and, abroad, respectful to his elders. He should be earnest and truthful. He should overflow in love to all, and cultivate the friendship of the good. When he has time and opportunity, after the performance of these things, he should employ them in polite studies. ¹"

07. Tsze-hsia said, "If a man withdraws his mind from the love of beauty, and applies it as sincerely to the love of the virtuous; if, in serving his parents, he can exert his utmost strength; if, in serving his prince, he can devote his life; if, in his intercourse with his friends, his words are sincere: —although men say that he has not learned, I will certainly say that he has. "

08. The Master said, "If the scholar be not grave, he will not call forth any veneration (敬意), and his learning will not be solid. Hold faithfulness and sincerity as first principles. Have no friends not equal to yourself². When you have faults, do not fear to abandon them. "

09. The philosopher Tsang said, "Let there be a careful attention to perform the funeral rites to parents, and let them be followed when long gone with the ceremonies of sacrifice; —then the virtue of the people will resume its proper excellence. "

10. Tsze-ch'in asked Tsze-kung saying, "When our master comes to any country, he does not fail to learn all about its government. Does he ask his information? Or is it given to him?" Tsze-kung said, "Our master is benign (仁慈), upright, courteous, temperate (温和), and complaisant (恭谨) and thus he gets his information. The master's mode of asking information! —is it not

different from that of other men?"

11. The Master said, "While a man's father is alive, look at the bent of his will[3]; when his father is dead, look at his conduct. If for three years he does not alter from the way of his father, he may be called filial. "

12. The philosopher Yû said, "In practicing the rules of propriety (礼节), a natural ease is to be prized. In the ways prescribed by the ancient kings, this is the excellent quality, and in things small and great we follow them. Yet it is not to be observed in all cases. If one, knowing how such ease should be prized, manifests it, without regulating it by the rules of propriety, this like-wise is not to be done. "

13. The philosopher Yû said, "When agreements are made according to what is right, what is spoken can be made good. When respect is shown according to what is proper, one keeps far from shame and disgrace. When the parties upon whom a man learns are proper persons to be intimate with, he can make them his guides and masters. "

14. The Master said, "He who aims to be a man of complete virtue in his food does not seek to gratify his appetite, nor in his dwelling place does he seek the appliances of ease[4]; he is earnest in what he is doing, and careful in his speech; he frequents the company of men of principle that he may be rectified (改正): —such a person may be said indeed to love to learn. "

15. Tsze-kung said, "What do you pronounce concerning the poor man who yet does not flatter, and the rich man who is not proud?" The Master replied, "They will do; but they are not equal to him, who, though poor, is yet cheerful, and to him, who, though rich, loves the rules of propriety. "

Tsze-kung replied, "It is said in the *Book of Poetry*, ' As you cut and then file (锉), as you carve and then polish. ' —The meaning is the same, I apprehend, as that which you have just expressed. " The Master said, "With one like Ts'ze, I can begin to talk about the odes[5]. I told him one point, and he knew its proper sequence. "

16. The Master said, "I will not be afflicted (难过) at men's not knowing me; I will be afflicted that I do not know men."

英译注释

1. polite studies：polite，有教养的，高雅的。原文"有余力，则学文"，此译本译作"如果有机会和实践，他再去进行高雅文化的学习"。

2. Have no friends not equal to yourself：祈使句，相当于 You should not have friends who are not equal to yourself. 原文"无友不如己者"中"无"通"毋"，"友"用作动词，译作"交朋友"。这句话的意思是"不要和志向不同的人交朋友"。

3. the bent of his will：他的志向爱好。bent，爱好，癖好。

4. He who aims to be a man of complete virtue in his food does not seek to gratify his appetite, nor in his dwelling place does he seek the appliances of ease：这里用了两个倒装结构，可还原为：He who aims to be a man of complete virtue does not seek to gratify his appetite in his food, nor does he seek the appliances of ease in his dwelling place.

5. the odes：颂歌，这里指的是收录在《诗经》（the *Book of Songs*, or the *Book of Poetry*）里的诗歌。

英译评述

理雅各是近现代第一个系统研究、翻译中国古代典籍的人。这位英国传教士从 1861 年到 1886 年的 25 年间，将"四书五经"等中国主要典籍全部译出，是海外汉学里程碑式的成就。1861—1872 年间，他所翻译的《中国经典》（*The Chinese Classics*）第一版在中国香港陆续出版。1861 年第一次出版的是"四书"，分两卷：第一卷包括《论语》（*Confucian Analects*）、《大学》（*The Great Learning*）和《中庸》（*The Doctrine of the Mean*）；第二卷是《孟子》（*The Works of Mencius*）的单行译本。他还是牛津大学的第一个汉学教授（1876—1897），数十年舌耕笔耘，使得中国思想精髓在西方得以传播。

本文选登的是《论语》第一篇《学而》的英译，是《论语》中脍炙人口的篇章，体现了孔子及其弟子的教育与学习理念以及儒家以仁、礼、孝、悌、诚、信为核心的修身治世原则。理雅各在英译时，保留了《论语》中排比、对仗、逐层递进的诗意语言。如第 4 句，"吾日三省吾身：为人谋而不忠乎？与朋友交而不信乎？传不习乎？"译为：I daily examine myself on three points：—whether, in transacting business for others, I may have been not faithful；—whether, in intercourse with friends, I may have been not sincere；—whether I may have not mastered and practiced the instructions of my teacher. 译者既能使译文句式与原文保持一致，又能根据原文的含义，适度添加字词。再比如"传不习乎？"这四字被译成了 whether I may have not mastered and practiced the instructions of my teacher，意思则更为明确。

又如第 13 句："信近于义，言可复也；恭近于礼，远耻辱也。因不失其亲，亦可宗也。"理雅各将其译为：When agreements are made according to what is right, what is spoken can be made good. When respect is shown according to what is proper, one keeps far from shame and disgrace. When the parties upon whom a man learns are proper persons to be intimate with, he can make them his guides and masters. 对仗工整，言辞信达，措辞雅致，"亦可宗也"四字译为 he can make them his guides and masters 把"宗"字译为 guides and masters，切合原意，与前文 shame and disgrace 在结构上相应和，读来朗朗上口。

鉴于中国典籍年代久远，字词句义常常有不同的阐释，译者采取了自己的解读。例如，"人不知而不愠，不亦君子乎？"译为 Is he not a man of complete virtue, who feels no discomposure though men may take no note of him? 其把"人不知"解读为"人们不关注他"，而其他阐释可能是"人们不了解他的才能""别人缺乏知识"等，译者在此取了简要的一种，不至于因为过度阐释而产生误导。

Ⅰ. **Translation Practice.**

Directions：Translate the following Analects into English.

1. 己所不欲，勿施于人。

2. 欲速则不达，见小利则大事不成。

3. 岁寒，然后知松柏之后凋也。

4. 君子成人之美，不成人之恶。

5. 有教无类。

Ⅱ. **Questions and Answers.**

<u>Directions：Answer the following questions according to the text.</u>

1. What can be concluded about Confucius' way of learning?

2. How do you describe Confucius as a common man and a statesman?

3. What are the most remarkable features of a Confucian scholar?

4. How do Confucius' disciples respond to the master's ideas?

5. How does Confucius teach his disciples?

第二节 《孟子》选译

 概 述

孟子（约前372—约前289），名轲，鲁国邹（今山东省邹城）人，是孔子之孙孔伋（子思）的再传弟子。相传他是鲁国姬姓贵族公子庆父的后裔，其父名激，母仉（zhǎng）氏。"孟母三迁"的著名故事讲的就是仉氏为孟子选择良好的教育环境而三次搬家的典故。后来，孟子成了战国时期伟大的思想家、教育家、儒家学派的代表人物，且与孔子并称"孔孟"，后世追封孟子为"亚圣公"，尊称为"亚圣"。

政治上，孟子主张法先王、行仁政；学说上，他推崇孔子，反对杨朱、墨翟。孟子继承并发展了孔子的思想，但较之孔子的思想，他又加入了自己对儒术的理解。他主张仁政，提出"民贵君轻"的民本思想，游历于齐、宋、滕、魏、鲁等诸国，希望效法孔子推行自己的政治主张，前后历时二十多年。但孟子的仁政学说被认为是"迂远而阔于事情"，没有得到实行。最后他与孔子一样，退居讲学，继承和发展了孔门学说，成为一代大儒。

孟子的言论主要收录在《孟子》一书中。这部语录体散文集是中国儒家典籍的主要组成部分，为"四书"之一。该书记录了孟子及其弟子有关政治、教育、哲学、伦理等学说和思想，据说是孟子和他的弟子万章、公孙丑等撰写、记录、整理而成。《孟子》在儒家典籍中占有很重要的地位，《汉书·艺文志》著录《孟子》十一篇，现存七篇十四卷，总字数三万五千余字。

　　本节选的是《孟子·告子章句》篇，是孟子与告子（据说是墨子的学生）之间的辩论。孟子持性善论，认为人性本善；告子持不善不恶说（即人生下来本无所谓善恶）。《告子章句》以两人的论辩开头，集中阐述了孟子关于人性、道德及其相关理论。这是孟子"性善论"思想较为完整的体现，对精神与物质、感性与理性、人性与动物性等问题亦做出了论述。全篇共 20 章，本节选取了其中最广为传颂的两章：《告子章句上》第十章"鱼我所欲也"和《告子章句下》第十五章"生于忧患、死于安乐"。这两章充分展示了孟子舍生取义的价值观，弘扬了他不畏艰险、奋发图强的浩然正气。

孟子·告子章句上·第十章

01. 孟子曰："鱼，我所欲也；熊掌，亦我所欲也，二者不可得兼，舍鱼而取熊掌者也。生，亦我所欲也；义，亦我所欲也，二者不可得兼，舍生而取义者也。

02. 生亦我所欲，所欲有甚于生者，故不为苟得[1]也；死亦我所恶，所恶有甚于死者，故患有所不辟[2]也。

03. 如使人之所欲莫甚于生，则凡可以得生者，何不用也？使人之所恶莫甚于死者，则凡可以辟患者，何不为也？

04. 由是则生而有不用也；由是则可以辟患而有不为也。

　　❶ 朱熹. 四书章句集注［M］. 北京：中华书局，2011：311–312，325–326.（根据英译本对原文略有改动，分小节加了序号）

05. 是故所欲有甚于生者，所恶有甚于死者，非独贤者有是心也，人皆有之，贤者能勿丧耳。

06. 一箪[3]食，一豆[4]羹，得之则生，弗得则死。呼尔而与之，行道之人弗受[5]；蹴[6]尔而与之，乞人不屑也。

07. 万钟[7]则不辩礼义而受之，万钟于我何加[8]焉？为宫室[9]之美、妻妾之奉、所识穷乏者[10]得我[11]与？

08. 乡[12]为身死而不受，今为宫室之美为之；乡为身死而不受，今为妻妾之奉为之；乡为身死而不受，今为所识穷乏者得我而为之，是亦不可以已乎？此之谓失其本心。"

孟子·告子章句下·第十五章

01. 孟子曰："舜发于畎亩之中[13]，傅说举于版筑之间[14]，胶鬲举于鱼盐之中[15]，管夷吾举于士[16]，孙叔敖举于海[17]，百里奚举于市[18]。

02. 故天将降大任于是人也，必先苦其心志，劳其筋骨，饿其体肤，空乏其身[19]，行拂乱[20]其所为，所以动心忍性[21]，曾益其所不能。

03. 人恒过，然后能改；困于心、衡于虑，而后作；征于色、发于声，而后喻。

04. 入则无法家拂士[22]，出则无敌国外患者，国恒亡。

05. 然后知生于忧患而死于安乐也。"

中文注释

[1] 苟得：苟且得到，以令人不齿的手段取得。

[2] 辟：躲避，通"避"。

[3] 箪：古代盛食物的圆竹器。

[4] 豆：古代一种木制的盛食物的器具。

[5] 呼尔而与之，行道之人弗受：吆喝着给他（吃喝），行路的人不会接受。尔，语气助词。这里用了《礼记·檀弓》中的典故："齐大饥。黔敖为食于路，以待饿者而食之。有饿者蒙袂辑屦，贸贸然来。黔敖左奉食，右执饮，

曰：'嗟！来食！'扬其目而视之，曰：'予惟不食嗟来之食，以至于斯也！'从而谢焉，终不食而死。"

[6] 蹴：用脚踢。

[7] 万钟：钟，古代的一种量器，六斛四斗为一钟。战国时期官员的俸禄以发多少粮食为单位。万钟指代的是高位厚禄。

[8] 何加：有什么益处。何，介词结构，后置。

[9] 宫室：住宅。

[10] 穷乏者：穷困的人。

[11] 得我：感激我。得：感激，通"德"。

[12] 乡：原先，从前，通"向"。

[13] 舜发于畎（quǎn）亩之中：大舜在田间被任用。舜本来是在历山耕田的农夫，因其贤明能服众，尧经过考验他，把帝位禅让给他。发：起，此处意指"任用"。畎亩：田亩，此处意为"耕田"。畎：田间水渠。

[14] 傅说（fù yuè）举于版筑之间：傅说在砌墙的时候受到重用。傅说原是殷商时的一名囚徒，商王武丁欲兴殷，梦得圣人，名曰说，视群臣皆非，使人求于野，得傅说。见武丁，武丁曰："是也。"与之语，果圣人，举以为相，殷国大治。事迹见于《史记·殷本纪》等。版筑：筑墙的时候在两块夹板中间放土，用杵捣土，使它坚实。筑：捣土用的杵。

[15] 胶鬲（gé）举于鱼盐之中：胶鬲是在海边捕鱼晒盐时被重用。胶鬲：商纣王大臣，与微子、箕子、比干同称贤人。

[16] 管夷吾举于士：管仲是在狱中被任用。管夷吾：管仲，战国时颖上（今河南许昌）人，家贫困。辅佐齐国公子纠，公子纠未能即位，公子小白即位，是为齐桓公。齐桓公知其贤，释其囚，用以为相，尊之为仲父。士：狱官。

[17] 孙叔敖（áo）举于海：孙叔敖在水滨得到重用。孙叔敖，蒍姓，名敖，字孙叔。春秋时为楚国令尹（宰相）。本为"期思之鄙人"，期思在今河南固始，河湖众多。偏僻之地称为鄙。海：水滨。

[18] 百里奚（xī）举于市：百里奚是在集市上被买来得到重用的。百里奚，又名百里傒。本为虞国大夫。晋国灭虞国，百里奚与虞国国君一起被俘

至晋国。晋国嫁女于秦，百里奚被当作媵臣陪嫁到秦国。百里奚逃往楚国，行至宛（今河南南阳），为楚国边界之鄙人所执。秦穆公闻其贤，欲重赎之，恐楚人不与，乃使人谓楚曰："吾媵臣百里奚在焉，请以五羖羊皮赎之。"楚人于是与之。时百里奚年已七十余，至秦，秦穆公亲释其囚，与语国事三日，大悦。授以国政，号称"五羖大夫"。市：集市。

［19］空乏其身：使他遭受贫困。空乏：使动用法，意为"使……穷困"。

［20］拂乱：使……颠倒错乱。

［21］动心忍性：让他的心智受到震动，让他的性情更为坚忍。

［22］法家拂（bì）士：有法度的世臣、能辅佐君主的贤士。拂：通"弼"，意为"辅佐"。

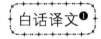

孟子·告子章句上·第十章

01. 孟子说："鱼是我喜欢吃的，熊掌也是我喜欢吃的；如果不能两样都吃，我就舍弃鱼而吃熊掌。生命是我想拥有的，正义也是我想拥有的；如果不能两样都拥有，我就舍弃生命而坚持正义。

02. 生命是我想拥有的，但是还有比生命更使我想拥有的，所以我不愿意苟且偷生；死亡是我厌恶的，但是还有比死亡更使我厌恶的，所以我不愿意因为厌恶死亡而逃避某些祸患。

03. 如果让人想拥有的没有超过生命的，那么，只要是可以活命，什么事情干不出来呢？如果让人厌恶的没有超过死亡的，那么，只要是可以逃避死亡的祸患，什么事情干不出来呢？

04. 但也有些人，照此做就可以拥有生命，却不照此做；照此做就可以逃避祸患，却不照此做。

05. 由此可知，的确有比生命更使人想拥有的东西，也的确有比死亡更使

---

❶ 古诗文网．《孟子·告子章句》译文 ［EB/OL］．［2015 - 08 - 12］. http://so.gushiwen.org/guwen/bfanyi_1123.aspx.（编者对译文有修改）

人厌恶的东西。这种心原本不只是贤人才有，而是人人都有，只不过贤人能够保持它罢了。

06. 一篮子饭，一碗汤，吃了便可以活下去，不吃就要饿死。如果吆喝着给人吃，过路的人虽然饿着肚子也不会接受；如果用脚踩踏后再给人吃，就是乞丐也不屑于接受。

07. 可是现在，万钟的俸禄却有人不问合乎礼义与否就接受了。万钟的俸禄对我有什么好处呢？为了华丽的住宅、妻妾的奉承以及我所认识的穷苦人感激我吗？

08. 过去宁肯死亡都不肯接受的，现在却为了华丽的住宅而接受了；过去宁肯死亡都不肯接受的，现在却为了妻妾的奉承而接受了；过去宁肯死亡都不肯接受的，现在却为了让所认识的穷苦人感激我而接受了。这些不是可以停止的吗？这种做法叫作丧失本性。"

孟子·告子下·第十五章

01. 孟子说："舜从田间劳动中成长起来，傅说从筑墙的工作中被选拔出来，胶鬲在海边捕鱼、卖盐时得到重用，管仲被提拔于囚犯的位置上，孙叔敖从水滨被发现，百里奚在集市上被买下得到重用。

02. 所以，上天要将重大使命降落到某人身上，一定要先使他的意志受到磨炼，使他的筋骨受到劳累，使他的身体忍饥挨饿，使他备受穷困之苦，做事总是不能顺利。这样来震动他的心志，坚韧他的性情，增长他的才能。

03. 人总是要经常犯错误，然后才能改正错误；心气郁结，殚思竭虑，然后才能奋发而起；显露在脸色上，表达在声音中，然后才能被人了解。

04. 一个国家，内没有守法的大臣和辅佐的贤士，外没有敌对国家的忧患，往往容易亡国。

05. 由此可以知道，忧患使人生存，安逸享乐却足以使人败亡。"

The Works of Mencius[1]

Translated by James Legge

Chapter 10, Part Ⅰ, Kao Tsze

That it is proper to man's nature to love righteousness more than life, and how it is that many act as if it were not so.

01. Mencius said, "I like fish, and I also like bear's paws. If I cannot have the two together, I will let the fish go, and take the bear's paws. So, I like life, and I also like righteousness. If I cannot keep the two together, I will let life go, and choose righteousness.

02. I like life indeed, but there is that which I like more than life, and therefore, I will not seek to possess it by any improper ways. I dislike death indeed, but there is that which I dislike more than death, and therefore there are occasions when I will not avoid danger.

03. If among the things which man likes there were nothing which he liked more than life, why should he not use every means by which he could preserve it? If among the things which man dislikes there were nothing which he disliked more than death, why should he not do everything by which he could avoid danger?

04. There are cases when men by a certain course might preserve life, and they do not employ it; when by certain things they might avoid danger, and they will not do them.

———————————

[1] James Legge. The Chinese Classics, Volume Ⅱ [M]. Taiper: SMC Publishing INC.: 1991: 411-414, 446-448. (为了便于对照阅读，编者对原文和译文加了章节序号，按原文的语句调整了译文的句序)

05. Therefore, men have that which they like more than life, and that which they dislike more than death. They are not men of distinguished (显著的) talents and virtue only who have this mental nature. All men have it; what belongs to such men is simply that they do not lose it.

06. Here are a small basket of rice and a platter (盘子) of soup, and the case is one in which the getting them will preserve life, and the want (缺乏) of them will be death; — if they are offered with an insulting voice, even a tramper (流浪汉) will not receive them, or if you first tread upon them, even a beggar will not stoop (弯腰) to take them.

07. And yet a man will accept of ten thousand chung, without any consideration of propriety or righteousness. What can the ten thousand chung add to him? When he takes them, is it not that he may obtain beautiful mansions (住宅), that he may secure the services of wives and concubines (妾), or that the poor and needy of his acquaintance may be helped by him?

08. In the former case the offered bounty was not received, though it would have saved from death, and now the emolument is taken for the sake of beautiful mansions. The bounty (赠物) that would have preserved from death was not received, and the emolument (报酬) is taken to get the service of wives and concubines. The bounty that would have saved from death was not received, and the emolument is taken that one's poor and needy acquaintance[2] may be helped by him. Was it then not possible likewise to decline this? This is a case of what is called — ' Losing the proper nature of one's mind. ' "

Chapter 15, Part Ⅱ, Kao Tsze

Trials and hardships are the way in which Heaven prepares men for great services.

01. Mencius said, "Shun rose from among the channelled fields[3]. Fû Yüeh was called to office from the midst of his building frames[4]; Chiao – ko from

his fish and salt; Kwan I-wu from the hands of his gaoler (监禁者); Sun – shû Âo from his hiding by the sea – shore; and Pâi-lî Hsî from the market-place.

02. Thus, when Heaven is about to confer a great office on any man, it first exercises his mind with suffering, and his sinews (肌腱) and bones with toil. It exposes his body to hunger, and subjects him to extreme poverty. It confounds his undertakings. By all these methods it stimulates his mind, hardens his nature, and supplies his incompetencies[5].

03. Men for the most part err, and are afterwards able to reform. They are distressed in mind and perplexed in their thoughts, and then they arise to vigorous reformation. When things have been evidenced in men's looks, and set forth in their words, then they understand them.

04. If a prince[6] have not about his court families attached to the laws and worthy counsellors (大臣), and if abroad there are not hostile States or other external calamities (敌人), his kingdom will generally come to ruin.

05. From these things we see how life springs from sorrow and calamity, and death from ease and pleasure. "

英译注释

1. 理雅各在翻译时为了对照方便，译文分成了小节，并且给每一章加了概述语，放在每章的前面。

2. poor and needy acquaintance：贫穷困苦的熟人。

3. channelled fields：有沟垄的田地。

4. building frames：建造框架。

5. supplies his incompetencies：弥补他能力不足的地方。

6. prince：这里指的是战国时期各诸侯国的国君。

英译评述

理雅各是学者型的汉学家。他在翻译《孟子》的过程中参照了东汉经学家赵歧的《孟子章句》、南宋理学家朱熹的《四书章句集注》、清朝哲学家焦循的《孟子正义》等儒学家对孟子的注疏，力求释义精确，行文流畅，用词典雅。理雅各把原文分成小节逐句对照翻译，便于阅读。原文还带有详尽的注释、索引和评述，限于篇幅，本文只节选了译文部分供比照赏析。

　　本文所选的两节是《孟子》中最广为传颂的段落，是孟子的人生观、价值观的集中体现，直言不讳地表明他对待生死、荣辱、义利等重大选择时的态度。理雅各在译文中忠实传递了孟子的理念，尽量按照原文字句进行了翻译。不过，理雅各为每一章加了一个概述性的英文总结，比如在"鱼与熊掌"一节加了 That it is proper to man's nature to love righteousness more than life, and how it is that many act as if it were not so（人的本性就应该是把义看得比生命还重，而为什么很多人的行为却与之相反）。在"生于忧患死于安乐"一章，他加了 Trials and hardships are the way in which Heaven prepares men for great services（艰难困苦是上天为那些做伟大事业的人设定的道路）。这样的"译者按"有利于读者很快把握整章的主要内容。

　　针对古汉语常常缺失主语的情况，理雅各自觉地添加了恰当的词汇以使得英文更为顺畅易懂。比如"入则无法家拂士，出则无敌国外患者，国恒亡"，译者译为 If a prince have not about his court families attached to the laws and worthy counsellors, and if abroad there are not hostile States or other external calamities, his kingdom will generally come to ruin，添加了 a prince 作为主语，把"国"与"国君"联系起来，使得整个表述有了行为者。

　　当然，由于古文年代久远，对很多字词含义的考证还难以定论，在翻译过程中也会出现争议。比如"孙叔敖举于海"一句，理雅各按照常规对"海"的理解，翻译成 Sun - shû Âo (was called to office) from his hiding by the sea-shore（孙叔敖从海边隐居之处被召来做官）。而根据史书中对孙叔敖生平的记载，他应该是河南淮滨县人。如《荀子·非相》篇："楚子孙叔敖，期思之鄙人也。"东汉邯郸淳《楚相孙叔敖碑》也提到："楚相孙君，讳饶，字叔敖，本是县人也，六国时期思属楚"。他是河南淮水沿岸的普通百姓，后来成为楚国贤相，最大的功业是治理淮河水患，修筑了我国历史上第一座水利工程——期思陂，借淮河古道泄洪，筑陂塘灌溉农桑，后来又修建了安丰塘等大量水利工程，造福淮河黎民。从他的生平来看，他与"海滨"并没有关系，"举于海"的"海"在先秦时期除了指"海洋"，还可以指代"偏僻荒野之地"，如《尔雅·释地》："九夷、八狄、七戎、六蛮谓之四海。"清段玉裁《说文解字注》引申为"凡地大物博者，皆得谓之海。"所以"孙叔敖举于海"翻译成 Sun - shū Âo（was called to office）from remote country 似乎更合适。

典籍英译不仅是语言层面的互换关系，更牵涉对古字词的考据、对所述文化背景的考察、对作者原意的把握等种种因素。理雅各作为严谨的汉学研究者，对中国典籍的英译做出了卓越的贡献，至今他的译文依然被视为经典之作，一百多年来继续受到汉学研究者们的评判与接受。

Ⅰ. **Translation Practice.**

Directions：Translate the following Mencius sayings into English.

1. 老吾老，以及人之老；幼吾幼，以及人之幼。

2. 民为贵，社稷次之，君为轻。

3. 穷则独善其身，达则兼济天下。

4. 尽信书，则不如无书。

5. 富贵不能淫，贫贱不能移，威武不能屈，此之谓大丈夫。

Ⅱ. **Oral Presentation.**

Directions：Choose one of the historical figures mentioned in the text, find his life and achievements, and accordingly present a report in class. You can make your presentation with the help of PPT.

1. 舜；2. 傅说；3. 胶鬲；4. 管仲；5. 孙叔敖；6. 百里奚

第三节　《大学》选译

　　《大学》是名列"五经"之三的《礼记》中的一个篇目，在南宋以前从未单独刊印，相传为孔子弟子曾参（前505—前434）所作。唐代大儒韩愈、李翱等把《大学》《中庸》看作与《孟子》《易经》同等重要的"经书"；宋代理学家程颐、程颢、朱熹祖述这种观点，竭力推崇其在经书中的地位，旨在弘扬理学。朱熹将《大学》与《中庸》《论语》《孟子》并称"四书"，于南宋绍熙元年（1190）刊刻成《四书章句集注》，因《论语》记载孔子言行，《孟子》记载孟子言行，《大学》为曾子所作，《中庸》为子思所作，故又称"四子书"。元朝延祐年间，朝廷规定科举考试必须在"四书"内出题，发挥题意必须以朱熹写的《集注》为根据。明清两朝的科举考试中都沿用了这种科举方法，并以八股文体相规范。从此，"四书"成为芸芸士子走向仕途之路之必读经典。

　　《大学》被朱熹排在"四书之首"，在顺序上超过了记录至圣先师孔子言行的《论语》和记述亚圣孟子思想的《孟子》。朱熹认为，《大学》是"为学纲目"，且"四书"中以《大学》最为易晓，故读"四书"要"先读《大学》，以定其规模；次读《论语》，以立其根本；次读《孟子》，以观其发越；次读《中庸》，以求古人之微妙处"。《大学》着重讨论个人修养与社会治乱的关系，以明明德、亲民、止于至善为修养的目标，后人称之为"三纲领"；又提出实现天下大治的八个步骤：格物、致知、诚意、正心、修身、齐家、治国、平天下，后人称之为"八条目"。为进一步服务于理学思想，朱熹加了"格物致知"一章，为《大学》原文所无。可以说，《大学》是朱熹悉心编撰的儒学经典读本，贯彻了理学对儒家思想的领悟和阐发。《大学》虽然没有《论语》《孟子》的影响力大，但因其提纲挈领的概要内涵、言简意赅的格言特征，成为儒家脍炙人口的必读典籍。

中文原文

大学❶（节选）

01. 大学之道，在明明德，在亲民[1]，在止于至善。

02. 知止[2]而后有定，定而后能静，静而后能安，安而后能虑，虑而后能得。

03. 物有本末，事有终始，知所先后，则近道[3]矣。

04. 古之欲明明德于天下者，先治其国；欲治其国者，先齐其家[4]；欲齐其家者，先修其身；欲修其身者，先正其心；欲正其心者，先诚其意；欲诚其意者，先致其知；致知在格物[5]。

05. 物格而后知至，知至而后意诚，意诚而后心正，心正而后身修，身修而后家齐，家齐而后国治，国治而后天下平。

06. 自天子以至于庶人，壹是皆以修身为本。

07. 其本乱而末治者否矣[6]，其所厚者薄，而其所薄者厚，未之有也。此谓知本、此谓知之至也。

08. 所谓诚其意者，毋自欺也，如恶恶臭、如好好色[7]，此之谓自谦[8]，故君子必慎其独也。

09. 小人闲居为不善，无所不至，见君子而后厌然[9]，掩其不善、而著其善。人之视己，如见其肺肝然，则何益矣。此谓诚于中，形于外，故君子必慎其独也。

10. 曾子曰："十目所视，十手所指，其严乎！富润屋，德润身，心广体胖[10]，故君子必诚其意。"

11. 子曰："听讼、吾犹人也[11]。必也使无讼乎。"无情者不得尽其

---

❶ 参照英译对照文本 A. Charles Muller. Great Learning［EB/OL］.（2013-07-04）［2015-11-02］. http://www.acmuller.net/con-dao/greatlearning.html. 句读参考朱熹. 四书章句集注［M］. 北京：中华书局，2011：1-10.（鉴于《大学》的句序素有争议，本书选择了说理性较强的名言进行汉英对照，并根据英译本对原文加了编号）

辞[12]。大畏民志。此谓知本。

12．所谓修身在正其心者，身有所忿懥[13]，则不得其正；有所恐惧，则不得其正；有所好乐，则不得其正；有所忧患，则不得其正。心不在焉，视而不见，听而不闻，食而不知其味。此谓修身在正其心。

13．所谓齐其家在修其身者：人之其所亲爱而辟[14]焉，之其所贱恶而辟焉，之其所畏敬而辟焉，之其所哀矜[15]而辟焉，之其所敖惰[16]而辟焉。故好而知其恶，恶而知其美者，天下鲜矣！故谚有之曰："人莫知其子之恶、莫知其苗之硕。"此谓身不修不可以齐其家。

中文注释

[1] 亲民：以仁爱之心爱护百姓。还有一种解释是"亲"通"新"，即革新、弃旧图新。亲民，也就是新民，使人弃旧图新、去恶从善。译文采用了第一种解释。

[2] 知止：知道最终目标所在。

[3] 近道：接近天道，靠近真理。

[4] 齐其家：管理好自己的家庭或家族。齐，使……齐整、有秩序。

[5] 致知在格物：使自己获得知识在于认识、研究万事万物。格：分析、研究。

[6] 否（fǒu）矣：不行，不可能。

[7] 如恶（wù）恶（è）臭（xiù），如好（hào）好（hǎo）色：如同讨厌恶劣的味道，喜欢美丽的颜色。

[8] 自谦：心安理得的样子。

[9] 厌然：躲躲闪闪的样子。

[10] 心广体胖（pán）：心胸宽广，身体就舒泰安康。胖：大，舒坦。

[11] "子曰"句：引自《论语·颜渊》。听讼：听诉讼，即审案子。犹人：与别人一样。

[12] 无情者不得尽其辞：使隐瞒真实情况的人不敢花言巧语。

[13] 忿懥（zhì）：愤怒。

［14］辟：偏颇，偏向。

［15］哀矜：哀怜，怜悯。

［16］敖惰：骄傲怠慢。

大学（选译）

01. 大学的宗旨在于弘扬光明正大的品德，在于让百姓仁爱敦睦、明理向善，在于使人达到最完善的境界。

02. 知道应达到的境界才能够有坚定的志向；志向坚定才能够镇静不躁；镇静不躁才能够心安理得；心安理得才能够思虑周详；思虑周详才能够达到最完善的境界。

03. 每样东西都有根本有枝末，每件事情都有开始有终结。明白了这本末始终的道理，就接近事物发展的规律了。

04. 古代那些要想在天下弘扬光明正大品德的人，先要治理好自己的国家；要想治理好自己的国家，先要管理好自己的家庭或家族；要想管理好自己的家庭或家族，先要修养自身的品性；要想修养自身的品性，先要端正自己的心思；要想端正自己的心思，先要使自己的意念真诚；要想使自己的意念真诚，先要使自己获得知识；获得知识的途径在于认识、研究万事万物。

05. 通过对万事万物的认识、研究后才能获得知识；获得知识后意念才能真诚；意念真诚后心思才能端正；心思端正后才能修养品性；品性修养后才能管理好家庭或家族；管理好家庭或家族后才能治理好国家；治理好国家后天下才能太平。

06. 上至天子，下至平民百姓，人人都要以修养品性为根本。

07. 若这个根本被扰乱了，家庭、家族、国家、天下要治理好是不可能的。不分轻重缓急，本末倒置却想做好事情，这也是不可能的！这就叫作抓

---

❶ 古诗文网.《大学》译文［EB/OL］.［2015-08-20］. http：//so. gushiwen. org/gu-wen/book_20. aspx. 编者对译文有所修改。

住了根本，这就叫知识达到极致了。

08. 使意念真诚的意思是说，不要自己欺骗自己。要像厌恶腐臭的气味一样，要像喜爱美丽的颜色一样，一切都发自内心。所以，品德高尚的人哪怕是在一个人独处的时候，也一定要谨慎。

09. 品德低下的人在私下里无恶不作，一见到品德高尚的人便躲躲闪闪，掩盖自己所做的坏事而自吹自擂。殊不知，别人看你自己，就像能看见你的心肝肺腑一样清楚，掩盖有什么用呢？这就叫作内心的真实一定会表现到外表上来。所以，品德高尚的人哪怕是在一个人独处的时候，也一定要谨慎。

10. 曾子说："十只眼睛看着，十只手指着，这难道不令人畏惧吗？财富可以装饰房屋，品德却可以修养身心。心胸宽广，身体就舒泰安康。所以，品德高尚的人一定要使自己的意念真诚。"

11. 孔子说："听诉讼审理案子，我也和别人一样，目的在于使诉讼不再发生。"使隐瞒真实情况的人不敢花言巧语，使人心畏服，这就叫作抓住了根本。

12. 之所以说修养自身的品性要先端正自己的心思，是因为心有愤怒就不能够端正；心有恐惧就不能够端正；心有喜好就不能够端正；心有忧虑就不能够端正。心思不端正就像心不在自己身上一样：虽然在看，但却像没有看见一样；虽然在听，但却像没有听见一样；虽然在吃东西，但却一点也不知道是什么滋味。所以说，要修养自身的品性必须先端正自己的心思。

13. 之所以说管理好家庭或家族要先修养自身，是因为人们对于自己亲爱的人会有偏爱；对于自己厌恶的人会有偏恨；对于自己敬畏的人会有偏向；对于自己同情的人会有偏心；对于自己轻视的人会有偏见。因此，很少有人喜爱某人又看到那人的缺点，厌恶某人又看到那人的优点。所以有谚语说："人都不知道自己孩子的坏，人都不满足自己庄稼的好。"这就是不修养自身就不能管理好家庭或家族的道理。

英文译本

The Great Learning

Translated by A. Charles Muller

A. The Text

01. The way of great learning consists in manifesting one's bright virtue, consists in loving the people, consists in stopping in perfect goodness.

02. When you know where to stop, you have stability. When you have stability, you can be tranquil. When you are tranquil, you can be at ease. When you are at ease, you can deliberate (仔细考虑). When you can deliberate, you can attain your aims.

03. Things have their roots and branches, affairs have their end and beginning. When you know what comes first and what comes last, then you are near the Way.

04. The ancients who wanted to manifest their bright virtue to all in the world first governed well their own states. Wanting to govern well their states, they first harmonized (使……和谐) their own clans (家族). Wanting to harmonize their own clan, they first cultivated themselves. Wanting to cultivate themselves, they first corrected their minds. Wanting to correct their minds, they first made their wills sincere. Wanting to make their wills sincere, they first extended their knowledge. Extension of knowledge consists of the investigation of things.

05. When things are investigated, knowledge is extended. When knowledge is extended, the will becomes sincere. When the will is sincere, the mind

---

❶ 本译文选自 A. Charles Muller. Great Learning [EB/OL]. (2013-07-04) [2015-08-26]. http://www.acmuller.net/con-dao/greatlearning.html. [A 部分为总纲（经），B 部分是曾子记述的孔子之言（传），是对总纲的注解，节选时对编号有所改动]

is correct. When the mind is correct, the self is cultivated. When the self is cultivated, the clan is harmonized. When the clan is harmonized, the country is well governed. When the country is well governed, there will be peace throughout the land.

06. From the king down to the common people, all must regard the cultivation of the self as the most essential thing.

07. It is impossible to have a situation wherein the essentials are in disorder, and the externals are well－managed. You simply cannot take the essential things as superficial, and the superficial things as essential. This is called "Knowing the root". This is called "The extension of knowledge."

B. The Traditional Commentary, Attributed to Confucius, Through the Transmission of Cengzi

08. "Making the will sincere," means "no self-deception." Like when we allow ourselves to be disgusted by a bad smell or become infatuated (着迷) with an attractive appearance. This is called "self-satisfaction." Therefore the Superior Man must be watchful over himself when he is alone.

09. When the inferior man is at leisure, there is no limit to the extent of his evil. But when he sees a Superior Man, he will be ashamed; he will cover his evil and show his goodness. When people observe you, they see right to your core. So what's the use of being deceitful? Therefore we say: "internal sincerity expresses itself outwardly." Therefore the Superior Man must be watchful over himself when he is alone.

10. Cengzi said, "What ten eyes see, what ten fingers indicate, is this not to be taken seriously? Rich land makes a house luxurious, virtue makes a person shine; when the mind is expanded, the body is enriched. Therefore the Superior Man must make his will sincere."

11. Confucius said, "In hearing legal cases I am just like anyone else.

What we really need is to not have legal cases. " Those who lack sincerity should not be allowed to speak on and on. They should also have a great awe for the will of the people. This is called knowing the basis.

12. "The cultivation of the person lies in the correction of the mind. " When you are angry, you cannot be correct. When you are frightened, you cannot be correct; when there is something you desire, you cannot be correct; when there is something you are anxious about, you cannot be correct. When the mind is not present, we look, but do not see. We listen, but do not hear; we eat, but don't taste our food. This is the meaning of "the cultivation of the person lies in the correction of the mind. "

13. "The regulation of the family lies in the cultivation of the person. " When there is someone you love, you are biased. When there is something you hate, you are biased. When there is something you are in awe of, you are biased. When there is someone you pity, you are biased. When you are lazy, you are biased. Those who love someone and yet know their bad points, or who hate someone and yet know their good points, are few and far between. Hence there is the proverb: "The man does not know of his own son's evil, or the richness of his own corn. " This shows that if you do not cultivate yourself, you cannot regulate your family.

英译评述

　　《大学》是"四书"中篇幅最短的一部，只有一千七百余字，总纲（经）二百零五字，评述（传）分十章一千五百余字。本文选择了总纲的全部与评述十章中的四章，以说理为主，去掉了引用《诗经》等古籍中的文字。译者 A. Charles Muller（1953—）是美国汉学家，先后在纽约州立大学、东京大学任教，主攻佛教研究和东亚文化。他翻译了中国的六部典籍："四书"和《道德经》《庄子》。他是数字化研究资源的积极推动者，他的译文与研究资料都在网上公开展示，以此推动东方文化研究的发展。（参见网址：http：//www. acmuller. net/）

鉴于译本为当代译者所做，所以句式简洁，用词易懂，尽可能采取了直译的策略。《大学》作为儒家理学纲领性文本，在说理过程中多次出现排比句式，层层递进，逐步说明理学所秉持的"正心、修身、齐家、治国、平天下"的君子理念，译文也按照原文句式，采用排比句式，尽可能保留了原文风味。如"知止而后有定，定而后能静，静而后能安，安而后能虑，虑而后能得"的译文为：When you know where to stop, you have stability. When you have stability, you can be tranquil. When you are tranquil, you can be at ease. When you are at ease, you can deliberate。以这样的直译手法，最大程度地重现了儒家理学所蕴含的从内心开始、从自身做起、然后再惠及国邦和天下的为人处世之道。

整个《大学》篇章中最有争议的是开篇总纲"大学之道，在明明德，在亲民，在止于至善"。古今中外的研究者们对此有不同的解读，在翻译时也有不同的阐释。本文译者将之译成：The way of great learning consists in manifesting one's bright virtue, consists in loving the people, consists in stopping in perfect goodness，而理雅各的译本则是：What the Great Learning teaches, is to illustrate illustrious virtue; to renovate the people; and to rest in the highest excellence。除了因为时代的久远，理雅各用词更为古雅外，最大的分歧在于"亲民"和"止于至善"这两处。Muller 将前者译为 loving the people，理雅各则译为 renovate the people（新民），是对"亲"字的不同解读。"止于至善"一句，Muller 译为 stopping in perfect goodness，理雅各译为 rest in the highest excellence。相较而言，理雅各所译更为贴近，"止于至善"不是停止，而是以至善为目标。

由于《大学》在中国思想史上的重要地位，许多中外学者都对其进行过英译，著名的译者有马礼逊（Robert Morrison）、马歇曼（Joshua Marshman）、理雅各、辜鸿铭、林语堂等。而对这篇不到两千字的短文进行解读，对照起来看则别有一番意味。

Ⅰ. **Translation Practice**.

Directions：Translate the following into English.

1. 格物致知。

2. 苟日新，日日新，又日新。

3. 仁者以财发身，不仁者以身发财。

4. 正心、修身、齐家、治国、平天下。

5. 心不在焉，视而不见，听而不闻，食而不知其味。

Ⅱ. **Translation Comparison.**

Directions：Read the following translation of the opening lines of *The Great Learning* and compare it with Muller's text.

The principles of the higher education consist in preserving man's clear character, in giving new life to the people, and in dwelling (or resting) in perfection, or the ultimate good. Only after knowing the goal of perfection where one should dwell, can one have a definite purpose in life. Only after having a definite purpose in life, can one achieve calmness of mind. Only after having achieved calmness of mind, can one have peaceful repose. Only after having peaceful repose, can one begin to think. Only after one has learned to think, can one achieve knowledge. There are a foundation and a super-structure in the constitution of things, and a beginning and an end in the course of events. Therefore to know the proper sequence or relative order of things is the beginning of wisdom. (Translated by Lin Yutang, *The Wisdom of Confucius*, London：Random House, 1938：122.)

第四节　《中庸》选译

　　《中庸》原为《礼记》中一篇，由孔子后裔子思所作，宋代朱熹将其抽出独立成篇，作《中庸章句》，与《大学》《论语》《孟子》合称为"四书"。全书共有三十三章，三千五百余字，言简意赅，哲学意味浓厚。按照朱熹的解释："中者，无过无不及之名也。庸，平常也。"不偏不倚，平和中正，是儒家的道德标准，是解决一切问题的最高智慧，至今仍有其现实意义。

　　据传《中庸》是"子思忧道学之失其传而作也"。子思通过引用孔子与

· 34 ·

《诗经》中的话语，围绕"中""和"二字展开论述。首句"天命之谓性，率性之谓道，修道之谓教"点出全篇要义，表明这是一篇关于如何修得"中""和"之道的文章。"天命之谓性"就是指"中"，即此章中指出的"喜、怒、哀、乐之未发，谓之中"，人性平和时原本的状态；"率性之谓道"是指"和"，即后文的"发而皆中节，谓之和"，事物变化引发情绪之后，人对心境进行调整后达到的平衡状态；"修道之谓教"表明这是一篇关于修行"中""和"之道的论著。

全书可分为四部分。第一章为第一部分，指出全书要义。第二章至十一章为第二部分，子思通过对舜、颜回、子路的描述表达出"知""仁""勇"这"三大德"，将其作为入道之门。第十二章至第二十章是第三部分，子思通过援引孔子之言阐明"道不可离"，所以君子慎独。第二十一章至第三十三章为第四部分，主要是子思的论述部分。它围绕"诚"展开，说明人非圣贤，生来就可以达到真实无妄的境界，但是人可以通过修行，"择善而固执之"就可以将自己提升到接近自然的境界。全书言简意赅，指近而寓远，是儒家要籍。英国汉学家理雅各和民国怪杰辜鸿铭都曾倾注心血翻译这部儒经，是对儒家思想的再现与重新阐释，折射出中西学者对这部经书的重视，并借此来反映本身对儒家哲思的理解与传承。本篇选用的是辜鸿铭译本。

中文原文

中庸❶（节选）

第一章

天命之谓性，率性之谓道，修道之谓教。

道也者，不可须臾离也，可离非道也。是故君子戒慎乎其所不睹，恐惧乎其所不闻。

---

❶　朱熹. 四书章句集注［M］. 北京：中华书局，2011：19-22.（根据英译版对章节和句读略有修改）

莫见乎隐，莫显乎微，故君子慎其独也。

喜怒哀乐之未发，谓之中；发而皆中节，谓之和。中也者，天下之大本也；和也者，天下之达道也。

致中和，天地位焉，万物育焉。

第二章

仲尼曰："君子中庸；小人反中庸。

君子之中庸也，君子而时中；小人之反中庸也，小人而无忌惮也。"

第三章

子曰："中庸其至矣乎！民鲜能久矣。"

第四章

子曰："道之不行也，我知之矣，知者过之，愚者不及也；道之不明也，我知之矣，贤者过之，不肖者不及也。人莫不饮食也，鲜能知味也。"

第五章

子曰："道其不行矣夫！"

第六章

子曰："舜其大知也与！舜好问而好察迩言，隐恶而扬善，执其两端，用其中于民，其斯以为舜乎！"

中庸❶（节选）

第一章

人的自然禀赋叫作"性"，顺着本性行事叫作"道"，按照"道"的原则修养叫作"教"。

"道"是不可以片刻离开的，如果可以离开，那就不是"道"了。所以，

---

❶ 古诗文网．《中庸》译文［EB/OL］．［2015-08-29］．http：//so. gushiwen. org/guwen/book_21. aspx. 编者有修改，并按照英译重新划分了段落。

品德高尚的人在没有人看见的地方也是谨慎的，在没有人听见的地方也是有所戒惧的。

越是隐蔽的地方越是明显，越是细微的地方越是显著。所以，品德高尚的人在一人独处的时候也是谨慎的。

喜怒哀乐没有表现出来的时候，叫作"中"；表现出来以后符合节度，叫作"和"。"中"，是人人都有的本性；"和"，是大家遵循的原则。

达到"中和"的境界，天地便各在其位了，万物便生长繁育了。

第二章

仲尼说："君子守中庸之道，小人违背中庸。

君子之所以守中庸之道，是因为君子随时做到适中，无过无不及；小人之所以违背中庸，是因为小人肆无忌惮，专走极端。"

第三章

孔子说："中庸之道大概是最高的德行了吧！大家缺乏它已经很久了！"

第四章

孔子说："中庸之道不能实行的原因，我知道了：聪明的人自以为是，认识过了头；愚蠢的人智力不及，不能理解它。中庸之道不能弘扬的原因，我知道了：贤能的人做得太过分；不贤的人根本做不到。就像人们每天都要吃喝，但却很少有人能够真正辨别滋味。"

第五章

孔子说："中庸之道恐怕不能够实行了啊！"

第六章

孔子说："舜可真是具有大智慧的人啊！他喜欢向人问问题，又善于分析别人浅近话语里的含义。隐藏人家的坏处，宣扬人家的好处。过与不及两端的意见他都掌握，采纳适中的用于老百姓。这就是舜之所以为舜的地方吧！"

The Conduct of Life❶ (An Excerpt)

Translated by Ku Hungmin

I

The ordinance of God[1] is what we call the law of our being (性). To fulfill the law of our being is what we call the moral law (道). The moral law when reduced to a system is what we call the religion (教).

The moral law is a law from whose operation we cannot for one instant in our existence escape. A law from which we may escape is not the moral law. Wherefore it is that the moral man (君子) watches diligently over what his eyes cannot see and is in fear and awe of what his ears cannot hear.

There is nothing more evident than that which cannot be seen by the eyes and nothing more palpable [显而易见] than that which cannot be perceived by the senses[2]. Wherefore the moral man watches diligently over his secret thought.

Modern Science, which is supposed to teach Materialism, on the contrary really teaches the existence, reality and inexorability [顺理成章] of law, which is not material but something which the eyes cannot see and the ears cannot hear. It is because he knows and is impressed with the reality and inexorability of law that the moral man lives a spiritual life and thereby becomes a moral man.

"Keep thy heart with all diligence, for out of it are the issues of life. " —Prov. Ⅳ.[3]

When the passions, such as joy, anger, grief and pleasure, have not awakened, that is our true self (中) or moral being. When these passions

---

❶ Ku, Hungming. The Conduct of Life [M]. Shanghai: Shanghai Mercury, 1906: 1–9. (译文中的汉字是译者自加，编者所加的注解已用方括号括起来；译文有所改动。)

awaken and each and all attain due measure and degree, that is the moral order (和). Our true self or moral being is the great reality (大本 lit. great root) of existence, and moral order is the universal law (达道) in the world.

"Our true self" —literally our central (中) inner self, or as Mr. Matthew Arnold[4] calls it, "the central clue in our moral being which unites us to the universal order". Mr. Arnold also calls it our "permanent self". Hence, the text above says, it is the root of our being. Mr. Arnold says, "All the forces and tendencies in us are like our proper central moral tendency, in themselves beneficent, but they require to be harmonized with this central (moral) tendency." —*St. Paul and Protestantism.*[5]

When true moral being and moral order are realized, the universe then becomes a cosmos [宇宙] and all things attain their full growth and development.

II

Confucius remarked: "The life of the moral man is an exemplification [例证] of the universal moral order. The life of the vulgar person, on the other hand, is a contradiction of the universal moral order.

"The moral man's life is an exemplification of the universal order, because he is a moral person who constantly lives his true self or moral being. The vulgar person's life is a contradiction of the universal order, because he is a vulgar person who in his heart has no regard for, or fear of, the moral law."

"The fool hath said in his heart: There is no God."[6]

III

Confucius remarked: "To find and get into the true central (中) balance of our moral being, i. e., our true moral ordinary (庸) self, that indeed is the highest human attainment. People are seldom capable of it for long."

Emerson[7] says: "From day to day the capital facts of human life are hidden

from our eyes. Suddenly the mist rolls up and reveals them, and we think how much good time is gone that might have been saved had any hint of these things been shown. "[8]

IV

Confucius remarked: "I know now why there is no real moral life. The wise mistake moral law to be something higher than what it really is; and the foolish do not know enough what moral law really is. I know now why the moral law is not understood. The noble natures want to live too high, high above their moral ordinary self; and the ignoble [无知的] natures do not live high enough, i. e., not up to their moral ordinary true self. "

"There is no one who does not eat and drink. But few there are who really know the taste of what they eat and drink. "

Goethe[9] says: "O needless strictness of morality while nature in her kindly way trains us to all that we require to be! O strange demand of society which first perplexes and misleads us, then asks of us more than Nature herself!" —The moral law is the law of our moral nature; and moral nature, what we call our moral being, is nothing else but our true or ordinary self.

V

Confucius remarked: "There is in the world now really no moral social order at all. "

The word Tao here means the moral law finding its expression in social order. Confucius in his time, as Carlyle[10] or Ruskin[11] in modern Europe, considered the world to have gone on a wrong track; the ways of men and constitution of society to be radically wrong.

VI

Confucius remarked: "There was the Emperor Shun. He was perhaps what may be considered a truly great intellect. Shun had a natural curiosity of mind and he loved to inquire into near facts (literally 'near words', meaning here ordinary topics of conversation in every-day life.) He looked upon evil merely as something negative; and he recognized only what was good as having a positive existence. Taking the two extremes of negative and positive, he applied the mean between the two extremes in his judgment, employment and dealings with people. This was the characteristics of Shun's great intellect."

What is here said of the Emperor Shun in ancient China may be also said of the two greatest intellects in modern Europe—Shakespeare[12] and Goethe. The greatness of Shakespeare's intellect is to be seen in this: that in all his plays there is not one essentially bad man. Seen through Shakespeare's intellect, such a monster of wickedness of the popular imagination as King Richard the Hunchback[13], becomes not a villain who makes "damnable faces," not even a really despicably bad man, but, on the contrary, a brave heroic soul who is driven by his strong, ill‐regulated, vindictive (怀恨的) passions to awful acts of cruelty and finally himself to a tragic end.

Goethe elsewhere says: "What we call evil in human nature is merely a defective or incomplete development, a deformity or malformation—absence or excess of some moral quality rather than anything positively evil."

⬚ 英译注释

1. The ordinance of God: 上帝的旨意。

2. There is nothing more evident that which cannot be seen by the eyes and nothing more palpable than that which cannot be perceived by the senses: 莫见乎隐，莫显乎微。最能表现出本质的是看不见的地方，最能彰显真理的是不能明显察觉的地方。

3. "Keep thy heart with all diligence, for out of it are the issues of life." —Prov. IV.: "你要谨守你的心，胜过谨守一切，因为生命的泉源由此而出。" 出自圣经中的《旧约·箴言》第四节。

4. Matthew Arnold：马修·阿诺德（1822—1888），英国维多利亚时期著名文化批评家、诗人，其作品针砭时弊，对文化、教育、道德、政治等问题予以理性批判。代表作有《文化与无政府主义》（*Culture and Anarchy*，1869）、《多佛海滩》（*Dover Beach*，1867）等。

5. *St. Paul and Protestantism*：《圣保罗与新教主义》，是马修·阿诺德于1870年撰写的一部关于宗教文化的著作。

6. The fool hath said in his heart：There is no God.：愚顽人心里说："没有上帝。"这是《圣经·旧约·诗篇》中的话。

7. Emerson：爱默生（Ralph Waldo Emerson，1803—1882），美国思想家、随笔作家、诗人、美国"先验主义"运动领袖，代表作有《论自然》（*Nature*，1836）等。

8. 以上引言出自爱默生的随笔《幻觉》（*Illusions*），收入随笔集《生活的准则》（*Conduct of Life*，1860）中。

9. Goethe：歌德（Johann Wolfgang Von Goethe，1749—1832），德国思想家、作家、科学家，代表作有《少年维特之烦恼》（*Die Leiden des jungen Werthers*，1774）、《浮士德》（*Faust*，1805）等。

10. Carlyle：卡莱尔（Thomas Carlyle，1795—1881），英国维多利亚时期历史学家、评论家，代表作有《法国大革命》（*The French Revolution：A History*，1837）等。

11. Ruskin：拉斯金（John Ruskin，1819—1900），英国作家、艺术家、艺术评论家，代表作有《时间与潮流》（*Time and Tide*，1867）等。

12. Shakespeare：威廉·莎士比亚（William Shakespeare，1564—1616），英国最伟大的剧作家、诗人之一，现存三十七部戏剧、两首长诗，以及一百五十四首十四行诗。代表作有《哈姆雷特》（*Hamlet*）、《罗密欧与朱丽叶》（*Romeo and Juliet*）等。

13. King Richard the Hunchback：驼背国王理查三世（Richard Ⅲ，1452—1485），英格兰国王，1483—1485年在位；爱德华四世之弟，1483年摄政。传闻其杀害侄子爱德华五世即位，后来在与里士满伯爵亨利·都铎（Henry Tutor）的交战中失利被杀。莎士比亚据此创作了剧本《理查三世》（*Richard*

Ⅲ，1591）。

英译评述

《中庸》作为儒家经典著作，有多种英译版本，单是国外译者就有理雅各、修中诚（E. R. Hughes）、安乐哲（Roger T. Ames）、浦安迪（Andrew H. Plaks）等人。华裔译者有辜鸿铭、陈荣捷等。本章节选的是 1906 年出版的我国近代著名学者辜鸿铭的译本。

辜鸿铭的《中庸》译本强调传递中国典籍的内在含义，并尝试站在西方读者的立场上，以他们既知的西方文化来阐释中国典籍中的思想。他的语言极具文学性，并充分体现了典籍的哲学内涵。为了体现典籍的内在逻辑性和完整性，他不惜变换原文位置，以求内在含义的统一。

对于不言鬼神的儒家常提到"天命"这样一个概念，辜鸿铭以 The ordinance of God 来翻译，把"修道之谓教"译成 The moral law when reduced to a system is what we call the religion，以便让熟悉基督教义的西方读者跨越文化障碍，理解儒家思想与西方思想的相通之处。

与坚持直译的西方汉学家不同，辜鸿铭作为中国人，采用了归化策略来翻译儒家典籍，力求沟通中西文化，达到共鸣。为了实现这一目标，他在翻译原文之外，还补充了西方文化中与儒家思想相一致的阐释，在西方文学、哲学和宗教中引经据典，来沟通中西方相近的思想源流。例如，在解读《中庸》的总纲中对"道"这一核心理念的"莫见乎隐，莫显乎微"特质时，译者将之与西方现代科学（Modern Science）相比较，指出科学所探究的"无形无闻"抽象道理，正是与儒家所说的"道"不谋而合。他还引用了《圣经·旧约·箴言》中的话 Keep thy heart with all diligence, for out of it are the issues of life 来证明君子"慎独"的道理与基督教中"守心"的训诫如出一辙。在下文中，辜鸿铭用英国文化学者马修·阿诺德对于基督教的阐释来对应《中庸》中合乎道德规范的自我（"守中"）的意义，以《圣经》中不信上帝的傻瓜（The fool hath said in his heart：There is no God.）来对应反中庸的小人；以美国哲学家爱默生的对现实真理（the capital facts of human life）不被人早些知晓而发出的感叹，来响应孔子对中庸之道不能为民所长久秉持的叹息；将德国文学家歌德关于道德与天性的统一与孔子所说的过犹不及是道之不行的原因相联系；用卡莱尔和拉斯金的"人心不古"悲观论调，来呼应孔子"道其不行矣夫"的哀叹；用莎士比亚对邪恶的英国国王理查三世的人性描写，来证明"性相近、习相远"，从而阐释孔子对舜的赞颂。

　　辜鸿铭的《中庸》译本出版于 1906 年，当时清王朝已处在风雨飘摇之中，中国传统文化正遭到西方文化的强烈挑战。在这剧烈变革的时代中，辜鸿铭虽然受过西方教育，却坚定地守护本国传统，他的翻译是为了在西方宣扬中国儒家思想的深厚底蕴和文化优越性，因此在翻译过程中把中国圣贤思想与西方思想尽量做比较，并在注释中让西方学者巨匠们围绕儒家的思想做阐发，大力推崇中国古代哲学思想。这样的翻译手法的确可以让西方人很快了解中国儒家文化，但也难免有言过其实、过度比附的地方。尽管如此，辜鸿铭对儒家文化的外译和传播起到了重要作用，为我国的典籍英译增添了一抹强烈的个人色彩，至今依然堪称归化翻译的典范。

Ⅰ. Translation Practice.

Directions：Translate the following into English.

1. 不偏之谓中，不易之谓庸。中者，天下之正道；庸者，天下之定理。

2. 凡事豫则立，不豫则废。

3. 好学近乎知，力行近乎仁，知耻近乎勇。

4. 博学之，审问之，慎思之，明辨之，笃行之。

5. 自诚明，谓之性；自明诚，谓之教。诚则明矣，明则诚矣。

Ⅱ. Translation Comparison.

Directions：Compare the following two versions of translated text from Zhong Yong.

　　"诚者，天之道也。诚之者，人之道也。诚者，不勉而中，不思而得，从容中道，圣人也。诚之者，择善而固执之者也。"（中庸·第二十章）

　　"Truth is the law of God. Acquired truth is the law of man. He who intuitively apprehends truth, is one who, without effort, hits what is right and without thinking, understands what he wants to know; whose life easily and naturally is in harmony with the moral law. Such a one is what we call a saint or a man of divine nature. He who acquires truth is one who finds out what is good and holds fast to it. " (Gu Hongming)

"Sincerity is the way of Heaven. The attainment of sincerity is the way of man. He who possesses sincerity, is he who, without an effort, hits what is right, and apprehends, without the exercise of thought – he is the sage who naturally and easily embodies the right way. He who attains to sincerity, is he who chooses and what is good, and firmly holds it fast. " (James Legge)

第二章

道家经典

导 读

　　道家思想以老庄著作为主体，两千多年来在中国哲学体系中占据着极其重要的地位，与儒家思想共同成为古代最重要的思想流派。不同于儒家一以贯之的社会使命感，道家更重视个人思想的解放、心灵的自由，并将之应用于治国理政、为人处世等现实层面，是对儒家思想的有力校正和有益补充，形成了我国儒道互补的哲学源流。本章节选了道家典籍中最重要的两部著作——春秋时期老子的《道德经》和战国时期庄周的《庄子》，结合两位外国汉学家对这两部哲学著作的翻译，探讨两位先贤的入世之思、出世之想，学习如何从汉英角度对道家思想进行阐发译介。

第一节　《道德经》选译

　　《道德经》又称《道德真经》《老子》《五千言》《老子五千文》，是我国先秦诸子百家的典籍之一，传说由春秋时期的老子所撰写，是道家哲学思想的重要来源。《道德经》分上下两篇，原文上篇《德经》、下篇《道经》，不分章，后改为《道经》三十七章在前，第三十八章之后为《德经》，共分为八十一章。《道德经》是道家哲学流派的奠基之作，也是中国历史上首部完整的哲学著作。

　　关于《道德经》与其作者老子有多种传说，目前采纳最多的是《史记·

老子韩非列传》的记载："老子者，楚苦县厉乡曲仁里人也，姓李氏，名耳，字聃，周守藏室之史也。……老子修道德，其学以自隐无名为务。居周久之，见周之衰，乃遂去。至关，关令尹喜曰：'子将隐矣，强为我著书。'于是老子乃著书上下篇，言道德之意五千余言而去，莫知其所终。"由此可知，老子是今天的河南鹿邑人，据考证他的生卒年代大约是在公元前 580 年至公元前 500 年，他做过东周王室管理藏书的史官，在归隐之前写下了《道德经》五千言。由于老庄学派的深远影响，他被道教奉为道祖太上老君。

《道德经》虽然只有五千余字，却文字简约、含义深邃，涵盖哲学、政治、伦理等诸多学科，博大精深，包容万象。由于《道德经》成书在两千多年前，版本屡经变异，至今研究者们对该典籍的字词句读有着诸多争议。通行的文本是三国时经学家王弼的《道德经注》，1973 年马王堆汉墓出土的《道德经》帛书，与王弼的版本有很多出入。无论如何，老子对"道"与"德"的描述，是从立体面的多层次剖析了宇宙、万物、人类以及人本身的种种内涵，在后世更是被从多种视角加以解读，莫衷一是。这为解读和翻译这部道家典籍增添了很多困难，也增加了诸多魅力，是哲学论辩的好素材，也是译本比较的好范例。

道德经[1]（节选）

老子

第一章

道可道，非常道；名可名，非常名。无名，天地之始；有名，万物之

---

❶ 老子，庄子. 老子·庄子 [M]. 傅云龙，陆钦，注释. 北京：华夏出版社，2000：15-21.（此版按照马王堆帛书定版，编者根据理雅各英译本对中文原文略有修订）

母。故常无欲，以观其妙；常有欲，以观其徼[1]。两者同出，异名同谓，玄之又玄，众妙之门。

第二章

天下皆知美之为美，斯恶已。皆知善之为善，斯不善已。故有无相生，难易相成，长短相形，高下相倾，音声相和，前后相随。常也。是以圣人处无为之事，行不言之教。万物作焉而弗辞。生而弗有，为而弗恃[2]，功成而弗居。夫唯弗居，是以不去。

第三章

不尚贤，使民不争。不贵难得之货，使民不为盗。不见可欲，使民心不乱。是以圣人之治也，虚其心，实其腹，弱其志，强其骨，常使民无知无欲，使夫智者不敢为也。为无为，则无不治。

第四章

道冲，而用之又弗盈也。渊兮似万物之宗。挫其锐，解其纷；和其光，同其尘。湛[3]兮似或存。吾不知其谁之子也，象帝之先。

第五章

天地不仁，以万物为刍狗[4]。圣人不仁，以百姓为刍狗。天地之间，其犹橐籥[5]乎？虚而不屈，动而愈出。多言数穷，不如守中。

第六章

谷神不死，是谓玄牝[6]。玄牝之门，是谓天地之根。绵绵兮其若存，用之不勤。

第七章

天长地久。天地所以能长且久者，以其不自生也，故能长生。是以圣人后其身而身先，外其身而身存。非以其无私邪？故能成其私。

第八章

上善若水。水善利万物而不争，处众人之所恶，故几于道矣。居善地，心善渊，与善仁，言善信，正善治，事善能，动善时。夫唯不争，故无尤。

第九章

执而盈之，不如其已。揣而锐之，不可长保。金玉满堂，莫之能守。富贵而骄，自遗其咎。功遂身退，天之道也。

第十章

载营魄抱一，能无离乎？抟气致柔，能如婴儿乎？涤除玄览，能无疵乎？爱国治民，能无为乎？天门开阖，能为雌乎？明白四达，能无知乎？生而畜之，生而不有，为而不恃，长而不宰，是谓玄德。

中文注释

[1] 徼（jiào）：边界，引申为表面。

[2] 恃（shì）：依赖，仗着。

[3] 湛（zhàn）：清澈，透明，无影无形。

[4] 刍（chú）狗：草做的狗，古代祭祀用的是草做的狗，用完即弃。

[5] 橐籥（tuó yuè）：风箱，古代鼓风吹火用的器具。

[6] 玄牝（pìn）：牝，雌性，化生万物之所在。玄牝，微妙化生之意。

道德经❶（节选）

老子

第一章

"道"如果可以践行，那它就不是永恒不变的"道"；"名"如果可以用文辞去命名，那它就不是永恒不变的"名"。"无名"，是天地混沌未开之际的状

况；而"有名"，则是宇宙万物产生之本原。因此，只有心中无欲，才能领悟"道"的奥妙；而心中有欲，看到的是"道"的端倪。"无欲"与"有欲"这两者，来源相同而名称相异，都可以称之为玄妙、深远。它不是一般的玄妙、深奥，而是玄妙又玄妙、深远又深远，是宇宙天地万物之奥妙的总法门。

第二章

天下人都知道美之所以为美，于是就有了令人嫌恶的丑；都知道善之所以为善，于是就有了反面的恶。所以，"有"与"无"相互凸显，"难"与"易"相互促成，"长"与"短"相互显现，"高"与"下"相依而存，"音"与"声"相互陪衬，"前"与"后"相互照应。因此，圣人从事于无所成名的事务，施行无须仗名立言的劝教，坦荡迎候万物的涌现与流变而不抵触畏避，创造了一切而并不据为己有，做成了什么并不仗恃，成就了事业并不矜居功名。就是因为他不矜居功名，所以他不会遭到贬黜。

第三章

不崇尚贤才异能，使人民不至于炫技逞能而争名逐利；不看重稀有珍贵之物，使人民不做盗贼。不显露足以引起贪欲的物事，使人民的心思不至于被扰乱。因此，圣人治理天下的原则是：排弃充斥于人民心中的各种成见，满足人民的温饱需求，弱化人民的贪念欲望，强健人民的筋骨；常让人民不执成见、不生贪欲，使那些聪明人不敢为所欲为。信奉无为之治，即可以得到全面的治理。

第四章

道是虚无的，但它的作用却似乎无穷无尽。它是那样的幽深莫测，像是一切存在的本原依归。它消磨了锋角，排解了纠纷，柔和了光芒，混同于尘俗。它无形无迹呵，像是很不确定的存在。我不知道在它之上还能有什么更本原的存在，只觉得它存在于天帝之前。

第五章

天地无所谓仁爱之心，把万物都当作草狗来看待；圣人也不执求仁爱之心，把百姓当作草狗来看待。天地之间，不正像风箱或空管那样的大空泡吗？

它虽空虚但却不会塌缩，运行之中生化不息。孜孜于仗名立言往往行不通，不如持守空虚而顺其自然。

第六章

虚神永远存在，可以称它为无比幽深的生殖之源。通向这个无比幽深的生殖之源的门径，就是这个天地世界的根本。它绵延存在而又若有若无，它施展的作用无穷无尽。

第七章

天长地久。天地所以能够长久，是因为它们不去强求一种非其不可的状况维持，所以能够长久。因此，圣人把自己的切身利益置后，反而成了人群的首领；把自己的身家性命置之度外，反而更好地保护了自己的身家性命。不正是因为他对自己很无所谓吗？这样反而可以更好地成就他自己。

第八章

最好的行为典范就像水一样。水，善于利导万物而不与之争，处守于众人所不愿处的低下处，所以，接近于道。水，善于择下而居，心幽深而明澈，交游共处谐和相亲，言行表里如一，公共关系易于清静太平，办事能干，行动善于应机顺势而行。正因为水总是利导万物而不与之争，所以，它很少患过失。

第九章

保持盈满，不如适可而止。锋芒毕露，难以长久。金玉满堂，谁能守藏？富贵而骄横，自埋祸殃。功成身退，是最应该奉行的行为准则。

第十章

保持神魂与体魄的谐和统一，能不崩解离散吗？圆融气质以致柔顺随和，能像婴儿一样吗？清理幽深而明澈的自体，能没有任何瑕疵吗？爱民治国，能不执着于名而顺其自然吗？在展身作为、功成身退的循环中，能安居于柔雌的状态吗？明于道而"发光"行进于一切领域，都能无须向显学成见"借光"吗？生它，养它，生了它并不拘系自有，成就了什么并不执为仗恃，虽获取较高的资格权能却不肆行宰制，这就叫作无限深得于道的"玄德"。

The Tao Teh King❶ (An Excerpt)

by Lao – Tse

Translated by James Legge

Chapter One

The Tao that can be trodden[1] is not the enduring and unchanging Tao. The name that can be named is not the enduring and unchanging name. (Conceived of as) having no name, it is the Originator of heaven and earth; (conceived of as) having a name, it is the Mother of all things.

Always without desire we must be found[2],

If its deep mystery we would sound;

But if desire always within us be,

Its outer fringe[3] is all that we shall see.

Under these two aspects, it is really the same; but as development takes place, it receives the different names. Together we call them the Mystery. Where the Mystery is the deepest is the gate of all that is subtle and wonderful.

Chapter Two

All in the world know the beauty of the beautiful, and in doing this they have (the idea of) what ugliness is; they all know the skill of the skilful, and in doing this they have (the idea of) what the want of skill is. So it is that existence and non – existence give birth the one to (the idea of) the other; that

---

❶ 本文选用的是理雅各的英译本，选取的是《道德经》八十一章中前十章的内容。(James Legge. The Texts of Taoism, Part I [M]. New York: Dover Publications, Inc.: 1962: 47–54.)

difficulty and ease produce the one (the idea of) the other; that length and shortness fashion out the one the figure of the other; that (the ideas of) height and lowness arise from the contrast of the one with the other; that the musical notes and tones become harmonious through the relation of one with another; and that being before and behind give the idea of one following another. Therefore the sage manages affairs without doing anything, and conveys his instructions without the use of speech. All things spring up, and there is not one which declines to show itself; they grow, and there is no claim made for their ownership; they go through their processes, and there is no expectation (of a reward for the results) . The work is accomplished, and there is no resting in it (as an achievement) .

The work is done, but how no one can see;

'Tis[4] this that makes the power not cease to be.

Chapter Three

Not to value and employ men of superior ability is the way to keep the people from rivalry among themselves; not to prize articles which are difficult to procure is the way to keep them from becoming thieves; not to show them what is likely to excite their desires is the way to keep their minds from disorder. Therefore the sage, in the exercise of his government, empties their minds, fills their bellies, weakens their wills, and strengthens their bones. He constantly (tries to) keep them without knowledge and without desire, and where there are those who have knowledge, to keep them from presuming to act (on it) . When there is this abstinence (节制) from action, good order is universal.

Chapter Four

The Tao is (like) the emptiness of a vessel; and in our employment of it we must be on our guard against all fullness. How deep and unfathomable it

is, as if it were the Honoured Ancestor of all things! We should blunt our sharp points, and unravel the complications of things; we should attemper (缓和) our brightness, and bring ourselves into agreement with the obscurity of others. How pure and still the Tao is, as if it would ever so continue! I do not know whose son it is. It might appear to have been before God.

Chapter Five

Heaven and earth do not act from (the impulse of) any wish to be benevolent; they deal with all things as the dogs of grass are dealt with. The sages do not act from (any wish to be) benevolent; they deal with the people as the dogs of grass are dealt with. May not the space between heaven and earth be compared to a bellows?

'Tis emptied, yet it loses not its power;

'Tis moved again, and sends forth air the more.

Much speech to swift exhaustion lead we see;

Your inner being guard, and keep it free.

Chapter Six

The valley spirit[5] dies not, aye the same;

The female mystery[6] thus do we name.

Its gate, from which at first they issued forth,

Is called the root from which grew heaven and earth.

Long and unbroken does its power remain,

Used gently, and without the touch of pain.

Chapter Seven

Heaven is long-enduring and earth continues long. The reason why heaven and earth are able to endure and continue thus long is because they do not live of, or for, themselves. This is how they are able to continue and endure. Therefore the sage puts his own person last, and yet it is found in the foremost place; he treats his person as if it were foreign to him, and yet that person is preserved. Is it not because he has no personal and private ends[7], that therefore such ends are realized?

Chapter Eight

The highest excellence is like (that of) water. The excellence of water appears in its benefiting all things, and in its occupying, without striving (to the contrary), the low place which all men dislike. Hence (its way) is near to (that of) the Tao. The excellence of a residence is in (the suitability of) the place; that of the mind is in abysmal (深不可测的) stillness; that of associations is in their being with the virtuous; that of government is in its securing good order; that of (the conduct of) affairs is in its ability; and that of (the initiation of) any movement is in its timeliness. And when (one with the highest excellence) does not wrangle (争斗) (about his low position), no one finds fault with him[8].

Chapter Nine

It is better to leave a vessel unfilled, than to attempt to carry it when it is full. If you keep feeling a point that has been sharpened, the point cannot long preserve its sharpness. When gold and jade fill the hall, their possessor cannot keep them safe. When wealth and honours lead to arrogancy (傲慢), this brings its evil on itself. When the work is done, and one's name is becoming distinguished, to withdraw into obscurity is the way of Heaven.

Chapter Ten

When the intelligent and animal souls[9] are held together in one embrace, they can be kept from separating. When one gives undivided attention to the (vital) breath, and brings it to the utmost degree of pliancy, he can become as a (tender) babe. When he has cleansed away the most mysterious sights (of his imagination), he can become without a flaw. In loving the people and ruling the state, cannot he proceed without any (purpose of) action? In the opening and shutting of his gates of heaven, cannot he do so as a female bird? While his intelligence reaches in every direction, cannot he (appear to) be without knowledge? (The Tao) produces (all things) and nourishes them; it produces them and does not claim them as its own; it does all, and yet does not boast of it; it presides over all, and yet does not control them. This is what is called "The mysterious Quality"[10] (of the Tao).

英译注释

1. trodden：踩，踏（tread 的过去分词）。理雅各将"道可道"译成"可以走的路"。

2. Always without desire we must be found：倒装句，即 We must always be found without desire，理雅各用韵文翻译《道德经》中押韵的部分，倒装句是为了照顾韵脚，下文中也出现了多次倒装。

3. outer fringe：外部的装饰。在原文中"徼"意为"边界"，引申为"表面"。

4. 'Tis：It is 的缩写形式。

5. The valley spirit：谷神，理雅各直译为"山谷之神"，另一解释是"空间的神奇作用"。

6. The female mystery：玄牝，玄妙的母体，译者将之解释为"雌性的神秘"。

7. personal and private ends：个人的、私人的目的；ends：目的，企图。

8. no one finds fault with him：无尤，没有过错。理雅各译为"没人能找出他的错误"。

9. the intelligent and animal souls：智慧的与本能的灵魂，指的是原文中"营魄"。"营"指身体，生命的寄居之所；"魄"指灵魂。也有把"营魄"理解为"灵魂"的。理雅各在翻译中把灵魂分成"智性"（intelligent）和"本能"（animal）的两种。

10. The mysterious Quality："玄德"，高尚的品德，理雅各将之阐释为"神秘的德性"。

英译评述

言简意深的《道德经》千百年来引起了众多学者的阐释。《道德经》是道家最重要的典籍，很早就引起了西方传教士和汉学家的注意。从 16 世纪《道德经》被翻译成多种文字开始，至今已有 250 多种版本，据称是世界上除了《圣经》之外译成外国文字发行量最多的世界文化名著。在众多译本中，理雅各的这个 19 世纪 70 年代的译本被认为是极具权威性的经典版本，至今依然有极高的阅读和研究价值。

理雅各译《道德经》，如同他翻译《中国经典》（*Chinese Classics*）中的四书五经一样，以西方传教士的视角来解读和译介中国古典哲学思想，让西方了解中国思维脉络，以达到思想融通、有利于传教的目的。理雅各在翻译中采取归化和异化相结合的策略，以归化为主、异化为辅的方法，力求以正规典雅的英文，诠释出奥妙无穷的老子思想。例如，理雅各把"道"直接音译为 the Tao，而将"德"视上下文内容译为 operation、quality 等多个对应词。针对多个含义模糊的名词，则尽量用英文阐释出来，如把"谷神"译为 the valley spirit，"玄牝"译为 the female mystery，以求让英文读者做到无障碍阅读。

在句式上，虽然理雅各秉承忠实于原文的直译法，但为了达到句法上的通顺流畅，译者增加了英文顺接关系的连词、代词等关联词汇，打通了句子之间的逻辑联系。他用括号的方式标注出添加的部分，以示与原文区别。例如"无名，天地之始；有名，万物之母"译为（Conceived of as）having no name, it is the Originator of heaven and earth；（conceived of as）having a name, it is the Mother of all things。原文极简洁，译者从英语句式的完整性考虑，加上 conceived of as 以表达句子语法与逻辑关系，通顺且意思明确。

这个译本的卓越之处还在于：译者用诗体韵文来翻译《道德经》中押韵的部分。由于文体的限定和韵脚的变化，很多研究者没有注意到《道德经》中有大量的押韵表述。理雅各在翻译时不仅注意到了押韵，还忠实地用流畅

的诗体翻译出了这些韵文。这些韵文有的藏在一章之内，如第一章的后半部分："故常无欲，以观其妙；常有欲，以观其徼。两者同出，异名同谓，玄之又玄，众妙之门。"有的整章都是，如第六章："谷神不死，是谓玄牝。玄牝之门，是谓天地之根。绵绵兮其若存，用之不勤。"理雅各都用英文诗体准确无误地译出了这些韵文，殊为不易。理雅各用19世纪的英文来表述公元前6世纪前后的中国古文，在用词和句式方面达到了融会贯通，风格一致。

后世的翻译批评者们会指出理雅各在翻译中国典籍时没有顾及某些词汇的意义分歧，以及他为了传播基督教思想而把中国哲学思想向西方归化的倾向。这在《道德经》的译本中表现得并不明显。跟后来 Arthur Waley、林语堂、许渊冲等的译本相比，理雅各的译本以其令人信服的阐释、流畅的语言，成为《道德经》最为经典的英译本之一。

第二节　《庄子》选译

庄子（约公元前369—公元前286），名周，字子休，战国时宋国蒙地人。先秦时期思想家、哲学家和文学家，道家学派的代表人物，道家学说的主要创始人之一，与老子合称"老庄"。据《史记·老子韩非列传》记载，庄子曾做过宋国蒙地的漆园吏，蔑视功名利禄，推崇老子学说，著书十余万言，即为《庄子》。此书如今尚存三十三篇，六万五千多字，分"内篇""外篇""杂篇"三部分，其中的名篇有《逍遥游》《秋水》《齐物论》等，多以寓言说理，表达了他"等生死而齐万物""顺自然而尚无为"的恬退思想。

《逍遥游》是《庄子·内篇》的首篇，想象雄奇，文采瑰丽，是理解庄子思想的入门之匙。开篇即以鲲鹏之高飞与鷃雀之低徊做对比，反映了世界之无穷无尽，世间万物的大小寿夭都是相对而言，唯有追求顺其自然无所依，忘却名利自我，去命去功，才能最终获得纯粹的逍遥自由。

逍遥游❶（节选）

庄子

北冥有鱼，其名为鲲。鲲之大，不知其几千里也；化而为鸟，其名为鹏。鹏之背，不知其几千里也；怒而飞，其翼若垂天之云。是鸟也，海运则将徙于南冥。南冥者，天池也。

《齐谐》者，志怪者也。《谐》之言曰："鹏之徙于南冥也，水击三千里，抟扶摇[1]而上者九万里，去以六月息者也。"野马也，尘埃也，生物之以息相吹也。天之苍苍，其正色邪？其远而无所至极邪？其视下也，亦若是则已矣。

且夫水之积也不厚，则其负大舟也无力。覆杯水于坳堂之上，则芥为之舟；置杯焉则胶，水浅而舟大也。风之积也不厚，则其负大翼也无力。故九万里，则风斯在下矣，而后乃今培风；背负青天而莫之夭阏[2]者，而后乃今将图南。

蜩与学鸠[3]笑之曰："我决起而飞，枪榆枋[4]，时则不至而控于地而已矣；奚以之九万里而南为？"适莽苍者，三飡而反，腹犹果然；适百里者，宿舂粮；适千里者，三月聚粮。之二虫又何知！

小知不及大知，小年不及大年。奚以知其然也？朝菌不知晦朔[5]，蟪蛄[6]不知春秋，此小年也。楚之南有冥灵者，以五百岁为春，五百岁为秋；上古有大椿者，以八千岁为春，八千岁为秋。而彭祖乃今以久特闻，

---

❶　老子，庄子. 老子·庄子 [M]. 傅云龙，陆钦，注释. 北京：华夏出版社，2000：85-88.（编者根据英译本对中文原文略有修订）

众人匹之，不亦悲乎？

汤之问棘^[7]也是巳："穷发之北，有冥海者，天池也。有鱼焉，其广数千里，未有知其修者，其名为鲲。有鸟焉，其名为鹏，背若太山，翼若垂天之云；抟扶摇、羊角而上者九万里，绝云气，负青天，然后图南，且适南冥也。斥鷃^[8]笑之曰：'彼且奚适也？我腾跃而上，不过数仞而下，翱翔蓬蒿之间，此亦飞之至也。而彼且奚适也？'"此小大之辩也。

故夫知效一官、行比一乡、德合一君而征一国者，其自视也亦若此矣。而宋荣子犹然笑之。且举世而誉之而不加劝，举世而非之而不加沮，定乎内外之分，辩乎荣辱之境，斯巳矣。彼其于世，未数数然^[9]也。虽然，犹有未树也。夫列子御风而行，泠然^[10]善也，旬有五日而后反。彼于致福者，未数数然也。此虽免乎行，犹有所待者也。若夫乘天地之正，而御六气之辩，以游无穷者，彼且恶乎待哉？

故曰：至人无己，神人无功，圣人无名。

中文注释

[1] 抟（tuán）扶摇：扶摇，海上飓风。抟：回旋而上；一作"搏"（bó），拍击，凭借。

[2] 莫之夭阏（yāo è）：没有什么将之阻碍。夭阏，又写作"夭遏"，意思是遏阻、阻拦。

[3] 蜩（tiáo）与学鸠：蝉与小鸠。蜩：蝉；学鸠：小斑鸠。

[4] 枪榆枋：碰到榆树和枋树。枪：通"抢"，碰撞。榆、枋是两种小树。

[5] 晦朔（huì shuò）：中国农历每月末一日及初一日，指代一个月的时间。晦：阴历每月末的一天；朔：阴历月初的一天。

[6] 蟪蛄（huì gū）：又名"知了"，一种蝉科昆虫。

[7] 汤之问棘（jí）：商汤曾经请教过棘。汤：商朝开国之君；棘：汤时贤人。

［8］斥鴳（chì yàn）：鴳雀，小鸟。斥：小泽。

［9］数（shuó）数然：刻意追求，急促地。

［10］泠（líng）然：轻妙飘然。

白话译文❶

北海有条大鱼名字叫鲲，鲲有多大，不知道它到底有几千里长。这鲲一变就成鹏鸟。这鹏鸟也不知道有多大，只知道当它张开翅膀、奋起而飞时，它的翅膀像遮天蔽日的云彩。这只鸟，当海动风起时就飞往南海。南海就是那天池了。

《齐谐》是一本记载怪异事物的书。《齐谐》上说："鹏鸟飞往南海时，激溅起来的水花达三千里，翼拍旋风而直上九万里高空。它飞了六个月才停歇下来。"游气、尘埃，都是有生命的物体呼出呼入的气息。天空苍苍茫茫，这是它的真正本色吗？还是高远无穷，不能看到它的至极深处呢？高飞九万里的大鹏往下看地面的景象，也不过是这样的情形。

而且，如果水不是很深，那大船在水里肯定也浮不起来。将一杯水倒在庭前的凹陷处，小草可以化为一叶扁舟，浮游在那水里了。如果将杯子放到水里，杯子肯定就沉了，不能动了，那是因为水很浅而船很大。风如果不是很大的话，也肯定难使大鸟飞起来。所以大鹏飞在九万里的高空中，正是有大风在下面衬着大鹏的翅膀，它才可以凭借着风力，背负着这苍苍青天，一路畅通，然后才能飞到那南海去。

蝉和斑鸠讥笑大鹏说："我们什么时候愿意飞就一下子飞起来，碰到榆树、枋树就停落在上边；有时力气不够、飞不到，落到地上就是了。何必要高飞九万里而到那遥远的南海呢？"去近郊旅行的人，只带三餐饭，当天回来，肚子还饱饱的；作百里之远旅行的人，需要花一夜工夫舂米面准备干粮；准备远行千里的人，准备三个月的粮食了。这两只小虫鸟又知道什么呢？

小聪明赶不上大智慧，寿命短比不上寿命长。怎么知道是这样的呢？清

---

❶ 古诗文网．《逍遥游（节选）》译文及注释［EB/OL］．［2015-09-18］．http：//www.jy135.com/guwen/160402_1fanyi.html．（编者根据英语译文有所修改）

晨的菌类不会懂得什么是晦朔，寒蝉也不会懂得什么是春秋，这就是短寿。楚国南边有叫冥灵的树木，它把五百年当作春，把五百年当作秋；上古有叫大椿的古树，它把八千年当作春，把八千年当作秋，这就是长寿。可是彭祖到如今还是以年寿长久而闻名于世，人们与他攀比，岂不可悲可叹吗？

商汤问棘，谈的也是这件事。棘说："在草木不生的极远北方，有个大海，叫天池。里面有条鱼，它的身子有几千里宽，没有人知道它有多长，它的名字叫作鲲。有一只鸟，它的名字叫作鹏。鹏的背像泰山，翅膀像天边的云；借着旋风盘旋而上九万里，超越云层，背负青天，然后向南飞翔，飞到南海去。小泽里的麻雀讥笑鹏说：'它要飞到哪里去呢？我一跳就飞起来了，不过数丈高就落下来了，在蓬蒿丛中盘旋，这也是极好的飞行了。而它还要飞到哪里去呢？'"这是大和小的分别。

所以，那些才智能胜任一官的职守、行为能够庇护一乡百姓的、德行能投合一个君王心意的、能力能够取得全国信任的，他们看待自己，也像上面说的那只小鸟一样。而宋荣子对这种人加以嘲笑。宋荣子这个人，世上所有的人都称赞他，他并不因此就特别奋勉；世上所有的人都诽谤他，他也并不因此就感到沮丧。他认定了对自己和对外物的分寸，分辨清楚了荣辱的界限，觉得不过如此罢了。对待人世间的一切，他都没有急切地去追求。即使如此，他还是有未达到的境界。列子乘风而行，飘然自得，驾轻就熟。十五天以后返回；对于求福的事，他没有急迫地去追求。这样虽然免了步行，还是有所凭借的。倘若顺应天地万物的本性，驾驭着六气的变化，遨游于无穷的境地，他还要凭借什么呢？

所以说：修养最高的人能任顺自然、忘掉自己，修养达到神化不测境界的人无意于求功，有道德学问的圣人无意于求名。

Excursions Into Freedom❶ (an Excerpt)

By Zhuangzi

Translated by Ernest Richard Hughes

In the Northern Ocean there is a fish, its name the Kun (Leviathan[1]), its size I know not how many li[1]. By metamorphosis[2] it becomes a bird called the P'eng [Roc[3]], with a back I know not how many li in extent. When it rouses itself and flies, its wings darken the sky like clouds. With the sea in motion this bird transports itself to the Southern Ocean, the Lake of Heaven.

In the words of Ch'i Hsieh[4], a recorder of marvels, "When the P'eng transports itself to the Southern Ocean, it thrashes the water for three thousand li, and mounts in a whirlwind to the height of ninety thousand li, and flies continuously for six months before it comes to rest". A mote[5] in a sun-beam (that in one sense is all that this vast Roc is): flying dust which living creatures breathe—in and out! And that blueness of the sky! Is it an actual colour, or is it the measureless depth of the heavens which we gaze at from below and see as "blue," just like that and nothing more?

Again take water, without the dense accumulation of which there is no power for the floating of a great ship. And (think of) a cup of water upset in a corner of the hall. A tiny mustard seed becomes a ship (afloat), but the cup which held the water will remain aground because of the shallowness of the water and the size of the cup as a ship. So with the accumulation of wind,

---

❶《庄子》的英译本很多，此处选取的是英国汉学家 Ernest Richard Hughes（中国名为修中诚，1883—1956）的译本。译文选自《中国古代哲学》（Ernest Richard Hughes. Chinese Philosophy In Classical Times [M]. London: J. M. Dent & Sons Ltd., 1942: 166-168. 段落已根据原文重新划分）

without sufficient density[②] it has no power to float huge wings. Thus it is that the P'eng has to rise ninety thousand li and cut off the wind beneath it. Then and not before, the bird, borne up by the down-pressed wind, floats in the azure heavens with secure support. Then and not before, it can start on its journey south.

A cicada and a young dove giggled together over the P'eng. The cicada said, "When we exert ourselves to fly up on to the tall elms, we sometimes fail to get there and are pulled back to the ground; and that is that. Why then should any one mount up ninety thousand li in order to go south?" Well, the man who goes out to the grassy country near by takes only three meals with him and comes back with his stomach well filled. But the man who has to travel a hundred li grinds flour for one night on the way; and the man who has to travel a thousand li requires food for three months. These two little creatures (the cicada and the dove), what can they know?

Small knowledge is not equal to great knowledge, just as a short life is not equal to a long one. How do we know this to be so? The mushroom with one brief morning's existence has no knowledge of the duration of a month. The chrysalis[6] knows nothing of the spring and the autumn. This is due to their short life. In the south of Ch'u State there is a Ming-ling[7] tree whose springs and autumns make five hundred years. In the old days there was a Ta-ch'un tree whose springs and autumns made eight thousand years. Right down to the present Grandfather P'eng[③][8] is famed for his immense age—although if all man matched him, how wretched they would be!

A variant version of the story of the Leviathan and the Roc is here given[9], winding up with a quail laughing at the P'eng and describing its flight among the bushes as "the perfection of flight". Chuang Chou says that this is due to the difference between small and great. He then continues:

Thus it is that the knowledge of some men qualifies them for a small office and for effecting unity in one district, whilst the moral power of another man fits him to be a ruler and proves itself throughout a whole country. These men have a view of themselves which is like the quail's view of himself. On the other hand, Master Yung of Sung State[10] just laughs at these men. If the whole world should admire or criticize him, he would neither be encouraged nor discouraged. Having determined the difference between what is intrinsic and what extrinsic, he disputed the accepted boundaries of honour and dishonour. In this he was himself, and there are very few such men in the world. Nevertheless he was not really rooted. Take Master Lieh[11]. He could drive the wind as a team and go, borne aloft, away for fifteen days before returning. Such a man attains a happiness which few possess. Yet in this, although he had no need to walk, there was still something on which he was dependent [viz. [12] the wind]. Supposing, however, that he were borne on the normality of the heavens and earth, driving a team of the six elements in their changes, and thus wandered freely in infinity-eternity, would there be anything then on which he was dependent?

Thus it is that I say, "The perfect man has no self, the spirit-endowed man no achievements, the sage no reputation".

译文原注

① Li: the Chinese mile, roughly a third of the English mile.

② "Density" seems the only word to represent the Chinese. This is an admirable example of the realistic way in which a really great poet's imagination works.

③ Grandfather P'eng: the Methuselah of Chinese tradition.

英译注释

1. Leviathan：利维坦，《圣经》中所记载的海洋中最大的生物，是上帝在创世的第六天所造。

2. metamorphosis：变形，通常指动物在形体上出现了生理突变。

3. Roc：大鹏鸟，阿拉伯神话传说中的一种巨型的猛禽，可以猎食大象和其他大型动物。

4. Ch'i Hsieh：《齐谐》，相传是战国时齐国人所著的记载奇闻逸事的书籍，原作今已失传。

5. mote：尘埃，微尘。

6. chrysalis：蛹，茧。原文里的"蟪蛄"指的是寒蝉，春生夏死，夏生秋死。

7. Ming-ling：冥灵，有两种阐释：一种指的是冥海灵龟，另一种认为是树木的名字。该译本采用的是第二种。

8. Grandfather Peng：彭祖，古代传说中最长寿的人，年达八百岁。译者在注释中采用了《圣经·创世记》中最长寿的人物 Methuselah（玛士撒拉），据传享年965岁，后来指代非常高寿的人。

9. 这里译者简化了部分内容，避免重复叙说鲲鹏和鷃雀的故事。

10. Master Yung of Sung State：宋荣子，公元前400至前320年间宋国人，杰出的反战思想家，倡导淡泊名利，上下均平，去除人心的闭塞。

11. Master Lieh：列子，即列御寇，春秋时代郑国思想家，传说能乘风而行。

12. viz.：拉丁语 videlicet 的简写，翻译成英语是 namely，意为"即、就是"。

英译评述

《逍遥游》是中国典籍中的名篇，语言优美，气势雄伟，典故繁多，寓意深远，备受阐释者和译介者青睐。鉴于篇幅所限，本文选取了《逍遥游》的第一部分，也是《庄子》中最脍炙人口的开篇。英国汉学家修中诚所做的翻译，达到了"信、达、雅"三种要求，对原文理解正确，用词到位，忠实而流畅地再现了庄子笔下鲲鹏展翅的气势与内涵，读来如行云流水，毫无滞涩，是《庄子》英译中的上乘之作。

在翻译策略上，他较好地结合了归化和异化两种手法，比如说，他用《圣经》中的利维坦（Leviathan）这一海洋最大生物来指"鲲"，用阿拉伯神话中的猛禽大鹏鸟（Roc）来指"鹏"，让西方读者能立即获取认知，树立了鲜活的形象。在解释"彭祖"这一中国寿星形象时，译者加了注释，用《圣经》中寿命最长的人玛士撒拉（Methuselah）来类比，与西方文化接洽。而对于"里"这个计量距离的单位，译者反而没有将之翻译成 mile 这个西方更好理解的词，而是直译成 li，在译文中加注释来说明 li 是中国的距离单位，大约等于英里的 1/3，以此来保留译文对原作描述习惯的尊重。

在原文出现跳跃性较大的陈述时，译者加了说明，以让读者更好地追随作者的思路，如在第一段"野马也，尘埃也，生物之以息相吹也"之后加了 (that in one sense is all that this vast Roc is)，为读者解释了鲲、鹏相对于天地之大来说，只不过像尘埃一样渺小。这样可以引导读者顺利跨越到庄子对相对而言的思辨中来，使得译文所呈现的庄子思想更有逻辑关系，易于为读者所接受。对于原文中重复述说的部分，译文予以简化，以保全叙事的完整、简洁。

当然，译文也有不尽如人意的地方，主要体现在文化意象的差异上。比如利维坦这一形象在西方文化中是邪恶海怪的代名词，大鹏鸟（Roc）在阿拉伯神话中以善于抓攫巨兽为特征，与我们中国文化中的鲲、鹏概念相去甚远，就像 dragon 和我国的"龙"相比，前者令人可怖，后者令人可敬，不可同日而语。在翻译中国典籍时，译者用归化手法谋求相通形象的同时，还须关注这些形象背后各自的文化含义，必要时辅以注释和说明，考虑文化差异，以免造成误解和过度阐释。

Ⅰ. **Translation Practice.**

Directions：Translate the following into English.

1. 人法地，地法天，天法道，道法自然。（《道德经》第 25 章）

2. 知人者智，自知者明；胜人者有力，自胜者强；知足者富，强行者有志；不失其所者久，死而不亡者寿。（《道德经》第 33 章）

3. 姓朱者学屠龙于支离益，殚千金之家，三年技成，而无所用其巧。《庄子·列御寇》

4. 寿陵余子之学行于邯郸，未得国能，又失其故行矣，直匍匐而归耳。
《庄子·秋水》

Ⅱ. **Translation Comparison.**

Directions: Compare the following Lin Yutang's translation of the second chapter of *Dao De Jing* with James Legge's in terms of interpretation, style, strategy, etc.

原文：天下皆知美之为美，斯恶已；皆知善之为善，斯不善已。有无相生，难易相成，长短相形，高下相盈，音声相和，前后相随。常也。是以圣人处无为之事，行不言之教，万物作而弗始，生而弗有，为而弗恃，功成而弗居。夫唯弗居，是以不去。

Lin Yutang's translation：

When the people of the Earth all know beauty as beauty,

There arises (the recognition of) ugliness.

When the people of the Earth all know the good as good,

There arises (the recognition of) evil.

Therefore：

Being and non-being interdepend in growth；

Difficult and easy interdepend in completion；

Long and short interdepend in contrast；

High and low interdepend in position；

Tones and voice interdepend in harmony；

Front and behind interdepend in company.

Therefore the Sage：

Manages affairs without action；

Preaches the doctrine without words；

All things take their rise, but he does not turn away from them；

He gives them life, but does not take possession of them；

He acts, but does not appropriate；

Accomplishes, but claims no credit.

It is because he lays claim to no credit

That the credit cannot be taken away from him.

Ⅲ. **Oral Presentation**.

Directions：Read the book *Zhuangzi*, select two pieces of fable or story, and present them in class with the help of PPT.

Ⅳ. **Writing Practice**.

Directions：Write an essay of about 200 words, stating your understanding of Daoism and its relationship with Confucianism.

第三章

《史记》选译

导　读

　　《史记》是我国的第一部纪传体通史，分十二本纪、十表、八书、三十世家、七十列传，共约五十二万六千五百字。记载了上自上古传说中的黄帝时代，下至汉武帝元狩元年间共三千多年的历史（涵盖哲学、政治、文学、经济、军事等），由西汉太史公司马迁撰写，又称《太史公书》。此书叙述生动，语言精妙，不仅是史书之典范，也是不朽的文学名著，鲁迅先生赞其为"史家之绝唱，无韵之离骚"。司马迁著述此书的目的是"究天人之际，通古今之变，成一家之言"，他的历史观和价值观深刻影响了中国传统文化的风骨与审美。本章所选的两则传记——卜式和汲黯，典型地体现了《史记》所秉承的个人品行、君王意志、国家利益三者之间的关系。

第一节　《平准书·卜式传》选译

　　《平准书》是《史记》中的八书之一，这八书分别是：礼、乐、律历、天、官、封禅、河渠、平准，记述的是礼乐制度、天文律法、社会经济、河渠地理等诸方面内容。其中《平准书》叙述的是汉武帝时期产生的平准均输政策的由来，介绍自西汉建国以来到汉武帝即位时的经济状况，以推求社会演变和社会风气的变化情形。

　　本篇选自卜式传。卜式本是布衣百姓，不贪财货，勤劳智慧，以牧羊致富。汉武帝时，匈奴屡犯边疆，他上书朝廷，愿以一半家财捐给国家抵御外侮。武帝授他官职，他辞而不受。他又斥巨资救济家乡贫民。朝廷闻其乐善好施，赏以重金，召拜为中郎，布告天下。他把赏金都捐给府库。他虽然身为中郎，仍然穿布衣为皇家牧羊于山中。武帝封其为缑氏县令，以试其治羊之法，因有政绩，又赐爵关内侯。元鼎中，官至御史大夫。后来他因为反对由官府经营盐和铁，又不喜欢作文章，被贬为太子太傅，得养天年。

卜式在《史记》所记录的众多王侯将相、英雄人物中并不算出名的。他的事迹没有列入"世家""列传"这些专门记载重要人物的篇章中，而是出现在以经济为主题的《平准书》中。然而，他却是司马迁所景仰的人之一，因为他不慕名利、忠勇孝悌，安身乡野不忘为国解忧，身居高位不忘布衣本分。这样的品行使得司马迁在《平准书》中详细叙述了卜式的生平。

史记·平准书·卜式传❶（节选）

天子乃思卜式之言，召拜式为中郎[1]，爵左庶长[2]，赐田十顷[3]，布告天下，使明知之。

初，卜式者，河南[4]人也，以田畜为事。亲死，式有少弟，弟壮，式脱身出分[5]，独取畜羊百馀，田宅财物尽予弟。式入山牧十馀岁，羊致千馀头，买田宅。而其弟尽破其业，式辄复分予弟者数矣。

是时汉方数使将击匈奴[6]，卜式上书，原输家之半县官助边。天子使使问式："欲官乎？"

式曰："臣少牧，不习仕宦，不原也。"

使问曰："家岂有冤，欲言事乎？"

---

❶ 司马迁. 史记 [M]. 北京：中华书局，1959：1431–1432. （此版本根据英译本划分了段落）

式曰："臣生与人无分争。式邑人[7]贫者贷之，不善者教顺之，所居人皆从式，式何故见冤於人！无所欲言也。"

使者曰："苟如此，子何欲而然？"

式曰："天子诛匈奴，愚以为贤者宜死节於边，有财者宜输委[8]，如此而匈奴可灭也。"

使者具其言入以闻。天子以语丞相弘[9]。弘曰："此非人情。不轨之臣，不可以为化而乱法，愿陛下勿许。"

於是上久不报式，数岁，乃罢式。式归，复田牧。

岁馀，会军数出，浑邪王[10]等降，县官[11]费众，仓府空。其明年，贫民大徙，皆仰给县官，无以尽赡。卜式持钱二十万予河南守，以给徙民。河南上富人助贫人者籍[12]，天子见卜式名，识之，曰"是固前而欲输其家半助边"，乃赐式外徭四百人[13]。式又尽复予县官。是时富豪皆争匿财，唯式尤欲输之助费。天子於是以式终长者，故尊显以风[14]百姓。

初，式不愿为郎。上曰："吾有羊上林[15]中，欲令子牧之。"式乃拜为郎，布衣屩[16]而牧羊。岁馀，羊肥息。上过见其羊，善之。式曰："非独羊也，治民亦犹是也。以时起居；恶者辄斥去，毋令败群。"上以式为奇，拜为缑氏令[17]试之，缑氏便之。迁为成皋[18]令，将漕最[19]。上以为式朴忠，拜为齐王太傅[20]。

中文注释

[1] 中郎：汉朝武官官衔，主要统领禁宫、皇室的护卫。

[2] 左庶长：秦汉时期的爵位名，在二十等爵位中列第十位。

[3] 顷：古代田地面积计量单位，一顷等于一百亩（1亩等于666.66667平方米）。

[4] 河南：指的是黄河以南，在今天的洛阳附近。

[5] 出分：父子兄弟分配财产，使其自立门户。

[6] 匈奴：古代蒙古大漠和草原上的游牧民族。自汉武帝元光六年（前129）起开始受到汉朝军队的攻击，汉武帝元朔六年（前123）匈奴将主力撤

回漠北地区，至汉武帝元狩四年（前119）匈奴国已经完全退出漠南地区。

[7] 邑（yì）人：指同县之人。

[8] 输委：捐献财物。

[9] 丞相弘：当时任丞相的平津侯公孙弘（前200—前121）。

[10] 浑邪（hún yé）王：浑邪是汉代匈奴的一支。汉武帝元狩二年（前121年），汉大将军霍去病破陇西，俘虏浑邪王子及相国、都尉。匈奴单于欲杀浑邪王，浑邪王和休屠王等遂降汉，武帝封浑邪王万户，为漯［luò］阴侯。

[11] 县官：官府。

[12] 籍：登记的名册。

[13] 赐式外徭四百人：天子赐给卜式对在外服徭役的四百人的处理权。卜式有权免除他们的徭役，当然是有代价的，即需交钱，按当时的规定，每人三百钱，共十二万钱。

[14] 风：通"讽"，用含蓄的方式劝告、教化。

[15] 上林：上林苑，汉武帝刘彻于建元三年（前138）在秦代的一个旧苑址上扩建而成的宫苑，跨长安、咸阳等境，纵横300里，规模宏伟，园林广袤，宫室众多。

[16] 屩（jué）：草鞋。

[17] 缑［gōu］氏令：缑氏的县令。缑氏：县名，在今河南偃师县东南。

[18] 成皋：县名，在今河南荥阳县西北。

[19] 将漕最：让他掌管漕运（利用水道转运粮食供应京城或接济军需），业绩考核为最佳。

[20] 齐王太傅：给齐王当老师。齐王是汉武帝的次子刘闳。

白话译文

皇帝想到卜式说的话，下诏拜卜式为中郎官，赐爵左庶长，赏田十顷，

● 译文参照：刘洪涛.《史记·平准书》译文［EB/OL］.［2015-09-20］http://so.gushiwen.org/guwen/bfanyi_106.aspx.（编者对译文做了修改）

布告天下，让天下人都知道他。

卜式，河南人（黄河以南人），以种田畜牧为生。双亲已故去，仅有年少的弟弟，弟弟成年后，卜式分家出来，自己只带走一百多头羊，把田宅财物全部留给了弟弟。卜式进山牧羊，十多年后，羊达到了一千多头。而他的弟弟却将所有财产都败光了，卜式就又多次分给弟弟一些羊。

那时候汉朝数度对匈奴用兵，卜式上书，愿意捐出一半家财支援边疆。

天子派人问卜式："你想做官吗？"

卜式说："我自小牧羊，不习惯做官，不想做。"

使者说："你家里有冤情，希望申诉出来吗？"

卜式说："我生来跟人没有争斗，同乡的人贫穷，我救济他们；对于不善良的人，我教育他们；去到哪里，人们都顺从我，我又怎么会有冤情呢？"

使者说："那么，你想要什么呢？"

卜式说："皇上讨伐匈奴，我认为贤能的人应该誓死保边，有钱的人应该捐钱助边，这样的话匈奴就可以灭掉了。"

使者把他的话转陈天子，天子向丞相公孙弘说起此事。公孙弘说："这不是人之常情。如果任用不守规矩的子民，会使法令混乱，希望陛下不要允许。"

于是天子许久都没给卜式答复，过了几年，斥退了他。卜式回到故乡，又到田里牧羊了。

一年多后，汉军几次征战，匈奴浑邪王等人投降之后，官府开支很大，国库空虚。又过了一年，贫民大迁徙，所有费用皆由官府支出，朝廷负担不起。卜式又拿了二十万钱给河南太守，用来发给迁徙的民众。河南把帮助贫民的富人名单登记了上报，皇帝看到卜式的名字，说："是以前希望捐出一半家产支援边疆的那个人！"，就下诏赐给卜式对在外服徭役的四百人的处理权。但卜式把这些奖赏全部还给了官府。那时候，富豪都争相把财产藏起来，唯有卜式还想给朝廷捐钱。汉武帝认为他的确具有长者风范，就赐官加爵来使他尊贵显赫，用来激励天下人。

初时，卜式不愿意做官，皇帝说："我在上林苑养有羊群，希望你去帮我放牧。"卜式才做了官，穿着布衣、草鞋就去牧羊。一年多后，羊都很肥美。

皇帝探访他牧羊的地方，对这儿很满意。卜式说："不仅仅是羊，治理人民也是这样。按时起居，把凶恶者赶走，不要让整个群体败坏。"皇帝对他的话很惊奇，想让他试着治理人民，任命他为缑氏县令。缑氏得到了很好的治理。朝廷又让他到成皋任县令，他管理漕运政绩最佳。皇帝由此认为卜式质朴、忠诚，于是任命他为齐王太傅。

Pu Shih❶

Translated by Burton Watson

The emperor, impressed by the words of a man named Pu Shih, summoned him to court and made him a palace attendant, giving him the honorary rank of tso-shu-ch'ang and presenting him with ten ch'ing of land. These rewards were announced throughout the empire so that everyone might know of Pu Shih's example.

Pu Shih was a native of Honan, where his family made a living by farming and animal raising. When his parents died, Pu Shih left home handing over the house, the lands, and all the family wealth to his younger brother, who by this time was full grown. For his own share he took only a hundred or so of the sheep they had been raising, which he led off into the mountains to pasture (放牧). In the course of ten years or so, Pu Shih's sheep had increased to over a thousand and he had bought his own house and fields. His younger brother in the meantime had failed completely in the management of the farm, but Pu Shih promptly handed over to him a share of his own wealth. This happened several times.

---

❶ Ssuma Chi'en. Records of the Grand Historian of China Vol II ［M］. trans. by Burton Watson. New York：Columbia University Press, 1961；//Mark A. Kishlansky, ed. , Sources of World History Volume I ［M］. New York：HarperCollins College Publishers, 1995：88-91.

Just at that time the Han was sending its generals at frequent intervals to attack the Hsiung-nu. Pu Shih journeyed to the capital and submitted a letter to the throne, offering to turn over half of his wealth to the district officials to help in the defense of the border. The emperor dispatched an envoy (使臣) to ask if Pu Shih wanted a post in the government.

"From the time I was a child," Pu Shih replied, "I have been an animal raiser. I have had no experience at government service and would certainly not want such a position."

"Perhaps then your family has suffered some injustice that you would like to report?" inquired the envoy.

But Pu Shih answered, "I have never in my life had a quarrel with anyone. If there are poor men in my village, I lend them what they need, and if there are men who do not behave properly, I guide and counsel them. Where I live, everyone does as I say. Why should I suffer any injustice from others? There is nothing I want to report!"

"If that is the case," said the envoy, "then what is your objective in making this offer?"

Pu Shih replied, "The Son of Heaven has set out to punish the Hsiung-nu. In my humble opinion, every worthy man should be willing to fight to the death to defend the borders, and every person with wealth ought to contribute to the expense. If this were done, then the Hsiung-nu could be wiped out!"

The envoy made a complete record of Pu Shih's words and reported them to the emperor. The emperor discussed the matter with the chancellor (首相) Kung-sun Hung, but the latter said, "The proposal is simply not in accord with human nature! Such eccentric (古怪的) people are of no use in guiding the populace (民众), but only throw the laws into confusion. I beg Your Majesty not to accept his offer!"

For this reason the emperor put off answering Pu Shih for a long time, and finally, after several years had passed, turned down the offer, whereupon Pu Shih went back to his fields and pastures.

A year or so later the armies marched off on several more expeditions, and the Hun-yeh king and his people surrendered to the Han. As a result the expenditures of the district officials increased greatly and the granaries (谷仓) and treasuries were soon empty. The following year a number of poor people were transferred to other regions, all of them depending upon the district officials for their support, and there were not enough supplies to go around. At this point Pu Shih took two hundred thousand cash of his own and turned the sum over to the governor of Ho-nan to assist the people who were emigrating to other regions. A list of the wealthy men of Ho-nan who had contributed to the aid of the poor was sent to the emperor and he recognized Pu Shih's name. "This is the same man who once offered half his wealth to aid in the defense of the border!" he exclaimed, and presented Pu Shih with a sum of money equivalent to the amount necessary to buy off four hundred men from military duty. Pu Shih once more turned the entire sum over to the district officials. At this time the rich families were all scrambling (抢着) to hide their wealth; only Pu Shih, unlike the others, had offered to contribute to the expenses of the government. The emperor decided that Pu Shih was really a man of exceptional (出类拔萃的) worth after all, and therefore bestowed upon him the honors mentioned above in order to hint to the people that they might well follow his example.

At first Pu Shih was unwilling to become a palace attendant, but the emperor told him, "I have some sheep in the Shang-lin Park which I would like you to take care of." Pu Shih then accepted the post of palace attendant and, wearing a coarse robe and straw sandals, went off to tend the sheep. After a year or so, the sheep had grown fat and were reproducing at a fine rate. The emperor, when he visited the park and saw the flocks, commended Pu Shih on his work. "It is not only with sheep," Pu Shih commented. "Gov-

erning people is the same way. Get them up at the right time, let them rest at the right time, and if there are any bad ones, pull them out at once before they have a chance to spoil the flock!"

The emperor, struck by his words, decided to give him a trial as magistrate (行政官) of the district of Kou-shih. When his administration proved beneficial to the people of Kou-shih, the emperor transferred him to the post of magistrate of Ch'eng-kao and put him in charge of the transportation of supplies, where his record was also outstanding. Because of his simple, unspoiled ways and his deep loyalty, the emperor finally appointed him grand tutor to his son Liu Hung, the king of Ch'i.

第二节　《汲郑列传》选译

　　《汲郑列传》位于《史记》第一百二十卷，第六十列传，是西汉两位大臣汲黯与郑庄的合传。列传是我国纪传体史书的体裁之一，司马迁撰《史记》时首创。他在《史记》索引里言道："列传者，谓列叙人臣事迹，令可传于后世。"汲黯与郑庄是与司马迁同时代的名臣。郑庄是汲黯的好友，两人为人处世有相似之处，但郑庄不如汲黯耿直敢言，所以司马迁把他的传记置于汲黯之后，叙述从略。

　　汲黯是太史公笔下首屈一指的忠直之臣。他出身官宦世家，仕途沉浮多年，曾位列九卿。他为人倨傲严正，率性敢言，从不屈从权贵、谄媚主上，以此令朝中上下皆感敬畏。他数次犯颜武帝、斥骂丞相公孙弘和御史大夫张汤，言辞尖锐，不留情面。武帝虽在背后骂他愚直，甚至起过杀心，但又不得不承认他是"社稷之臣"而宽容几分。司马迁怀着极其钦敬的心情为汲黯树碑立传，不多叙政绩，而倾全力表彰他秉正疾恶、忠直敢谏的杰出品格。同时，汲黯多病，又信仰黄老学说，崇尚无为清静，这样的性情并没有使他成为一个无所作为的庸吏，却让他成了所到之处政治清明的贤吏。这和武帝崇尚儒学、重用酷吏、好大喜功、扰乱民生的"多欲"政治正好相反。司马迁在汲黯身上寓托了自己对时政的不平与不忿。清代学者牛运震曾在《史记评注》中评说："汲黯乃太史公最得意之人,故特出色写之。当其时,势焰横赫如田蚡,阿谀固宠怀诈饰智如公孙弘、张汤等,皆太史公所深嫉痛恶而不忍见者,故于灌夫骂坐,汲黯面诋弘、汤之事,皆津津道之,如不容口,此太史公胸中垒块借此一发者也。"太史公在对汲黯品性言行的细致描写中,对权贵与时政做了鲜明而强烈的批判。

汲郑列传❶(节选)

汲黯字长孺,濮阳[1]人也。其先有宠於古之卫君[2]。至黯七世,世为卿大夫。

黯以父任,孝景[3]时为太子洗马[4],以庄见惮[5]。孝景帝崩,太子即位,黯为谒者[6]。

东越[7]相攻,上使黯往视之。不至,至吴而还,报曰:"越人相攻,固其俗然,不足以辱天子之使。"

河内[8]失火,延烧千馀家,上使黯往视之。还报曰:"家人失火,屋比延烧,不足忧也。臣过河南,河南贫人伤水旱万馀家,或父子相食,臣谨以便宜,持节[9]发河南仓粟以振贫民。臣请归节,伏矫制之罪。"

上贤而释之,迁为荥阳[10]令。黯耻为令,病归田里。上闻,乃召拜为中大夫。以数切谏,不得久留内,迁为东海[11]太守。

黯学黄老[12]之言,治官理民,好清静,择丞史而任之。其治,责大

---

❶ 司马迁. 史记 [M]. 北京:中华书局,1959:3105-3107.(此版本根据英译本划分了段落,并根据译本内容做了修订)

指而已，不苛小。黯多病，卧闺阁[13]内不出。岁馀，东海大治。称之。

上闻，召以为主爵都尉，列於九卿[14]。治务在无为而已，弘大体，不拘文法。

黯为人性倨，少礼，面折，不能容人之过。合己者善待之，不合己者不能忍见，士亦以此不附焉。然好学，游侠，任气节，内行脩絜[15]，好直谏，数犯主之颜色，常慕傅柏[16]、袁盎[17]之为人也。……

天子方招文学儒者，上曰吾欲云云，黯对曰："陛下内多欲而外施仁义，奈何欲效唐虞[18]之治乎！"

上默然，怒，变色而罢朝。公卿皆为黯惧。上退，谓左右曰："甚矣，汲黯之戆也！"

群臣或数黯，黯曰："天子置公卿辅弼之臣，宁令从谀承意，陷主於不义乎？且已在其位，纵爱身，奈辱朝廷何！"

上曰："汲黯何如人哉？"庄助[19]曰："使黯任职居官，无以逾人。然至其辅少主，守城深坚，招之不来，麾之不去，虽自谓贲、育[20]亦不能夺之矣。"

上曰："然。古有社稷之臣，至如黯，近之矣。"

中文注释

[1] 濮阳：今河南省濮阳县。

[2] 古之卫君：战国时期的卫国国君。

[3] 孝景：汉景帝刘启的谥号，汉武帝的父亲。

[4] 太子洗马：辅佐太子从事政务、学习文理的官员。洗马可能原作"冼马"，在马前驱使之意。

[5] 以庄见惮：（汲黯）因为为人严肃而使人觉得敬畏。

[6] 谒者：皇帝近侍官，执掌文书。

[7] 东越：族名，古代越人的一支，相传为越王勾践的后裔，秦汉时分布在今浙江省东南部、福建省北部一带。汉武帝元鼎六年（前111）东越王馀善反汉，旋被其部属所杀。部分族人被迫迁入江淮地区。司马迁写有《史

记·东越列传》。

[8]河内：河内郡，郡治在今河南武涉县。

[9]持节：拿着使臣的符节，作为调动地方官员的凭证。

[10]荥阳：今河南省荥阳县，郑州附近的一个县。

[11]东海：东海郡，汉时又称郯郡，其时辖地在今山东省郯城一带，下辖三十七县，跨山东、江苏两省。

[12]黄老：黄老之术，中国战国时的哲学、政治思想流派。尊传说中的黄帝和老子为创始人，故名。黄老之术始于战国，盛于西汉，假托黄帝和老子的思想，实为道家和法家思想相结合，并兼采阴阳、儒、墨等诸家观点而成，讲究无为而治、贵柔守雌。

[13]闺閤：内室。

[14]九卿：亦称九寺大卿，职能相当于后世六部尚书，分为太常、光禄勋、卫尉、太仆、廷尉、大鸿胪、宗正、大司农、少府九大官职。

[15]脩絜（xiū jié）：高尚、纯洁。

[16]傅柏：汉朝梁孝王刘武手下的大将，以正直刚正著称。

[17]袁盎：汉文帝时大臣，敢于犯颜直谏，后因被梁王所派的刺客暗杀而死。

[18]唐虞：唐尧与虞舜的并称，亦指尧与舜的时代，古人以为尧舜时代政治清明，是太平盛世。

[19]庄助：又名严助，西汉中期会稽郡吴县（今江苏省苏州市）人，在汉武帝时任中大夫，其后任会稽太守，后受淮南王刘安造反牵连而被诛。

[20]贲（bēn）、育：战国时勇士孟贲和夏育的并称。

╭┄┄┄┄┄┄┄┄┄┄╮
┆ 白话译文❶ ┆
╰┄┄┄┄┄┄┄┄┄┄╯

汲黯，字长孺，河南濮阳县人。他的祖先曾受先前卫国国君恩宠。到他已是第七代，代代都在朝中荣任卿、大夫之职。

————————————

❶ 史有为.《史记·七十列传·汲郑列传第六十》译注［EB/OL］.［2015-09-28］. http：//www. ziyexing.com/ files-5/shiji/Shiji_120. htm.

汲黯在父亲的保举下，在孝景帝时当了太子洗马。因他为人严正而被人敬畏。景帝死后，太子继位，任命他做谒者之官。

东越人发生攻战，皇上派汲黯前往视察。他未到达东越，行至吴县便折返而归，禀报说："东越人相攻，是由于当地的民俗本来就如此好斗，不值得烦劳天子的使臣去过问。"

河内郡发生了火灾，绵延烧及千余户人家，皇上又派汲黯去视察。他回来报告说："那里普通人家不慎失火，由于住房密集，火势便蔓延开去，不必多忧。我路过河南郡时，眼见当地贫民饱受水旱灾害之苦，灾民多达万余家，有的竟至于父子相食，我就趁便凭所持的符节，下令发放了河南郡官仓的储粮，赈济当地灾民。现在我请求缴还符节，承受假传圣旨的罪责。"

皇上认为汲黯贤良，赦他无罪，贬为荥阳县令。汲黯耻于当县令，便称病辞官还乡。皇上闻讯，召汲黯回朝任中大夫。由于他屡次向皇上直言谏诤，仍不得久留朝中，被外放当了东海郡太守。

汲黯崇仰道家学说，治理官府和处理民事，喜好清静少事，把事情都交托自己挑选出的得力的郡丞和书史去办。他治理郡务，不过是督查下属按大原则行事罢了，并不苛求小节。他体弱多病，经常躺在卧室内休息不出门。一年多的时间，东海郡便十分清明太平，人们都很称赞他。

皇上得知后，召汲黯回京任主爵都尉，比照九卿的待遇。他为政力求无为而治，弘其大要而不拘守法令条文。

汲黯与人相处很傲慢，不讲究礼数，当面顶撞人，容不得别人的过错。与自己心性相投的，他就亲近友善；与自己合不来的，连见面都不耐烦，士人也因此不愿依附他。但是汲黯好学，又好行侠仗义，很注重志气节操。他平日居家，品行美好纯正；入朝，喜欢直言劝谏，屡次触犯皇上的龙颜。他时常仰慕傅柏和袁盎的为人。……

这时皇上正在招揽文学之士和崇奉儒学的儒生，说我想要如何如何，汲黯便答道："陛下心里欲望很多，只在表面上施行仁义，怎么能真正仿效唐尧虞舜的政绩呢！"

皇上沉默不语，心中恼怒，脸一变就罢朝了，公卿大臣都为汲黯惊恐、担心。皇上退朝后，对身边的近臣说："太过分了，汲黯太愚直！"

群臣中有人责怪汲黯，汲黯说："天子设置公卿百官这些辅佐之臣，难道是让他们一味屈从讨好，阿谀奉迎，将君主陷于违背正道的窘境吗？何况我已身居九卿之位，纵然爱惜自己的生命，但要是损害了朝廷大事，那可怎么办！"

皇上问道："汲黯这个人怎么样？"庄助说："让汲黯当官执事，没有过人之处。然而他能辅佐年少的君主，坚守已成的事业，以利诱之他不会来，以威驱之他不会去，即使有人自称像孟贲、夏育一样勇武非常，也不能憾夺他的志节。"

皇上说："是的。古代有所谓安邦保国的忠臣，汲黯跟他们很相似了。"

Chi An❶

Translated by Burton Watson

Chi An, whose polite name was Chi Ch'ang-ju, was a native of P'u-yang. His ancestors won favor with the rulers of the state of Wei and for seven generations, down to the time of Chi An, served without break as high officials.

During the reign of Emperor Ching, Chi An, on the recommendation of his father, was appointed as a mounted guard to the heir apparent（有确定继承权的人）. Because of his stern bearing he was treated with deference. Later, when Emperor Ching passed away and the heir apparent ascended the throne, Chi An was appointed master of guests.

When the tribes of Eastern and Southern Yueh began to attack each other, the emperor dispatched Chi An to go to the area and observe the situation. He did not journey all the way, however, but went only as far as

---

❶ Ssuma Chi'en. Records of the Grand Historian of China Vol Ⅱ ［M］. trans. by Burton Watson. New York：Columbia University Press, 1961；//In Mark A. Kishlansky, ed. Sources of World History Volume I ［M］. New York：HarperCollins College Publishers, 1995：91-93.

Wu and then turned around and came back to the capital to make his report. "The Yueh people have always been in the habit of attacking each other," he said. "There is no reason for the Son of Heaven's envoy to trouble himself about such matters!"

When a great fire broke out in Ho-nei and destroyed over a thousand houses, the emperor once more sent Chi An to observe the situation. On his return he reported, "The roofs of the houses were so close together that the fire spread from one to another; that is why so many homes were burned. It is nothing to worry about. As I passed through Ho-nan on my way, however, I noted that the inhabitants (居民) were very poor, and over ten thousand families had suffered so greatly from floods and droughts that fathers and sons were reduced to eating each other. I therefore took it upon myself to use the imperial seals to open the granaries of Ho-nan and relieve the distress of the people. I herewith return the seals and await punishment for overstepping (僭越) my authority in this fashion."

The emperor, impressed with the wisdom he had shown, overlooked the irregularity of his action and transferred him to the post of governor of Ying-yang. Chi An, however, felt that he was unworthy of a governorship[1] and, pleading illness, retired to his home in the country. When the emperor heard of this, he summoned him to court again and appointed him a palace counselor. But because he sharply criticized the emperor on several occasions, it proved impossible to keep him around the palace for long. The emperor therefore transferred him to the post of governor of Tung-hai.

Chi An studied the doctrines of the Yellow Emperor and Lao Tzu. In executing his duties and governing the people he valued honesty and serenity (安详), selecting worthy assistants and secretaries and leaving them to do as they saw fit. In his administration he demanded only that the general spirit of his directives be carried out and never made a fuss over minor details. He was sick a great deal of the time, confined to his bed and unable to go out, and yet after only a year or so as governor of Tung-hai he had succeeded in setting the affairs of the Province in perfect order and winning the acclaim of the people.

The emperor, hearing of his success, summoned him to court and appointed him master of chief commandant（司令官）, promoting him to one of the nine highest offices in the government. In this post, as well, Chi An emphasized a policy of laissez-faire[2], interpreting his duties very broadly and not bothering with the letter of the law.

Chi An was by nature very haughty and ill-mannered. He could not tolerate the faults of others and would denounce（斥责）people to their faces. Those who took his fancy[3] he treated very well, but those who didn't he could not even bear to see. For this reason most men gave him a wide berth[4]. On the other hand he was fond of learning and liked to travel about doing daring and generous things for others, and his conduct was always above reproach[5]. He was also fond of outspoken criticism and his words frequently brought scowls（怒容）to the emperor's face. His constant ambition was to be as direct and outspoken as the Liang general Fu Po and Emperor Ching's minister Yuan Ang.

The emperor at the time was busy summoning scholars and Confucians to court and telling them, "I want to do thus-and-so. I want to do thus-and-so." Commenting on this, Chi An said to the emperor, "On the surface Your Majesty is practicing benevolence and righteousness, but in your heart you have too many desires. How do you ever expect to imitate the rule of the sage emperors Yao and Shun in this way?"

The emperor sat in silence, his face flushed with anger, and then dismissed the court. The other high officials were all terrified of what would happen to Chi An. After the emperor had left the room, he turned to his at-

tendants and said, "Incredible—the stupidity of that Chi An!"

Later, some of the officials reproached Chi An for his behavior, but he replied, "Since the Son of Heaven has gone to the trouble of appointing us as his officials and aides, what business have we in simply flattering his whims[6] and agreeing with whatever he says, deliberately leading him on to unrighteous deeds? Now that we occupy these posts, no matter how much we may value our own safety, we cannot allow the court to suffer disgrace, can we?"

"What sort of man is Chi An anyway?" the emperor asked, to which Chuang Chu replied, "As long as he is employed in some ordinary post as an official, he will do no better than the average person. But if he were called upon to assist a young ruler or to guard a city against attack, then no temptation could sway him from his duty, no amount of entreaty could make him abandon his post. Even the bravest men of antiquity, Meng Pen and Hsia Yuh could not shake his determination!"

"Yes." said the emperor. "In ancient times there were ministers who were deemed worthy to be called the guardians of the altars[7] of the nation. And men like Chi An come near to deserving the same appellation (称谓)."

英译注释

1. he was unworthy of a governorship：不适合做县令。

2. a policy of laissez-faire：放任自由的政策。laissez-faire：法语词，意为"自由放任主义，无干涉主义"。

3. took his fancy：take one's fancy，引起某人的兴趣。

4. gave him a wide berth：与他保持相当的距离。berth：泊位。

5. above reproach：无可指责。

6. flattering his whims：迎合他（皇帝）的一时冲动。

7. the guardians of the altars：圣坛的护卫者，译者以 altar（圣坛，神坛）来翻译"社稷"一词。"社稷"原是土神和谷神的总称。由于古时的君主为了祈求国事太平，五谷丰登，每年都要到郊外祭祀土地和五谷神。社稷也就成了国家的象征，后来人们就用"社稷"来代表国家。

英译评述

本章所选《史记》的译者 Burton Watson（1925— ），中文名为华兹生。他是美国著名的汉学家，通晓中文和日文，翻译了大量的中国文史哲经典和诗词歌赋，多次获得国际翻译大奖。1956 年，他获得了哥伦比亚大学博士学位，博士论文研究的是太史公司马迁；1961 年，他翻译的《史记》英文版 *Records of the Grand Historian* 正式出版，使得他成为西方汉学届研究司马迁的主要译者和学术权威。

在选材上，华兹生并未翻译《史记》全部的 130 卷，1961 年出版的译本中只选译了 65 卷，翻译的是《史记》中具有重大历史意义和文学性的篇章。作为司马迁的研究者和仰慕者，华兹生非常认同司马迁的历史观和价值观，在英译过程中忠实地再现了《史记》中对人物的生动刻画，把太史公笔下的褒贬毁誉原汁原味地表现在英文译本中。华兹生在选材上更多地体现了司马迁作为一个卓越的文学家的才华、一个爱憎分明的个人主义者的评判，其史料的历史性和学术性并非重点。

本书所选的两篇人物传记——卜式和汲黯，鲜明地体现了译者对司马迁心中所赞赏的人物的认同。卜式和汲黯的出身和性格都截然不同，前者是乡下牧羊人，后者是簪缨世家子；前者淡泊名利、乐善好施，后者看重名位、傲慢无礼。但是两人都有着司马迁所赞赏的个人品质：卜式身在乡野，心系社稷，仗义疏财，主动捐献家产帮助国家抵御外族，且不慕荣利，当官之后保持质朴本色；汲黯坚持真理，直言敢谏，对待权贵绝不奴颜婢膝，即使触怒龙颜也毫不畏惧。华兹生在翻译中一字不漏地描述了这两位的言谈举止、为人处世。

就译者语言来看，华兹生所译《史记》，语言优美，措辞平易，可读性强，具有很高的文学性。他删除了一些人名和细节，使得故事更有可读性。他没有像很多汉学家译者那样，以直译加注释的方式来谨守古文典籍的学术性。华兹生选择的是以简洁的笔调、平实的英文将原文含义生动地展现出来，

不用大词、古词，没有繁复的句型结构，使得读者基本可以做到无障碍阅读。

在翻译一些专有名词时，译者采取了音译和意译相结合的策略。有些不影响理解或者前面篇章里提到的称谓，这里采用音译，如将"爵左庶长"译为 the honorary rank of tso-shu-ch'ang，"田十顷"译为 ten ch'ing of land，"匈奴"译为 the Hsiung-nu，"浑邪王"译为 the Hun-yeh king 等。而那些要体现含义的称谓，则通过意译来阐释，如将"中郎"译为 palace attendant，"天子"译为 The Son of Heaven，"主爵都尉"译为 master of chief commandant。在上下文需要的情况下，译者也会加词予以解释，如在翻译"贲、育"时就加了词，译为 the bravest men of antiquity, Meng Pen and Hsia Yuh（古代最勇敢的人，孟贲和夏育），以便读者直接从译文中得知原文所指。

当然，任何译文都难做到完美无缺，华兹生译《史记》也有值得商榷的地方。比如，译者把"太子洗马"（辅佐太子处理政事、文书的官员）译作 a mounted guard to the heir apparent（太子的骠骑侍卫）；谒者（执掌文书的近侍官）译为 master of guests（接待宾客的主管）就有望文生义之嫌。又如，同为县令之职，卜式任"缑氏县令"，译者译为 magistrate of the district of Kou-shih，汲黯被任命为"荥阳令"，译者译为 governor of Ying-yang，并把下文"黯耻为令"译为 he was unworthy of a governorship，原文意思为 he was ashamed of a county governorship（以做县令为耻），并非如译文所说"认为自己不适合做地方官"，如此等等。这可能是译者在翻译过程中未多方查找、核对研究资料所致。

综上所述，华兹生所译《史记》是典籍英译中的卓越之作，他在选材时抓住了《史记》的核心内容，在翻译风格中采用了贴近司马迁本人叙事风格的生动笔触，用英文再现了太史公的如椽之笔。虽然在字词考证和史料溯源的严谨性方面有所缺憾，但瑕不掩瑜，华兹生英译《史记》可作为典籍英译的范本，无论作为英语学习者的阅读资料，还是翻译学科的教学资源，都有其不可替代的价值。

Ⅰ. **Questions and Answers.**

Directions：Answer the following questions according to the two passages.

1. Why did the emperor's counselor think that Pu Shi was eccentric? What be-

havior did they think reasonable?

2. What were the values that make the shepherd Pu Shi suited to serve as grand tutor to the emperor's son?

3. Why did Chi An not bother to investigate the civil war in Yueh but did bother to distribute grain in Ho-nan?

4. What did Chi An think was the role of a counselor to the emperor?

Ⅱ. **Chinese-English Translation Practice**.

Directions：Translate the following into English.

1. 人固有一死，或重于泰山，或轻于鸿毛，用之所趋异也。

2. 非独羊也，治民亦犹是也。以时起居；恶者辄斥去，毋令败群。

3. 黯学黄老之言，治官理民，好清静，择丞史而任之。

4. 一死一生，乃知交情。一贫一富，乃知交态。一贵一贱，交情乃见。

Ⅲ. **English-Chinese Translation Practice**.

Directions：Translate the following back into Chinese. Find the original Chinese version and compare it with your translation.

The brave man does not always die for honor, while even the coward may fulfill his duty. Each takes a different way to exert himself. Though I might be weak and cowardly and seek shamefully to prolong my life, yet I know full well the difference between what ought to be followed and what rejected. How could I bring myself to sink into the shame of ropes and bonds if even the lowest slave and scullery maid can bear to commit suicide, why should not one like myself be able to do what has to be done? But the reason I have not refused to bear these ills and have continued to live, dwelling among this filth, is that I believe that I have things in my heart that I have not been able to express fully, and I am ashamed to think that after I am gone my writings will not be known to posterity.

I too have ventured not to be modest but have entrusted myself to my useless writings. I have gathered up and brought together the old traditions of the world which were scattered and lost. I have examined the deeds and events of the past and investigated the principles behind their success and failure, their rise and decay, in one hundred and thirty chapters. I wished to examine into all that concerns heaven

and man, to penetrate the changes of the past and present, completing all the work of one family. But before I had finished my rough manuscript, I met with this calamity. It is because I regretted that it had not been completed that I submitted to the extreme penalty without rancor. When I have truly completed this work, I shall deposit it in some safe place. If it may be handed down to men who will appreciate it and penetrate to the villages and great cities, then though I should suffer a thousand mutilations, what regret would I have? (excerpted from Sima Qian, "Letter to Ren An")

Ⅳ. **Oral Presentation.**

Directions: Read the *Records of Grand Historian*, select a historical figure or an important event, and present it in class with the help of PPT.

中篇

小说

第一章

唐传奇

导 读

唐传奇指唐代的文言短篇小说，是在六朝志怪小说的基础上发展起来的，其中不乏神灵鬼怪之说；除此之外，还有大量故事描写人情冷暖、世间百态，是了解唐代生活状态的宝贵资料。

鲁迅称唐传奇"叙述宛转，文辞华艳"，其故事情节往往一波三折，引人入胜，部分作品还塑造了鲜明生动的人物形象。唐传奇的出现，标志着中国古代短篇小说趋于成熟，对后代小说、戏曲及讲唱文学有较大的影响。主要代表作有元稹的《莺莺传》、白行简的《李娃传》、李公佐的《南柯太守传》、李朝威的《柳毅传》等。

第一节 《莺莺传》选译

元稹（779—831），字微之，别字威明，唐洛阳人（今河南洛阳），为北魏宗室鲜卑族拓跋氏后裔；唐朝著名诗人、宰相，与白居易共同倡导"新乐府运动"，被后世称为"元白"，诗作号为"元白体"。元稹虽自幼丧父，却早知发愤，一举及第。因触犯宦官权贵曾被贬参军，然苦心为文，诗文创作广受好评。代表诗作有《菊花》《离思五首》《遣悲怀三首》《菟丝》《莺莺传》等，语言优美，生动自然，表现出其细腻丰富的情感归属与寄托。

《莺莺传》，又名《会真记》，元曲《西厢记》也是由此改编而来。此传讲述了贫寒书生张生对没落士族之女崔莺莺始乱终弃的爱情悲剧故事，成功地塑造了崔莺莺这样一个单纯、善良、执着追求爱情却被封建闺训所束缚的经典形象，充分反映了历史上无数女性受封建礼教束缚而遭遇抛弃、讽刺的悲惨命运。而对张生负心薄幸的主观辩护为后世提供了创作动力，对戏曲创作影响深远。关于现实世界的描写在唐传奇的发展过程中具有里程碑意义，影响巨大，广为流传。

莺莺传❶（节选）

元稹

崔之婢曰红娘。生私为之礼者数四，乘间遂道其衷。婢果惊沮，腆然而奔。张生悔之。翼日，婢复至。张生乃羞而谢之，不复云所求矣。婢因谓张曰："郎之言，所不敢言，亦不敢泄。然而崔之姻族，君所详也。何不因其德而求娶焉？"张曰："余始自孩提，性不苟合。或时纨绮间居，曾莫流盼。不为当年，终有所蔽。昨日一席间，几不自持。数日来，行忘止，食忘饱，恐不能逾旦暮，若因媒氏而娶，纳采问名，则三数月间，索我于枯鱼之肆[1]矣。尔其谓何？"婢曰："崔之贞慎自保，虽所尊不可以非语犯之。下人之谋，固难入矣。然而善属文，往往沉吟章句，怨慕者久之。君试为喻情诗以乱之。不然，则无由也。"张大喜，立缀《春词》二首以授之。是夕，红娘复至，持彩笺以授张，曰："崔所命也。"题其篇曰《明月三五夜》。其词曰："待月西厢下，迎风户半开。拂墙花影动，疑是

---

❶ 元稹，等. 唐宋传奇［M］. 北京：华夏出版社，2015：100 - 103.

玉人来。"张亦微喻其旨。是夕，岁二月旬有四日矣。崔之东有杏花一株，攀援可逾。既望之夕，张因梯其树而逾焉。达于西厢，则户半开矣。红娘寝于床，生因惊之。红娘骇曰："郎何以至？"张因绐[2]之曰："崔氏之笺召我也，尔为我告之。"无几，红娘复来，连曰："至矣！至矣！"张生且喜且骇，必谓获济。及崔至，则端服严容，大数张曰："兄之恩，活我之家，厚矣。是以慈母以弱子幼女见托。奈何因不令之婢，致淫逸之词。始以护人之乱为义，而终掠乱以求之。是以乱易乱，其去几何？诚欲寝[3]其词，则保人之奸，不义；明之于母，则背人之惠，不祥。将寄与婢仆，又惧不得发其真诚。是用托短章，愿自陈启。犹惧兄之见难，是用鄙靡[4]之词，以求其必至。非礼之动，能不愧心。特愿以礼自持，毋及于乱！"言毕，翻然而逝。张自失者久之，复逾而出，于是绝望。数夕，张生临轩独寝，忽有人觉之。惊骇而起，则红娘敛衾携枕而至，抚张曰："至矣至矣！睡何为哉！"并枕重衾而去。张生拭目危坐久之，犹疑梦寐。然而修谨以俟。俄而红娘捧崔氏而至。至，则娇羞融冶，力不能运支体，曩[5]时端庄，不复同矣。是夕，旬有八日也。斜月晶莹，幽辉半床。张生飘飘然，且疑神仙之徒，不谓从人间至矣。有顷，寺钟鸣，天将晓。红娘促去。崔氏娇啼宛转，红娘又捧之而去，终夕无一言。张生辨色而兴，自疑曰："岂其梦邪？"及明，睹妆在臂，香在衣，泪光荧荧然，犹莹于茵席而已。是后又十余日，杳不复知。张生赋《会真诗》三十韵，未毕，而红娘适至，因授之，以贻崔氏。自是复容之。朝隐而出，暮隐而入，同安于曩所谓西厢者，几一月矣。张生常诘郑氏之情。则曰："我不可奈何矣。"因欲就成之。无何，张生将之长安，先以情喻之。崔氏宛无难词，然而愁怨之容动人矣。将行之再夕，不可复见，而张生遂西下。数月，复游于蒲，会于崔氏者又累月。崔氏甚工刀札[6]，善属文。求索再二，终不可见。往往张生自以文挑，亦不甚睹览。大略崔之出人者，艺必穷极，而貌若不知；言则敏辨，而寡于酬对。待张之意甚厚，然未尝以词继之。时愁艳幽邃，恒若不识，喜愠之容，亦罕形见。异时独夜操琴，愁弄[7]凄恻。张窃听之。求之，则终不复鼓矣。以是愈惑之。张生俄以文调[8]及期，又当西去。当去之夕，不复自言其情，愁叹于崔氏之侧。崔已阴知将诀矣，恭貌怡声，徐谓张曰："始乱之，终弃之，固其宜矣。愚不敢恨。必也君乱之，君终之，君之惠也。则没身之誓，其有终矣。又何必深感于此行？然而君既不怿，无以奉宁。君常谓我善鼓琴，向时羞颜，所不能及。今且往矣，既君此诚。"因命拂琴，鼓《霓裳羽衣》序，不数声，哀音怨乱，不复知其是曲也。左右皆歔欷[9]。崔亦遽止之，投琴，泣下流连，趋归郑所，遂不复至。明旦而张行。明年，文战不胜，张遂止于京，因贻书于崔，以广其意。崔氏缄[10]报之词，粗载于此。曰："捧览来问，抚爱过深。儿女之情，悲喜交集。兼惠花胜[11]一合，口脂五寸，致耀首膏唇之饰。虽荷殊恩，谁复为容？睹物增怀，但积悲叹耳。伏承使于京中就业，进修之道，固在便安。但恨僻陋之人，永以遐弃。命也如此，知复何言！自去秋已来，常忽忽如有所失。于喧哗之下，或勉为语笑，闲宵自处，无不泪零。乃至梦寐之间，亦多感咽，离忧之思，绸缪缱绻[12]，暂若寻常，幽会未终，惊魂已断。虽半衾如暖，而思之甚遥。一昨拜辞，倏逾旧岁。长安行乐之地，触绪牵情。何幸不忘幽微，眷念无斁[13]。鄙薄之志，无以奉酬。至于终始之盟，则固不忒[14]。鄙昔中表[15]相因，或同宴处，婢仆见诱，遂致私诚。儿女之心，不能自固。君子有抚琴之挑[16]，鄙人无投梭之拒[17]。及荐寝席，义盛意深。愚陋之情，永谓终托。岂期既见君子，而不能定情。致有自献之羞，不复明侍巾帻[18]。没身永恨，含叹何言！倘仁人用心，俯遂幽眇，虽死之日，犹生之年。如或达士略情[19]，舍小从大，以先配为丑行，以要盟为可欺。则当骨化形销，丹诚不泯，因风委露，犹托清尘。存没之诚，言尽于此。临纸呜咽，情不能申。千万珍重，珍重千万！玉环一枚，是儿婴年所弄，寄充君子下体所佩。玉取其坚润不渝，环取其终始不绝。兼乱丝一絇[20]，文竹茶碾子一枚。此数物不足见珍。意者欲君子如玉之真，弊志如环不解。泪痕在竹，愁绪萦丝。因物达情，永以为好耳。心迹身遐，拜会无期。幽愤所钟，千里神合。千万珍重！春风多厉，强饭为嘉。慎言自保，无以鄙为深念。"

中文注释

[1] 枯鱼之肆：卖干鱼的店铺，比喻无法挽救的绝境。

[2] 绐（dài）：欺骗；哄骗。

[3] 寝：停止，平息。

[4] 鄙靡（bǐ mí）：鄙俚柔弱。

[5] 曩（nǎng）：以往，从前，过去的。

[6] 刀札（zhá）：书写。

[7] 弄：奏乐或乐曲的一段、一章，如梅花三弄。

[8] 文调：举人赴京应试。

[9] 歔欷（xū xī）：悲泣；抽噎；叹息。

[10] 缄（jiān）：书信。

[11] 花胜：古代妇女的一种首饰，以剪彩为之。

[12] 绸缪（chóu móu）：缠绵，情意深厚。缱绻：（qiǎn quǎn）情意深笃，难以分舍。

[13] 斁（yì）：厌倦；懈怠；厌弃。

[14] 不忒（tè）：没有变更；没有差错。

[15] 中表：指与祖父、父亲的姐妹的子女的亲戚关系，或与祖母、母亲的兄弟姐妹的子女的亲戚关系。

[16] 抚琴之挑：据《史记·司马相如列传》记载，司马相如在卓府做客，弹唱了一曲《凤求凰》，挑动了卓文君的心弦，乃与其私奔。

[17] 投梭之拒：据《晋书·谢鲲传》，"邻家高氏女有美色，鲲尝挑之，女投梭，折其两齿"。后以"投梭折齿"为女子拒绝调戏的典故。

[18] 巾帻（zé）：古代的头巾。

[19] 略情：把事情看得很随便。

[20] 絇（qú）：古代量词，丝是五两为一絇。

中文译本

　　崔氏女的丫鬟叫红娘，张生私下里多次向她作揖行礼，趁机道出了自己的心事。丫鬟果然吓坏了，红着脸跑了，张生很后悔。第二天，丫鬟又来了，张生羞愧地道歉，不再提所求之事。丫鬟于是对张生说："你的话，我不敢转达，也不敢泄露，然而崔家的内外亲戚你是了解的，何不凭着你有恩于她家而向他们求婚呢？"张生说："我从孩童时候起，生性就不愿随便附合与人结交。有时和身着华服的女子一处，也不曾侧目顾盼。当年不肯做的事，如今终于还是被迷住。昨天在宴席间，我几乎不能控制自己。这些天来，走路忘了要到哪里停下来，吃饭也感觉不出是否吃饱，恐怕性命朝夕难保。如果让媒人去提亲，又要'纳采'，又要'问名'，少说也得三四个月，那时我恐怕已不在人世了。你告诉我该怎么办呢？"丫鬟说："崔小姐洁身自好，谨言慎行，很注意保护自己的名节，即使是她所尊敬的人也不能用非礼之辞冒犯她。下人的主意实在难使她接受。然而她很会写文章，常常低声吟诵诗句，久久地陷入爱恨情思之中。您可以试着写些情诗来挑动她的心思，否则，是没有别的办法了。"张生非常高兴，马上作《春词》两首，交给了红娘。当天晚上，红娘又来了，拿着彩色信纸交给张生说："这是崔小姐命我交给你的。"那篇诗的题目是《明月三五夜》，诗文写道：

"待月西厢下，迎风户半开。拂墙花影动，疑是玉人来。"

张生也略微明白了诗的含义，当天晚上是二月十四日。

崔莺莺厢房的东面有一棵杏花树，攀上它可以越过墙头。阴历十六晚上，张生以那棵树作梯子爬过墙去到了西厢房，门果然半开着。红娘躺在床上，于是张生唤醒红娘。红娘大吃一惊，问："你怎么来了？"张生骗她说："崔小姐的信中召我来的，你替我通报一下。"不一会儿，红娘回来了，连声说："来了！来了！"张生又高兴又害怕，以为一定会成功。等到崔小姐到了，只见她穿戴整齐，表情严肃，大声数落张生说："兄长救了我们全家，这是大恩大德，因此我的母亲才会把幼弱的子女托付给你，可你为什么叫不懂事的丫鬟，送来了淫秽诗词？你起初保护别人免受兵乱，这是义，可最终却乘危要挟索取，这是以淫乱代替暴乱，二者有几分差别呢？实在是想要把这淫诗压下不提，可这是包庇奸邪之行，不符合道义；若向母亲说明此事，就辜负了你的恩情，不吉祥；想让婢女转告又怕不能表达我的真实心意。因此借用短小的诗章，想要亲自来说明白，又怕兄长难堪，所以写了首鄙薄的诗，希望你一定会来到。如果做了不合乎礼的举动，难道能不问心有愧吗？我只希望你用礼约束自己，不要陷入淫乱之中。"说完，转身就走了。张生愣了老半天，怅然若失，只好又翻墙而出，彻底绝望。

一连几个晚上，张生都临窗而睡。忽然有人叫醒了他，张生惊恐地坐了起来，原来是红娘抱着被子带着枕头来了，安慰张生说："来了！来了！还睡什么？"把枕头和被子并排放置好就走了。张生揉了揉眼睛，端正地坐了半天，还疑心是在做梦，但是还是恭恭敬敬地等待着。不一会儿，红娘就扶着崔莺莺来了。来了后崔莺莺显得娇美羞涩、温和美丽，好像没有力气支持自己的肢体，跟从前的端庄完全不一样。那晚是十八日，皎洁的月亮斜挂天边，幽幽的月光撒满了半床。张生不禁飘飘然，简直疑心是神仙下凡，不觉得是从人间来的。过了一段时间，寺里的钟响了，天快亮了。红娘催促离开，崔小姐娇滴滴地低声哭泣，红娘又扶着她走了。整个晚上莺莺没说一句话。张生看到天蒙蒙亮时就起床了，心下怀疑，说："难道这是做梦吗？"等到天亮了，看到脂粉的痕迹还留在手臂上，衣服上还留有香气，亮晶晶的泪珠还在草席上微微闪光。

这以后又过了十几天，莺莺又杳无音信。张生作《会真诗》三十韵，还没作完，红娘正巧来了，于是交给了她，让她送给崔莺莺。从此莺莺又同意与他幽会了，晚上悄悄地进来，早上悄悄地离开，一块儿安寝在以前叫作"西厢"的地方，差不多有一个月的时间。张生常追问郑姨的态度，莺莺就说："我已经没有办法了，就这样吧。"不久，张生将去长安，先把情况告诉了崔莺莺。崔莺莺似乎没有怨言，然而忧愁、哀怨的表情令人动心。临行前的两个晚上，没有再见面。张生于是向西出发了。过了几个月，张生又来到蒲州，跟崔莺莺又相聚了几个月。崔莺莺字写得很好，还善于写文章，张生再三向她央求，但始终没见到她的字和文章。张生常常自己写文章挑逗，莺莺也不怎么看。大概崔莺莺的过人之处在于技艺达到了极高的程度，而表面上好像不懂；说话机敏善辩，却很少对答；对张生情深意厚，然而却从不用语言表达出来；美丽的面容常常带着深深的忧愁之色，却好像浑然不知的样子；喜怒之情，很少流露于外。有一天夜晚，独自弹琴，曲调哀怨凄恻动人。张生偷偷地听到了，请求她再弹奏一次，却始终没再弹奏过。因此张生更猜不透她的心事。

　　不久到了张生赴京赶考的日子，又当西行了。临走的晚上，张生不再诉说自己的心情，而在崔莺莺面前忧愁喟叹。崔莺莺暗自明白将要分别了，因而神情恭敬，声音柔和，慢慢地对张生说："你一开始挑逗玩弄，最后却抛弃我，本是自然，我不敢怨恨。假若你玩弄了我，又最终娶我，那是你的恩惠。就算是白首偕老的誓言，也有到头的时候，你又何必对这次的离去有这么多感触呢？然而你既然不高兴，我也没有什么安慰你的。你曾说我擅长弹琴，那时候害羞，没能给你弹。现在你要走了，就让我满足了你的心愿吧。"于是她开始弹琴，弹的是《霓裳羽衣曲序》，还没弹几声，琴声哀怨混乱，听不出弹的是什么曲子了。身边的人听了都悲泣，崔莺莺便突然停止演奏，扔下琴，泪流满面，急步回到了母亲的屋里，再也没有出来。第二天早上张生出发了。

　　第二年，考试不中，张生便留在了京城。于是给莺莺写了一封信，宽慰她的心。崔莺莺的回信，大致地记载于此，信中说：

　　"捧读来信，抚爱之意极为深厚。儿女之情的流露，使我悲喜交集。又送我一盒头饰，五寸唇膏，这些都是使头发增彩，使嘴唇润泽的。虽然承受特殊的恩惠，但打扮了又给谁看呢？看到这些东西更增加了想念，只会使悲伤叹息越来越多罢了。你既选择了到京城参加考试而进身的途径，研修学问之道，就应该安下心来。只遗憾粗鄙、浅陋的我，因为路远而与你离弃。是我的命该如此，还能说什么呢？自去年秋天以来，常常恍恍惚惚，若有所失。在喧闹的场合，有时勉强说笑，而夜深人静独处之时，无时无刻不双泪涟涟。甚至在睡梦当中，也常感叹呜咽。想到离别的忧愁，又情思缠绵、情深意浓，一时间仿佛又回到从前。秘密相会没有结束，却梦醒惊魂散。虽然半边的被衾余温犹在，可思念是那么遥远。昨天才分别，可是转眼就过去一年了。长安是个行乐的地方，触景生情，你还想着我这个微不足道的人，眷恋之情从未倦怠，我是何其有幸啊！我浅薄的心意，无法报答你。至于我们的山盟海誓，我从来没有改变。我从前跟你以表亲关系相接触，有时同桌吃饭。是婢女引诱我，于是就私下里付出一片痴心。青春男女的心思不能自我控制，你像司马相如弹琴挑逗卓文君那样来挑逗我，我却未能像高氏之女投梭拒绝谢鲲那样拒绝您。等到与你同衾共枕，情深义浓，我浅薄的心认为可以终生相托。哪里想到见了你以后，却不能缔结良缘！以至于我投怀送抱，并以此为羞耻，从而不能光明正大地侍奉你啦。这是毕生的遗憾，我只能心中叹息，还能说什么呢？如果仁义的人肯尽心尽力，能成就我卑微的心愿，那么即使我死了，也会像活着一样。如果旷达的人不屑私情，忽略小节追求大业，把先前的情分看成丑行，认为诱迫的誓盟是可以不用遵守，那么我将骨毁形销，但一片赤诚永不泯灭。凭着风，借着露，拜托清尘捎去我的诚心。生死至诚，全表达在这信上面了。面对信纸我泣不成声，感情也觉得抒发不出来。只是希望你千万保重，千万保重。玉环一枚是我儿时玩过的，寄给你佩带于腰间。'玉'表示坚固润泽不改变，'环'表示始终不断，加上乱丝一束、斑竹茶碾子一枚。这几个物件都不是什么珍贵的东西，取其用意，希望你如玉一般坚贞，而我的心意如环般永不改变。相思的泪痕落到了竹子上，愁思别绪像乱丝般剪不断理还乱。借物表达情意，永远相爱。心近身远，相会无期。幽恨凝聚，神驰千里与君相会。千万珍重。春风凌厉，你一定要好好吃饭，千万要爱惜自己，不要以我为念。"

The Story Of Ts'ui Ying-Ying[1] (An Excerpt)

By Yüan Chen

Translated by Arthur Waley

Ying-ying had a maid-servant called Hung-niang, whom Chang sometimes met and greeted. Once he stopped her and was beginning to tell her of his love for her mistress; but she was frightened and ran away. Then Chang was sorry he had not kept silence. Next day he met Hung-niang again, but was ashamed and did not say what was in his mind. But this time the maid herself broached the subject and said to Chang, "Master, I dare not tell her

[1]　译文选自著名英国汉学家和文学翻译家亚瑟·威利（Arthur Waley, 1888—1966）的《再译自中国人》（Arthur Waley. More Translations from the Chinese [M]. New York: Alfred A. Knopf, 1919）。

what you told me, or even hint at it. But since your mother was a kinswom-an[1] of the Ts'uis, why do you not seek my mistress's hand on that plea?"

Chang said, "Since I was a child in arms, my nature has been averse to intimacy. Sometimes I have idled with wearers of silk and gauze, but my fancy was never once detained. I little thought that in the end I should be en-trapped. Lately at the banquet I could scarcely contain myself; and since then, when I walk, I forget where I am going and when I eat, I forget to finish my meal, and do not know how to endure the hours from dawn to dusk. If we were to get married through a matchmaker and perform the ceremonies of Sending Presents and Asking Names[2], it would take many months, and by that time you would have to look for me 'in the dried-fish shop[3]'. What is the use of giving me such advice as that?"

The maid replied, "My mistress clings steadfastly to her chastity, and e-ven an equal could not trip her with lewd talk. Much less may she be won through the stratagems of a maid-servant. But she is skilled in composition, and often, when she has made a poem or essay, she is restless and dissatis-fied for a long while after. You must try to provoke her by a love-poem. There is no other way."

Chang was delighted and at once composed two Spring Poems to send her. Hung-niang took them away and came back the same evening with a coloured tablet, which she gave to Chang, saying, "This is from my mistress." It bore the title "The Bright Moon of the Fifteenth Night." The words ran:

"To wait for the moon I am sitting in the western parlour[4]; To greet the wind, I have left the door ajar.

When a flower's shadow stirred and brushed the wall. For a moment I thought it the shadow of a lover coming."

Chang could not doubt her meaning. That night was the fourth after the first decade of the second month. Beside the eastern wall of Ts'ui's apartments there grew an apricot-tree; by climbing it one could cross the wall. On the next night (which was the night of the full moon) Chang used the tree as a ladder and crossed the wall. He went straight to the western parlour and found the door ajar. Hung-niang lay asleep on the bed. He woke her, and she cried in a voice of astonishment, "Master Chang, what are you doing here?" Chang answered, half-truly: "Ts'ui's letter invited me. Tell her I have come. " Hung-niang soon returned, whispering, "She is coming, she is coming. " Chang was both delighted and surprised, thinking that his salvation was indeed at hand.

At last Ts'ui entered.

Her dress was sober and correct, and her face was stern. She at once began to reprimand Chang, saying, "I am grateful for the service which you rendered to my family. You gave support to my dear mother when she was at a loss how to save her little boy and young daughter. How came you to send me a wicked message by the hand of a low maid-servant? In protecting me from the license of others, you acted nobly. But now that you wish to make me a partner to your own licentious desires, you are asking me to accept one wrong in exchange for another. How was I to repel this advance? I would gladly have hidden your letter, but it would have been immoral to harbour a record of illicit proposals. Had I shown it to my mother, I should ill have requited the debt we owe you. Were I to entrust a message of refusal to a servant or concubine, I feared it might not be truly delivered. I thought of writing a letter to tell you what I felt; but I was afraid I might not be able to make you understand. So I sent those trivial verses, that I might be sure of your coming. I have no cause to be ashamed of an irregularity which had no other object but the preservation of my chastity. " With these words she vanished. Chang remained for a long while petrified with astonishment. At last he climbed back over the wall and went home in despair.

Several nights after this he was lying asleep near the verandah, when

someone suddenly woke him. He rose with a startled sigh and found that Hung-niang was there, with bedclothes under her arm and a pillow in her hand. She shook Chang, saying, "She is coming, she is coming. Why are you asleep?" Then she arranged the bedclothes and pillow and went away.

Chang sat up and rubbed his eyes. For a long while he thought he must be dreaming, but he assumed a respectful attitude and waited.

Suddenly Hung-niang came back, bringing her mistress with her. Ts'ui, this time, was languid and flushed, yielding and wanton in her air, as though her strength could scarcely support her limbs. Her former severity had utterly disappeared.

That night was the eighth of the second decade. The crystal beams of the sinking moon twinkled secretly across their bed. Chang, in a strange exaltation, half-believed that a fairy had come to him, and not a child of mortal men.

At last the temple bell sounded, dawn glimmered in the sky and Hung-niang came back to fetch her mistress away. Ts'ui turned on her side with a pretty cry, and followed her maid to the door.

The whole night she had not spoken a word.

Chang rose when it was half-dark, still thinking that perhaps it had been a dream. But when it grew light, he saw her powder on his arm and smelt her perfume in his clothes. A tear she had shed still glittered on the mattress.

For more than ten days afterwards he did not see her again. During this time he began to make a poem called "Meeting a Fairy[5]", in thirty couplets. It was not yet finished, when he chanced to meet Hung-niang in the road. He asked her to take the poem to Ts'ui.

After this, Ts'ui let him come to her, and for a month or more he crept out at dawn and in at dusk, the two of them living together in that western parlour of which I spoke before.

Chang often asked her what her mother thought of him. Ts'ui said, "I know she would not oppose my will. So why should we not get married at once?"

Soon afterwards, Chang had to go to the capital. Before starting, he tenderly informed her of his departure. She did not reproach him, but her face showed pitiable distress. On the night before he started, he was not able to see her.

After spending a few months in the west, Chang returned to Puchow and again lodged for several months in the same building as the Ts'uis. He made many attempts to see Ying-ying alone, but she would not let him do so. Remembering that she was fond of calligraphy and verse, he frequently sent her his own compositions, but she scarcely glanced at them.

It was characteristic of her that when any situation was at its acutest point, she appeared quite unconscious of it. She talked glibly, but would seldom answer a question. She expected absolute devotion, but herself gave no encouragement.

Sometimes when she was in the depth of despair, she would affect all the while to be quite indifferent. It was rarely possible to know from her face whether she was pleased or sorry.

One night Chang came upon her unawares when she was playing on the harp, with a touch full of passion. But when she saw him coming, she stopped playing. This incident increased his infatuation.

Soon afterwards, it became time for him to compete in the Literary Examinations, and he was obliged once more to set out for the western capital.

The evening before his departure, he sat in deep despondency by Ts'ui's side, but did not try again to tell her of his love. Nor had he told her that he was going away, but she seemed to have guessed it, and with submissive face and gentle voice, she said to him softly: "Those whom a man leads astray, he will in the end abandon. It must be so, and I will not reproach you. You

deigned to corrupt me and now you deign to leave me. That is all. And your vows of 'faithfulness till death⁶'— they too are cancelled. There is no need for you to grieve at this parting, but since I see you so sad and can give you no other comfort—you once praised my harp-playing; but I was bashful and would not play to you. Now I am bolder, and if you choose, I will play you a tune."

She took her harp and began the prelude to "Rainbow Skirts and Feather Jackets①⁷." But after a few bars the tune broke off into a wild and passionate dirge.

All who were present caught their breath; but in a moment she stopped playing, threw down her harp and weeping bitterly, ran to her mother's room.

She did not come back.

Next morning Chang left. The following year he failed in his examinations and could not leave the capital. So, to unburden her heart, he wrote a letter to Ts'ui. She answered him somewhat in this fashion: "I have read your letter and cherish it dearly. It has filled my heart half with sorrow, half with joy. You sent with it a box of garlands⁸ and five sticks of paste⁹, that I may decorate my head and colour my lips.

I thank you for your presents; but there is no one now to care how I look. Seeing these things only makes me think of you and grieve more.

You say that you are prospering in your career at the capital, and I am comforted by that news. But it makes me fear you will never come back again to one who is so distant and humble. But that is settled forever, and it is no use talking of it.

Since last autumn I have lived in a dazed stupor. Amid the clamour of the daytime, I have sometimes forced myself to laugh and talk; but alone at night I have done nothing but weep. Or, if I have fallen asleep my dreams have always been full of the sorrows of parting. Often I dreamt that you came to me as you used to do, but always before the moment of our joy your phantom[10] vanished from my side. Yet, though we are still bedfellows in my dreams, when I wake and think of it the time when we were together seems very far off. For since we parted, the old year has slipped away and a new year has begun. . . . Ch'ang-an[11] is a city of pleasure, where there are many snares to catch a young man's heart. How can I hope that you will not forget one so sequestered and insignificant as I? And indeed, if you were to be faithful, so worthless a creature could never requite you. But our vows of unending love—those I at least can fulfill.

Because you are my cousin, I met you at the feast. Lured by a maidservant, I visited you in private. A girl's heart is not in her own keeping. You tempted me by your ballads[②12], and I could not bring myself to 'throw the shuttle[③13] '.

Then came the sharing of pillow and mat, the time of perfect loyalty and deepest tenderness. And I, being young and foolish, thought it would never end.

Now, having 'seen my Prince[④14] ', I cannot love again; nor, branded by the shame of self-surrender, am I fit to perform 'the service of towel and comb[⑤15] '; and of the bitterness of the long celibacy which awaits me, what need is there to speak?

The good man uses his heart; and if by chance his gaze has fallen on the humble and insignificant, till the day of his death, he continues the affections of his life. The cynic[16] cares nothing for people's feelings. He will discard the small to follow the great, look upon a former mistress merely as an accomplice in sin, and hold that the most solemn vows are made only to be broken. He will reverse all natural laws as though Nature should suddenly let bone dissolve, while cinnabar[17] resisted the fire. The dew that the wind has shaken from the tree still looks for kindness from the dust; and such, too, is the sum of my hopes and fears.

As I write, I am shaken by sobs and cannot tell you all that is in my

heart. My darling, I am sending you a jade ring that I used to play with when I was a child. I want you to wear it at your girdle, that you may become firm and flawless as this jade, and, in your affections, unbroken as the circuit of this ring.

And with it I am sending a skein of thread and a tea-trough of flecked bamboo. There is no value in these few things. I send them only to remind you to keep your heart pure as jade and your affection unending as this round ring. The bamboo is mottled as if with tears, and the thread is tangled as the thoughts of those who are in sorrow. By these tokens I seek no more than that, knowing the truth, you may think kindly of me forever. Our hearts are very near, but our bodies are far apart. There is no time fixed for our meeting; yet a secret longing can unite souls that are separated by a thousand miles.

Protect yourself against the cold spring wind, eat well—look after yourself in all ways and do not worry too much about your worthless handmaid,

Ts'ui Ying-ying. "

译文原注

① A gay, court tune of the eighth century.

② As Ssū-ma tempted Cho Wēn-chün, second century b. c.

③ As the neighbour's daughter did to Hsieh Kun (a. d. fourth century), in order to repel his advances.

④ Odes I. 1., X. 2.

⑤ = become a bride.

英译注释

1. kinswoman：女性亲戚，这里是说崔莺莺的母亲与张生的母亲同姓郑，论亲戚，其为张生另一支派的姨母。

2. Sending Presents and Asking Names：西周"六礼"，从议婚至完婚过程

中的纳采、问名。纳采即男方家请媒人去女方家提亲，女方家答应议婚后，男方家备礼前去求婚。问名，即男方家请媒人去问女方的名字和出生年月日。

3. in the dried-fish shop：卖干鱼的店铺，即枯鱼之肆。出自《庄子·外物》中的"吾得斗升之水然活耳，君乃言此，曾不如早索我於枯鱼之肆矣！"，后引以为典，比喻无法挽救的绝境。

4. parlour：客厅，雅座。这里指古时位于正房前面两旁的房屋，即厢房。西厢房是张生与莺莺幽会的地方。

5. Meeting a Fairy：元稹作《会真诗》，共六段，描写的是张生在井桐庭竹声中遇一美人，二人一见钟情，继而交颈合欢，互换礼物许下誓言，永久相爱。

6. faithfulness till death：山盟海誓，表示盟约和誓言像山和海那样永恒不变。也指男女相爱时立下的誓言，表示爱情要像山和海一样永恒不变。多指男女发誓真诚相爱，永不变心。

7. Rainbow Skirts and Feather Jackets：《霓裳羽衣曲》，是唐朝大曲中的法曲精品，唐歌舞的集大成之作。直到现在，它仍无愧为音乐舞蹈史上一颗璀璨的明珠。

8. garlands：花胜，古代妇女的一种头饰，以剪彩为之。

9. paste：唇脂，古时化妆用的唇膏。

10. phantom：幽灵、幻影。这里指莺莺连做梦都是对张生的思念，已经深陷其中，不能自拔。

11. Ch'ang-an：长安，都城，汉唐时期西安的古称，十分繁华。

12. tempted me by your ballads：用歌谣引诱我。这里引用了公元前200年的一则典故。西汉风流才子司马相如以一曲《凤求凰》打动了才女卓文君的心，"文君夜亡奔相如"，演出了一幕传唱千古的私奔佳话。

13. throw the shuttle：扔梭子。公元400年，西晋谢鲲的邻居高氏有一女，颇有美色。谢鲲曾尝试挑逗，结果那女子向谢鲲扔梭子，把他的牙齿打掉了两颗。由此时人唱谣道："任达不已，幼舆折齿。"谢鲲听到后，得意洋洋地说："犹不废我啸歌"。

14. seen my Prince：遇到王子，这里指莺莺遇到了自己的心上人张生。

15. the service of towel and comb：侍候别人用毛巾和梳子。这里指为人

妻，用来形容古时妻子的义务。

16. cynic：犬儒主义者，这里指愤世嫉俗，好挖苦人者。

17. cinnabar：朱砂，古时称作"丹"，朱砂的粉末呈红色，可以经久不褪。

英译评述

《莺莺传》是唐传奇中影响最大、流传最广的一篇，鲁迅先生认为其"震撼文林，为力甚大"。文笔优美流畅，对人物形象的塑造传神，对年轻男女之间情与礼的矛盾描述生动，体现了作者的审美主张。其客观叙述和主观评价，启发读者深思，意义深远。由于篇幅有限，本文选取了《莺莺传》的高潮部分，即从牵线丫鬟红娘的出现一直至悲情结局的部分情节；英国汉学家亚瑟·威利所做的翻译，力求准确无误，忠实于原著，立足于再现原著风貌，达到了忠实、通顺、化境的要求，译文的风格和笔调也与原文的性质相同，读来生动流畅，一气呵成，是《莺莺传》英译中的佳作。

在翻译策略上，译者较好地结合了直译和意译两种手法，比如说，他将原文中意义独特而在英文中没有对应说法的成语"枯鱼之肆"，直接翻译成 in the dried-fish shop，让西方读者立即想象出那种处于绝境的场景，又达到了译文应有的表达效果。将《霓裳羽衣曲》直译成 Rainbow Skirts and Feather Jackets，更是生动形象，相比之下，译者没有将《会真诗》直译成 The Poem of Huizhen，而意译成 Meeting a Fairy，能让西方读者快速地理解其含义。倘若直译的话，译文读者根本无法理解其寓意，即张生与莺莺最美的相遇。

在原文叙述冗长的地方，译者进行了省译。比如在"然而崔之姻族，君所详也"中，省译为 since your mother was a kinswoman，完全可以概括出原文的意思。将"其去几何？"这样的没有太多实际意义的反问省去，更能言简意赅地达意，符合西方读者直接简洁的思维逻辑。另外，译文中对司马相如与卓文君、名士谢鲲等典故的运用，更显示出译者对中华博大精深传统文化知识的掌握与积累，引导西方读者更好地体会传统中华文化的魅力所在。

然而，译者在理解方面存在不准确之处。比如"张亦微喻其旨"，译文翻译为 Chang could not doubt her meaning，显然与原意相背，应该指"并不确定，只是略懂其意"，而不是"非常确定"。此外，译文也存在对保持源语风格的过于追求而过度异化的问题，比如文章开头"或时纨绮间居"，译为 Sometimes I have idled with wearers of silk and gauze，对于不熟悉中国文化的西方读者而言，很难体会其意义，不如归化译作易于理解的，Sometimes I have stayed with women。因此在翻译时，一定要注意理解准确，避免过度地异化，以免造成误解。

Ⅰ. **Translation Practice**.

Directions：Translate the following into English.

唐贞元中，有张生者，性温茂，美风容，内秉坚孤，非礼不可入。或朋从游宴，扰杂其间，他人皆汹汹拳拳，若将不及；张生容顺而已，终不能乱。以是年二十三，未尝近女色。知者诘之，谢而言曰："登徒子非好色者，是有凶行。余真好色者，而适不我值。何以言之？大凡物之尤者，未尝不留连于心，是知其非忘情者也。"诘者识之。

Ⅱ. **Oral Presentation**.

Directions：Read "The Story of Ts'ui Ying-ying", select the most impressive part in the story, and present it in class with the help of PPT.

Ⅲ. **Writing Practice**.

Directions：Write an essay of about 200 words, stating your understanding of the writer's opinion of Ts'ui Ying-ying.

第二节　《李娃传》选译

白行简（约776—826），唐代文学家，字知退，华州下邽（今陕西渭南）人，白居易之弟。其文辞简易，辞赋工整，当世文人纷纷效仿。白行简以传

奇著称于世，代表作为《李娃传》。

《李娃传》又名《汧国夫人传》，被收入《太平广记》484卷，是唐传奇中的名篇。全文不足5000字，但故事情节跌宕起伏，引人入胜，塑造了李娃这样一个敢爱，有担当、聪慧能干的鲜明形象；对某些具体场景的描绘细致逼真，体现了唐传奇写实手法的高度成就，也是研究了解唐代社会风貌的宝贵资料。《李娃传》是对后世"才子佳人"型故事影响最大的三大唐传奇故事之一，后世以此为蓝本改编了许多戏曲。

故事讲述荥阳公子郑生赴京赶考，在京城游玩时偶见"妖姿要妙，绝代未有"的长安名妓李娃而陷入热恋。不到一年，郑生财尽囊空，被老鸨设计逐出。悲痛饥饿使他重病不起，被人送到了丧肆，病愈后便在肆间唱挽歌谋生。在一次唱挽歌时郑生为其父发现，因其玷辱家门而被父亲鞭笞至昏死，此后郑生流落街头。乞讨时郑生再次遇到李娃。李娃对其悉心照顾，苦心督促，使其发愤用功，博得功名。当李娃欲功成身退时，公子之父现身，迎李娃为儿媳，后被封为"汧国夫人"。本书节选李娃再遇公子至公子得官赴任一段，是全书李娃形象塑造最为丰满的精彩篇章。

李娃传❶（节选）

白行简

自秋徂冬，夜入于粪壤窟室，昼则周游廛肆[1]。

一旦大雪，生为冻馁[2]所驱，冒雪而出，乞食之声甚苦。闻见者莫不凄恻。时雪方甚，人家外户多不发。至安邑东门，循里垣北转第七八，有

---

❶ 元稹，等．唐宋传奇［M］．北京：华夏出版社，2015：85-87.

一门独启左扇，即娃之第也。生不知之，遂连声疾呼"饥冻之甚"，音响凄切，所不忍听。娃自阁中闻之，谓侍儿曰："此必生也。我辨其音矣。"连步而出。见生枯瘠疥疠[3]，殆非人状。娃意感焉，乃谓曰："岂非某郎也？"生愤懑绝倒，口不能言，颔颐[4]而已。娃前抱其颈，以绣襦[5]拥而归于西厢。失声长恸曰："令子一朝及此，我之罪也！"绝而复苏。姥大骇，奔至，曰："何也？"娃曰："某郎。"姥遽[6]曰："当逐之，奈何令至此？"娃敛容却睇曰："不然。此良家子也。当昔驱高车，持金装，至某之室，不逾期而荡尽。且互设诡计，舍而逐之，殆非人。令其失志，不得齿于人伦。父子之道，天性也。使其情绝，杀而弃之。又困踬[7]若此。天下之人尽知为某也。生亲戚满朝，一旦当权者熟察其本末，祸将及矣。况欺天负人，鬼神不祐，无自贻其殃也。某为姥子，迨今有二十岁矣。计其赀[8]，不啻值千金。今姥年六十余，愿计二十年衣食之用以赎身，当与此子别卜所诣。所诣非遥，晨昏得以温清[9]。某愿足矣。"姥度其志不可夺，因许之。

给姥之余，有百金。北隅四五家税一隙院。乃与生沐浴，易其衣服；为汤粥，通其肠；次以酥乳润其脏。旬余，方荐水陆之馔[10]。头巾履袜，皆取珍异者衣之。未数月，肌肤稍腴；卒岁，平愈如初。异时，娃谓生曰："体已康矣，志已壮矣。渊思寂虑，默想曩昔之艺业，可温习乎？"生思之，曰："十得二三耳。"娃命车出游，生骑而从。至旗亭南偏门鬻坟典之肆[11]，令生拣而市之，计费百金，尽载以归。因令生斥弃百虑以志学，俾[12]夜作昼，孜孜矻矻[13]。娃常偶坐，宵分乃寐。伺其疲倦，即谕之缀诗赋。二岁而业大就；海内文籍，莫不该览。生谓娃曰："可策名试艺矣。"娃曰："未也，且令精熟，以俟百战。"更一年，曰："可行矣。"于是遂一上登甲科，声振礼闱[14]。虽前辈见其文，罔不敛衽[15]敬羡，愿友之而不可得。娃曰："未也。今秀士，苟获擢[16]一科第，则自谓可以取中朝之显职，擅天下之美名。子行秽迹鄙，不侔[17]于他士。当砻淬[18]利器，以求再捷。方可以连衡多士，争霸群英。"生由是益自勤苦，声价弥甚。

其年，遇大比，诏征四方之隽，生应"直言极谏"科[19]，策名第一，授成都府参军。三事以降[20]，皆其友也。将之官，娃谓生曰："今之复子本躯，某不相负也。愿以残年，归养老姥。君当结媛鼎族，以奉蒸尝[21]。中外婚媾，无自黩[22]也。勉思自爱。某从此去矣。"生泣曰："子若弃我，当自颈[23]以就死。"娃固辞不从，生勤请弥恳。娃曰："送子涉江，至于剑门，当令我回。"生许诺。

中文注释

[1] 廛（chán）肆：市肆；亦泛指街市。

[2] 馁（něi）：饥饿。

[3] 疥疠（jiè lài）：恶疮。疠：古同"癞"，癞病。

[4] 颔颐（hàn yí）：点头以示默认、承诺。

[5] 襦（rú）：短衣，短袄。

[6] 遽（jù）：急，仓猝。

[7] 困踬（zhì）：困顿阻厄；受挫折。

[8] 赀（zī）：财也。

[9] 温凊（wēn qìng）：冬温夏凊的省称。冬天温被使暖，夏天扇席使凉，侍奉父母之礼。

[10] 水陆之馔：水上和陆上出产的山珍海味；泛指山珍海味。

[11] 坟典之肆：书店。坟典，即"三坟""五典"，传说中的上古书籍，后转为古代典籍的通称。《三坟》即伏羲、神农、黄帝之书；《五典》即少昊、颛顼、高辛、尧、舜之书；《八索》乃八卦之说；《九丘》为九州之志等古书。

[12] 俾（bǐ）：【动】使，把。

[13] 孜孜矻矻（kū）：勤勉不懈的样子。

[14] 礼闱：指古代科举考试之会试，因其为礼部主办，故称礼闱。

[15] 敛衽：＜书＞整整衣襟，表示恭敬。

[16] 擢（zhuó）：提拔，提升。

[17] 侔（móu）：相等，齐。

[18] 砻淬（lóng cuì）：磨炼刀刃；比喻刻苦锻炼。

[19] 直言极谏科：唐代科举常选之外有制科。制科不定期举行，由天子亲策，专用于网罗选用特殊人才。类似汉代的举贤良文学、孝廉方正。其中，以贤良方正直言极谏科、才识兼茂明于体用科最为常见，宋代沿之。

[20] 三事以降：三公以下的官员。

[21] 蒸尝：本指秋冬二祭，后泛指祭祀。

[22] 黩（dú）：污辱，玷污。

[23] 颈（jǐng）：用刀割颈。

李娃传（节选）

从秋天到了冬天，公子夜晚钻进厕所、地窖中，白天就逗留于市场、店铺。有一天早上下起了大雪，公子被寒冷和饥饿逼迫，冒雪出去乞讨，乞讨的声音非常凄惨，凡听到的人无不因其凄悲而痛心的。当时雪下得正大，各家都大门紧闭。公子到了安邑里东门，沿着里墙向北走。过了七八户人家，有一户的左半边大门开着，这就是李娃的住宅。公子不知情，连声疾呼："饿煞啦！冻煞啦！"声音凄切，令人不忍心听。

李娃在房中听到，对婢女说："这一定是公子。我听出是他的声音了。"说完疾步跑了出来。只见公子骨瘦如柴，满身疥疮，已经不成人形了。李娃感到很心痛，就对他说："你难道不是某郎吗？"公子气愤得昏倒过去，口里一句话也说不出来，只是点头罢了。李娃上前抱住他的颈脖，给他披上绣花短袄，并扶他回到西厢房，失声恸哭道："使你落到今天这步田地，是我的罪过啊！"她哭昏过去，过了很久才醒过来。

老太婆大惊，奔跑过来，说："怎么啦！"李娃说："这是公子。"老太婆忙说："应当赶他走。怎么能让他到这里来！"李娃表情严肃，回头瞟了她一眼说："不该这样。他是好人家的子弟。想当初他驾着华丽的大车，带着满满的财宝，来到我的屋里，不到一年就花光了所有的钱。我们合伙设下诡计，抛弃并赶走了他，简直是非人道的行径。让他丧失志向，被亲戚朋友看不起。父子之道，是天性，他父亲却因此对他恩断情绝，狠命鞭打他后弃之荒野。公子如今沦落到这个地步，世上的人都知道是因为我。满朝廷都是公子的亲戚，有朝一日当权的亲戚查清原由，灾祸就会降到我们头上了。何况欺天负人，鬼神也不会保佑我们，不要自找祸殃吧。我做您女儿，至今有二十年了。算起来您为我花的钱，已不止千金。现在您六十多了，我愿供养您后二十年，承担您的吃穿用度，以此赎身。我要和他另找住处。那地方离您不会太远，早晚能够来问安侍候您，您若答应，我的心愿也就满足了。"老太婆料想李娃的心意已难改变，只得答应了。

李娃给了老太婆赎金之后，还剩下百金，便在北边隔四五家处租了一个空院子。她替公子洗了澡，换了衣服；做了汤粥，润通他的肠道；再用酥乳滋润他的肠胃。十多天后，才开始给公子吃些山珍海味。头巾鞋袜，都取精美的给他穿戴。没过几个月，公子肌肤丰满了些。过了一年，公子康复得像当年一样了。又过了些日子，李娃对公子说："你的身体已经康复了，志气已经旺盛了。你应该深思静虑，默想从前的学业，可以重新开始温书学习了吗?"公子想了想，说："只记得十分之二三了。"李娃吩咐驾车出门，公子骑马跟在后面。到了旗亭南偏门处的书店，她让公子挑选好一些书买下，算起来共费了百金，然后把书全都装上车运了回来。李娃叫公子抛弃杂念一心学习，不分白天黑夜，孜孜不倦。李娃经常陪坐在一旁，直到深夜才睡；每当看到公子疲倦了，就劝他练习诗文来调剂调剂。过了两年，公子学业大有所成，天下的典籍，没有一种没读过。

公子对李娃说："可以报名应考了。"李娃说："不行。还应让学业更加精通熟练，才能应对各种考试。"又过了一年，李娃说："可以应考了。"公子就一举考上了甲科。名声传遍了礼部。即使是老前辈看到他的文章，也无不肃然起敬，都想与他结交但又不能如愿以偿。李娃说："你现在还不行。现在的秀才，得了一次科名，就自以为可以得到朝廷的要职，美名扬天下。你过去行为不端，有不光彩的历史，不同于其他文人。你应当磨砺锋利的武器，以求再战再胜，才能结交众多文人，在名士中称雄。"公子从此越发勤奋刻苦，声望越来越高。那一年，正赶上科举考试的大比之年，诏令四方的才子应考，公子报考直言极谏科，名列第一，授予成都府参军的职位。三公以下的官员，都成了他的朋友。

公子将要去上任，李娃对他说："如今你恢复了本来的样子，我不再有负于你了。我愿以我有生之年，回去赡养老妈妈。你应当和高门大族的小姐缔结姻缘，让她主持家政。与你们的姻族或姻族外的高门大族通婚，不要糟蹋自己。努力自珍自爱。我就此离别了。"公子哭道："你如果抛下我，我就自刎而死。"李娃坚决推辞不从，公子苦苦请求，而且越来越恳切。李娃说："我送你渡江，到达剑门后，就回来。"公子只好答应。

The Story of Miss Li[1] (An Excerpt)

By Po Hsing-Chien

Translated by Arthur Waley

Autumn had now turned to winter. He spent his nights in public lavatories and his days haunting the markets and booths.

One day when it was snowing hard, hunger and cold had driven him into the streets. His beggar's cry was full of woe and all who heard it were heart-rent. But the snow was so heavy that hardly a house had its outer door open, and the streets were empty.

When he reached the eastern gate of An-i, about the seventh or eighth turning north of the Hsün-li Wall, there was a house with the double-doors half open.

---

[1] 著名汉学家亚瑟·威利翻译了《李娃传》。汉学家杜德桥（Glen Dudbridge）也翻译过这个唐传奇故事，译作 The Tale of Li Wa: Study and Critical Edition of a Chinese Story from the Ninth Century。本书所选为威利的译作，译文选自《再译自中国人》（More Translations from the Chinese [M]. edited and translated by Arthur Waley. New York: Alfred A. Knopf, 1919）。

It was the house where Miss Li was then living, but the young man did not know.

He stood before the door, wailing loud and long.

Hunger and cold had given such a piteous accent to his cry that none could have listened unmoved.

Miss Li heard it from her room and at once said to her servant, "That is so-and-so. I know his voice." She flew to the door and was horrified to see her old lover standing before her so emaciated by hunger and disfigured by sores that he seemed scarcely human. "Can it be you?" she said. But the young man was so overcome by bewilderment and excitement that he could not speak, but only moved his lips noiselessly.

She threw her arms round his neck, then wrapped him in her own embroidered jacket and led him to the parlour. Here, with quavering voice, she reproached herself, saying, "It is my doing that you have been brought to this pass." And with these words she swooned.

Her mother[1] came running up in great excitement, asking who had arrived. Miss Li, recovering herself, said who it was. The old woman cried out in rage: "Send him away! What did you bring him in here for?"

But Miss Li looked up at her defiantly and said: "Not so! This is the son of a noble house. Once he rode in grand coaches and wore golden trappings on his coat. But when he came to our house, he soon lost all he had; and then we plotted together and left him destitute. Our conduct has indeed been inhuman! We have ruined his career and robbed him even of his place in the category of human relationships. For the love of father and son is implanted by Heaven; yet we have hardened his father's heart, so that he beat him with a stick and left him on the ground.

"Every one in the land knows that it is I who have reduced him to his present plight. The Court is full of his kinsmen. Some day one of them will come into power. Then an inquiry will be set afoot, and disaster will overtake us. And since we have flouted Heaven and defied the laws of humanity, neither spirits nor divinities will be on our side. Let us not wantonly incur a further retribution!

"I have lived as your daughter for twenty years. Reckoning what I have cost you in that time, I find it must be close on a thousand pieces of gold. You are now aged sixty, so that by the price of twenty more years' food and clothing, I can buy my freedom. I intend to live separately with this young man. We will not go far away; I shall see to it that we are near enough to pay our respects to you both morning and evening."

The "mother" saw that she was not to be gainsaid and fell in with the arrangement. When she had paid her ransom, Miss Li had a hundred pieces of gold left over; and with them she hired a vacant room, five doors away. Here she gave the young man a bath, changed his clothes, fed him with hot soup to relax his stomach, and later on fattened him up with cheese and milk.

In a few weeks she began to place before him all the choicest delicacies of land and sea; and she clothed him with cap, shoes and stockings of the finest quality. In a short time he began gradually to put on flesh, and by the end of the year, he had entirely recovered his former health.

One day Miss Li said to him: "Now your limbs are stout again and your will strong! Sometimes, when deeply pondering in silent sorrow, I wonder to myself how much you remember of your old literary studies?" He thought and answered: "Of ten parts I remember two or three."

Miss Li then ordered the carriage to be got ready and the young man followed her on horseback. When they reached the classical bookshop at the side-gate south of the Flag-tower, she made him choose all the books he wanted, till she had laid out a hundred pieces of gold. Then she packed them in the cart and drove home. She now made him dismiss all other thoughts from his mind and apply himself only to study. All the evening he toiled at his books, with Miss Li at his side, and they did not retire till midnight. If ever she found that he was too tired to work, she made him lay down his classics and write a poem or ode.

In two years he had thoroughly mastered his subjects and was admired by all the scholars of the realm. He said to Miss Li, "Now, surely, I am ready for the examiners!" but she would not let him compete and made him revise all he had learnt, to prepare for the "hundredth battle." At the end of the third year she said, "Now you may go." He went in for the examination and passed at the first attempt. His reputation spread rapidly through the examination rooms and even older men, when they saw his compositions, were filled with admiration and respect, and sought his friendship.

But Miss Li would not let him make friends with them, saying, "Wait a little longer! Nowadays when a bachelor of arts has passed his examination, he thinks himself fit to hold the most advantageous posts at Court and to win a universal reputation. But your unfortunate conduct and disreputable past put you at a disadvantage beside your fellow-scholars. You must 'grind, temper and sharpen^2' your attainments, that you may secure a second victory. Then you will be able to match yourself against famous scholars and contend with the illustrious."

The young man accordingly increased his efforts and enhanced his value. That year it happened that the Emperor had decreed a special examination for the selection of candidates of unusual merit from all parts of the Empire. The young man competed, and came out top in the "censorial essay." He was offered the post of Army Inspector at Ch'ēng-tu Fu. The officers who were to escort him were all previous friends.

When he was about to take up his post, Miss Li said to him, "Now that you are restored to your proper station in life, I will not be a burden to you. Let me go back and look after the old lady till she dies. You must ally yourself with some lady of noble lineage, who will be worthy to carry the sacrificial dishes in your Ancestral Hall. Do not injure your prospects by an unequal union. Good-bye, for now I must leave you."

The young man burst into tears and threatened to kill himself if she left him, but she obstinately refused to go with him. He begged her passionately not to desert him, and she at last consented to go with him across the river as far as Chien-mēn.[1] "There," she said, "you must part with me." The young man consented and in a few weeks they reached Chien-mēn.

译文原注

[1] Chien-mēn: the "Sword-gate", commanding the pass which leads into Szechuan from the north.

英译注释

1. her mother：姥，即老鸨，并非母亲，但娼妓常以"妈妈"呼之。威利译为 mother 并以引号表示此母非亲母，但不以通常带有贬义色彩的 pimp 或 procuress 来翻译，使后文李娃愿"归养小姥"更便于读者理解译文。

2. grind, temper and sharpen：砻淬。temper 做动词，意为使（钢铁等）回火，锻炼。

英译评述

亚瑟·威利翻译了大量的中国古代文学作品，其译作忠实、流畅，深受读者喜爱，很多成了西方颇具影响的翻译名著。西方的翻译界人士对威利的翻译也给予了极高的评价，认为他对所译作品的语言有很深的造诣，对所译作品有透彻的研究。

威利对《李娃传》的翻译忠实、流畅，虽有一些误译之处，但它既忠实地还原了原作的内容，也像原作一样引人入胜。威利在处理直接引语时并非机械地对应直译，而是采用了灵活的变通手法，既忠实地表达了原作的内容，又使译文流畅易懂。其变通手法有：①原文的直接引语译为间接引语。如：姥大骇奔至，曰："何也?"娃曰："某郎"。威利译为：asking who had arrived 和 said who it was. 并且还在此处补充译出前文未译的"绝而复苏"中的"复苏"，前后衔接自然流畅。②原文中的直接引语有机地融入描述性的语言。如：遂连声疾呼："饥冻之甚。"音响凄切，所不忍听。句中的直接引语"饥冻之甚。"被威利巧妙地译为后一句的主语 hunger and cold（He stood before

the door, wailing loud and long. Hunger and cold had given such a piteous accent to his cry that none could have listened unmoved.)。③原文的直接引语变为半间接引语半直接引语。如：娃曰："送子涉江，至于剑门，当令我回。"生许诺。威利处理为 she at last consented to go with him across the river as far as Chien-mēn. "There," she said, "you must part with me."

威利对直接引语的灵活处理也体现了他高超的分句和合句能力，他能摆脱原作的句子单体限制，在充分理解原作的基础上，把原句分译成多个句子或者合译成一个句子。如上文最后一个例子中译为间接引语是为了与前一句"生勤请弥恳"相连。"生勤请弥恳"李娃才答应相送至剑门，清晰而流畅。缀补一例：原文"愿友之而不可得"被分译为"愿友之"（and sought his friendship）和"不可得"（But Miss Li would not let him make friends with them, saying...）根据后文李娃的劝诫可知，"不可得"乃因李娃所言，所以此处的补充很合理，李娃告诫之语随势而出。

Ⅰ. Translation Practice.

Directions：Translate the following into English.

1. 父子之道，天性也。

2. 况欺天负人，鬼神不佑，无自贻其殃也。

3. 所诣非遥，晨昏得以温凊，某愿足矣。

4. 体已康矣，志已壮矣。渊思寂虑，默想曩昔之艺业，可温习乎?

5. 愿以残年，归养小姥。

Ⅱ. Translation Study.

Directions：Study the excerpt, identify the incorrect translations and come up with your own translation.

如"循里垣，北转第七八"译为"about the seventh or eighth turning north of the Hsün–li Wall"，"里垣"和"第"理解错误。

Ⅲ. Writing Practice.

Directions：Read *the Story of Miss Li* and write an English play.

第二章

明清小说

导　读

　　明代小说是在宋元时期说话艺术的基础上发展起来的。从明代开始，小说这种文学形式才充分显示出它的社会作用和文学价值，打破了正统诗文的垄断地位，在文学史上取得了与唐诗、宋词、元曲相提并论的地位。在明代，小说出现了空前繁荣的局面，在四大名著中就占据三席。《三国演义》和《水浒传》是历史演义；《西游记》是神怪小说；还有拟话本"三言""二拍"，它们都是脍炙人口之作。

　　清代小说是中国古代小说发展史上的高峰，其品类繁多，不仅包容了各种传统的小说形式，而且有了大量的创新，精品名著倍出，取得了辉煌的成就。清初蒲松龄的《聊斋志异》把借鬼怪灵异之事抒发幽怀的志怪小说发挥到了极致，而清代小说成就最高者当属曹雪芹的《红楼梦》。本章摘选了《红楼梦》中的第二十三回。

第一节　《三国演义》选译

　　罗贯中（1330—1400），名本，字贯中，号湖海散人；元末明初著名小说家、戏曲家，是中国章回体小说的鼻祖。他一生著作颇丰，代表作《三国演义》讲述了东汉末年到西晋初年群雄逐鹿的谋略和智勇，体现出了罗贯中的博大精深之才、经天纬地之气。他不仅精通军事学、心理学、智谋学、公关学、人才学等，而且诗词造诣颇高。《三国演义》采用浅近的文言文，明快流畅，雅俗共赏，是中国古典文学之集大成者。

《三国演义》长于描述一幕幕惊心动魄的战争场面。全书共写大小战争四十多次，其中尤以官渡之战、赤壁之战、夷陵之战（又称猇亭之战）最为出色。其在惊心动魄的军事、政治斗争及尖锐复杂的矛盾冲突中，通过一系列的故事情节和人物语言，成功地塑造了众多的人物形象，其中主要人物都是性格鲜明、形象生动的艺术典型，最为突出的是人们所谓的"三绝"，即曹操的"奸绝"、关羽的"义绝"、孔明的"智绝"。书中的故事，如桃园结义、三英战吕布、煮酒论英雄、过五关斩六将、三顾茅庐、舌战群儒、单刀赴会、草船借箭、失街亭、空城计、斩马谡等，都脍炙人口。空城计等故事更是被改编成了经典的戏剧曲目。本书节选的正是"草船借箭"故事，其充分展示了诸葛亮超群的智慧和谋略。

用奇谋孔明借箭❶

却说鲁肃领了周瑜言语，径来舟中相探孔明。孔明接入小舟对坐。肃曰："连日措办军务，有失听教。"孔明曰："便是亮亦未与都督贺喜。"肃曰："何喜？"孔明曰："公瑾使先生来探亮知也不知，便是这件事可贺喜耳。"唬得鲁肃失色，问曰："先生何由知之？"孔明曰："这条计只好弄蒋干。曹操虽被一时瞒过，必然便省悟，只是不肯认错耳。今蔡、张二人既死，江东无患矣，如何不贺喜？吾闻曹操换毛玠、于禁为水军都督，则这两个手里，好歹送了水军性命。"鲁肃听了，开口不得，把些言语，支吾了半晌，别孔明而回。孔明嘱曰："望子敬在公瑾面前，勿言亮先知

---

❶ 罗贯中. 三国演义［M］. 北京：中华书局，2005：256-258.

此事。恐公瑾心怀妒忌，又要寻事害亮。"鲁肃应诺而去，回见周瑜，把上项事只得实说了。瑜大惊曰："此人决不可留，吾决意斩之。"肃劝曰："若杀孔明，却被曹操笑也。"瑜曰："吾自有公道斩之，教他死而无怨。"肃曰："何以公道斩之？"瑜曰："子敬休问，来日便见。"

次日，聚众将于帐下，教请孔明议事。孔明欣然而至。坐定，瑜问孔明曰："即日将与曹军交战，水路交兵，当以何兵器为先？"孔明曰："大江之上，以弓箭为先。"瑜曰："先生之言，甚合愚意。但今军中正缺箭用，敢烦先生监造十万枝箭，以为应敌之具。此系公事，先生幸勿推却。"孔明曰："都督见委，自当效劳。敢问十万枝箭何时要用？"瑜曰："十日之内，可完办否？"孔明曰："操军即日将至，若候十日，必误大事。"瑜曰："先生料几日可完办？"孔明曰："只消三日，便可拜纳十万枝箭。"瑜曰："军中无戏言。"孔明曰："怎敢戏都督？愿纳军令状：三日不办，甘当重罚。"瑜大喜，唤军政司当面取了文书，置酒相待曰："待军事毕后，自有酬劳。"孔明曰："今日已不及，来日造起，至第三日，可差五百小军，到江边搬箭。"饮了数杯，辞去。鲁肃曰："此人莫非诈乎？"瑜曰："他自送死，非我逼他。今明白对众要了文书，他便两胁生翅，也飞不去。我只分付军匠人等，教他故意迟延，凡应用物件，都不与齐备，如此必然误了日期，那时定罪，有何理说？公今可去探他虚实，却来回报。"

肃领命，来见孔明。孔明曰："吾曾告子敬休对公瑾说，他必要害我。不想子敬不肯为我隐讳，今日果然又弄出事来。三日内如何造得十万箭？子敬只得救我。"肃曰："公自取其祸，我如何救得你？"孔明曰："望子敬借我二十只船，每船要军士三十人，船上皆用青布为幔，各束草千余个，分布两边，吾别有妙用。第三日，包管有十万枝箭。只不可又教公瑾得知。若彼知之，吾计败矣。"肃应诺，却不解其意。回报周瑜，果然不提起借船之事，只言孔明并不用箭竹翎毛胶漆等物，自有道理。瑜大疑曰："且看他三日后如何回覆我。"

却说鲁肃私自拨轻快船二十只，各船三十余人，并布幔束草等物尽皆齐备，候孔明调用。第一日，却不见孔明动静；第二日亦只不动。至第三日四更时分，孔明密请鲁肃到船中。肃问曰："公召我来何意？"孔明曰："特请子敬同往取箭。"肃曰："何处去取？"孔明曰："子敬休问，前去便见。"遂命将二十只船，用长索相连，径望北岸进发。

是夜大雾漫天。长江之中雾气更甚，对面不相见。孔明促舟前进，果然是好大雾。前人有篇《大雾垂江赋》曰：

"大哉长江！西接岷峨，南控三吴，北带九河。汇百川而入海，历万古以扬波。至若龙伯、海若，江妃、水母，长鲸千丈，天蜈九首，鬼怪异类，咸集而有。盖夫鬼神之所凭依，英雄之所战守也。时而阴阳既乱，昧爽[1]不分。讶长空之一色，忽大雾之四屯。虽舆薪[2]而莫睹，惟金鼓之可闻。初若溟濛[3]，才隐南山之豹；渐而充塞，欲迷北海之鲲[4]。然后上接高天，下垂厚地，渺乎苍茫，浩乎无际。鲸鲵出水而腾波，蛟龙潜渊而吐气。又如梅霖收溽[5]，春阴酿寒，溟溟漠漠，浩浩漫漫。东失柴桑之岸，南无夏口之山。战船千艘，俱沉沦于岩壑；渔舟一叶，惊出没于波澜。甚则穹昊[6]无光，朝阳失色。返白昼为昏黄，变丹山为水碧。虽大禹之智，不能测其浅深；离娄[7]之明，焉能辨乎咫尺。于是冯夷[8]息浪，屏翳[9]收功，鱼鳖遁迹，鸟兽潜踪；隔断蓬莱之岛，暗围阊阖[10]之宫。恍惚奔腾，如骤雨之将至；纷纭杂沓，若寒云之欲同。乃能中隐毒蛇，因之而为瘴疠[11]；内藏妖魅，凭之而为祸害。降疾厄于人间，起风尘于塞外。小民遇之天伤，大人观之感慨。盖将返元气于洪荒，混天地为大块。"

当夜五更时候，船已近曹操水寨。孔明教把船只头西尾东，一带摆开，就船上擂鼓呐喊。鲁肃惊曰："倘曹兵齐出，如之奈何？"孔明笑曰："吾料曹操于重雾中必不敢出。吾等只顾酌酒取乐，待雾散便回。"

却说曹寨中听得擂鼓呐喊，毛玠、于禁二人慌忙飞报曹操。操传令曰："重雾迷江，彼军忽至，必有埋伏，切不可轻动。可拨水军弓弩手乱箭射之。"又差人往旱寨内唤张辽、徐晃，各带弓弩军三千，火速到江边助射。比及号令到来，毛玠、于禁怕南军抢入水寨，另差弓弩手，在寨前放箭。少项,旱寨内弓弩手亦到,约一万余人,尽皆向江中放箭,箭如雨发。孔明教把船调回,头东尾西,逼近水寨受箭,一面擂鼓呐喊。待至日高雾散,孔明令收船急回。二十只船,两边束草上,排满箭枝。孔明令各船上军士齐声叫曰:"谢丞相箭!"比及曹军寨内报知曹操时,这里船轻水急,已放回二十余里,追之不及。曹操懊悔不已。

却说孔明回船,谓鲁肃曰:"每船上箭约五六千矣。不费江东半分之力,已得十万余箭。明日即将来射曹军,却不甚便?"肃曰:"先生真神人也,何以知今日如此大雾?"孔明曰:"为将而不通天文,不识地利,不知奇门,不晓阴阳,不看阵图,不明兵势,是庸才也。亮于三日前已算定今日有大雾,因此敢任三日之限。公瑾教我十日完办,工匠料物都不应手,将这一件风流罪过,明白要杀我。我命系于天,公瑾焉能害我哉!"鲁肃拜服。

船到岸时,周瑜已差五百军在江边等候搬箭。孔明教于船上取之,可得十余万枝,都搬入中军帐交纳。鲁肃入见周瑜,备说孔明取箭之事。瑜大惊,慨然叹曰:"孔明神机妙算,吾不如也!"后人有诗赞曰:

"一天浓雾满长江,远近难分水渺茫。

　　骤雨飞蝗来战舰,孔明今日伏周郎。"

少项,孔明入寨见周瑜。瑜下帐迎之,称美曰:"先生神算,使人敬服。"孔明曰:"诡谲[12]小计,何足为奇。"

瑜邀孔明入帐共饮。瑜曰:"昨吾主遣使来催督进军,瑜未有奇计,愿先生教我。"孔明曰:"亮乃碌碌庸才,安有妙计?"瑜曰:"某昨观曹操水寨,极其严整有法,非等闲可攻。思得一计,不知可否。先生幸为我一决之。"孔明曰:"都督且休言。各自写于手内,看同也不同。"瑜大喜,教取笔砚来,先自暗写了,却送与孔明。孔明亦暗写了。两个移近坐榻,各出掌中之字,互相观看,皆大笑。原来周瑜掌中字,乃一"火"字,孔明掌中亦一"火"字。瑜曰:"既我两人所见相同,更无疑矣,幸勿漏泄。"孔明曰:"两家公事,岂有漏泄之理。吾料曹操虽两番经我这条计,然必不为备,今都督尽行之可也。"饮罢分散,诸将皆不知其事。

中文注释

[1] 昧爽：明暗。

[2] 舆薪：满车子的柴，比喻大而易见的事物。

[3] 溟濛（míng méng）：昏暗，模糊不清。

[4] 鲲（kūn）：传说中的一种大鱼。

[5] 溽（rù）：湿润。

[6] 穹昊（qióng hào）：天穹，苍天。

[7] 离娄：相传为黄帝时人，目力极强，能于百步之外望见秋毫之末。

[8] 冯夷：神话中的水神。

[9] 屏翳（yì）：神话中的风神。

[10] 阊阖（chāng hé）：传说中的天门。

[11] 瘴疬（zhāng lì）：恶性疾病。

[12] 诡谲（guǐ jué）：怪异。

英文译本

Using Strategy, Zhuge Liang Borrows Arrows[1]

By Luo Guanzhong

Translated by C. H. Brewitt-Taylor

Lu Su departed on his mission and found Zhuge Liang seated in his little craft.

"There has been so much to do that I have not been able to come to listen to your instructions," said Lu Su.

"That is truly so," said Zhuge Liang, "and I have not yet congratulated

---

[1] 国内外许多学者都尝试过把《三国演义》译成英文，但全译本只有两个：1925 年的 C. H. Brewitt-Taylor（邓罗）译本和 1991 年的 Moss Roberts 译本。本书所选的是邓罗的译本，译文源自 http://threekingdoms.com/046.htm，该网站改用了新的拼音记法。

the Commander-in-Chief. "

"What have you wished to congratulate him upon?"

"Why Sir, the matter upon which he sent you to find out whether I knew about it or not. Indeed I can congratulate him on that. "

Lu Su turned pale and gasped, saying, "But how did you know, Master?"

"The ruse succeeded well thus played off on Jiang Gan. Cao Cao has been taken in this once, but he will soon rise to it. Only he will not confess his mistake. However, the two men are gone, and the South Land is freed from a grave anxiety. Do you not think that is a matter for congratulation? I hear Mao Jie and Yu Jin are the new admirals, and in their hands lie both good and evil for the fate of the northern fleet. "

Lu Su was quite dumbfounded. He stayed a little time longer passing the time in making empty remarks, and then took his leave.

As he was going away, Zhuge Liang cautioned him, saying, "Do not let Zhou Yu know that I know his ruse. If you let him know, he will seek some chance to do me harm. "

Lu Su promised. Nevertheless he went straight to his chief and related the whole thing just as it happened.

"Really he must be got rid of," said Zhou Yu. "I have quite decided to put the man out of the way. "

"If you slay him, will not Cao Cao laugh at you?"

"Oh, no; I will find a legitimate way of getting rid of him so that he shall go to his death without resentment. "

"But how can you find a legitimate way of assassinating him?"

"Do not ask too much. You will see presently. "

Soon after all the officers were summoned to the main tent, and Zhuge Liang's presence was desired. He went contentedly enough.

When all were seated, Zhou Yu suddenly addressed Zhuge Liang, saying, "I am going to fight a battle with the enemy soon on the water. What weap-

ons are the best?"

"On a great river arrows are the best," said Zhuge Liang.

"Your opinion and mine agree. But at the moment we are short of them. I wish you would undertake to supply about a hundred thousand arrows for the naval fight. As it is for the public service, you will not decline, I hope. "

"Whatever task the Commander-in-Chief lays upon me, I must certainly try to perform," replied Zhuge Liang. "May I inquire by what date you require the hundred thousand arrows?"

"Could you have them ready in ten days?"

"The enemy will be here very soon. Ten days will be too late," said Zhuge Liang.

"In how many days do you estimate the arrows can be ready?"

"Let me have three days. Then you may send for your hundred thousand. "

"No joking, remember!" said Zhou Yu, "There is no joking in war time. "

"Dare I joke with the Commander-in-Chief? Give me a formal military order. If I have not completed the task in three days, I will take my punishment. "

Zhou Yu, secretly delighted, sent for the secretaries[1] and prepared the commission then and there.

Then he drank to the success of the undertaking and said, "I shall have to congratulate you most heartily when this is accomplished. "

"This day is too late to count," said Zhuge Liang. "On the third from tomorrow morning send five hundred small boats to the river side to convey the arrows. "

They drank a few more cups together, and then Zhuge Liang took his leave.

After he had gone, Lu Su said, "Do you not think there is some deceit about this?"

"Clearly it is not I! It is he who has signed his own death warrant," said Zhou Yu, "Without being pressed in the least, he asked for a formal order in the face of the whole assembly. Even if he grew a pair of wings, he could not escape. Only I will just order the workers to delay him as much as they can, and not supply him with materials, so that he is sure to fail. And then, when the certain penalty is incurred, who can criticize? You can go and inquire about it all and keep me informed."

So off went Lu Su to seek Zhuge Liang, who at once reproached him with having blabbed about the former business.

Zhuge Liang said, "He wants to hurt me, as you know, and I did not think you could not keep my secret. And now there is what you saw today, and how do you think I can get a hundred thousand arrows made in three days? You will simply have to rescue me."

"You brought the misfortune on yourself, and how can I rescue you?" said Lu Su.

"I look to you for the loan of twenty vessels, manned each by thirty people. I want blue cotton screens and bundles of straw lashed to the sides of the boats. I have good use for them. On the third day, I shall undertake to deliver the fixed number of arrows. But on no account must you let Zhou Yu know, or my scheme will be wrecked."

Lu Su consented, and this time he kept his word. He went to report to his chief as usual, but he said nothing about the boats.

He only said, "Zhuge Liang is not using bamboo or feathers or glue or varnish, but has some other way of getting arrows."

"Let us await the three days' limit," said Zhou Yu, puzzled though confident.

On his side Lu Su quietly prepared a score of light swift boats, each with its crew and the blue screens and bundles of grass complete and, when these

were ready, he placed them at Zhuge Liang's disposal.

Zhuge Liang did nothing on the first day, nor on the second. On the third day at the middle of the fourth watch, Zhuge Liang sent a private message asking Lu Su to come to his boat.

"Why have you sent for me, Sir?" asked Lu Su.

"I want you to go with me to get those arrows."

"Whither are you going?" "Do not ask. You will see."

Then the twenty boats were fastened together by long ropes and moved over to the north bank. The night proved very foggy and the mist was very dense along the river, so that one person could scarcely see another. In spite of the fog, Zhuge Liang urged the boats forward as if into the vast fairy kingdom.

There is a poem on these river fogs:

Mighty indeed is the Great River!

Rising far in the west, in the Emei and Min Mountains,

Plowing its way through Wu, east flowing, resistless,

Swelled by its nine tributary streams, rolling down from the far north,

Aided and helped by a hundred rivulets swirling and foaming,

Ocean receives it at last welcoming, joyful, its waters.

Therein abide sea nymphs and water gods,

Enormous whales a thousand fathoms long,

Nine-headed monstrous beasts, reptiles and octopi,

Demons and uncouth creatures wondrous strange.

In faith it is the home and safe retreat

Of devils and sprites, and wondrous growths,

And eke the battle ground of valiant humans.

At times occur strange strife of elements,

When darkness strives on light's domains that encroach,

Whereat arises in the vaulted dome of blue,

White wreaths of fog that toward the center roll.

Then darkness falls, too dense for any torch

Illumine; only clanging sounds can pass.

The fog at first appears, a vaporous wreath

Scarce visible. But thickening fast, it veils

The Southern Hills, the painted leopard's home.

And spreads afar, until the northern sea

Leviathans are amazed and lose their course.

And denser yet it touches on the sky.

And spreads a heavy mantle over the earth.

Then, wide as is the high pitched arch of heaven,

Therein appears no single rift of blue.

Now mighty whales lead up their spouses to sport

Upon the waves, the sinuous dragons dive

Deep down and, breathing, swell the heaving sea.

The earth is moist as with the early rains,

And spring's creative energy is chilled.

Both far and wide and high the damp fog spreads,

Great cities on the eastern bank are hid,

Wide ports and mountains in the south are lost,

Whole fleets of battle ships, a thousand keels,

Hide in the misty depths; frail fishing boats

High riding on a wave are seen — and lost.

The gloom increases and the domed sky

Grows dark and darker as the sun's light fails.

The daylight dies, dim twilight's reign begins,

The ruddy hills dissolve and lose their hue.

The skill of matchless King Yu would fail to sound

The depth and height; and Li Lou's eye, though keen,

Could never pierce this gloom.

Now is the time, O sea and river gods, to use your powers.

The gliding fish and creeping water folk

Are lost; there is no track for bird or beast.

Fair Penglai Isles are hidden from our sight,

The lofty gates of heaven have disappeared.

Nature is blurred and indistinct, as when

A driving rain storm hurries over the earth.

And then, perhaps, within the heavy haze,

A noisome serpent vents his venom foul

And plagues descend, or impish demons work

Their wicked wills.

Ills fall on humans but do not stay,

Heaven's cleansing breath sweeps them sway,

But while they last the mean ones cry,

The nobler suffer silently.

The greatest turmoil is a sign

Of quick return to state benign.

The little fleet reached Cao Cao's naval camp about the fifth watch, and Zhuge Liang gave orders to form a line lying prows west, and then to beat the drums and shout.

"But what shall we do if they attack us?" exclaimed Lu Su.

Zhuge Liang replied with a smile, "I think their fleet will not venture out in this fog. Go on with your wine, and let us be happy. We will go back when the fog lifts."

As soon as the shouting from the river was heard by those in the camp, the two admirals, Mao Jie and Yu Jin, ran off to report to Cao Cao, who said, "Coming up in a fog like this means that they have prepared an ambush for us. Do not go out, but get all the force together and shoot at them."

He also sent orders to the ground camps to dispatch six thousand of archers and crossbowmen to aid the marines.

The naval forces were then lined up shooting on the bank to prevent a landing. Presently the soldiers arrived, and ten thousand and more soldiers were shooting down into the river, where the arrows fell like rain. By and bye Zhuge Liang ordered the boats to turn round so that their prows pointed east and to go closer in so that many arrows might hit them.

Zhuge Liang ordered the drums to be kept beating till the sun was high and the fog began to disperse, when the boats got under way and sailed downstream. The whole twenty boats were bristling with arrows on both sides.

As they left, Zhuge Liang asked all the crews to shout derisively, "We thank you, Sir Prime Minister, for the arrows!"

They told Cao Cao, but by the time he came, the light boats helped by the swift current were seven miles long down the river and pursuit was impossible. Cao Cao saw that he had been duped and was very sorry, but there was no help for it.

On the way down Zhuge Liang said to his companion, "Every boat must have five or six thousand arrows and so, without the expenditure of an ounce of energy, we must have more than ten myriad arrows, which tomorrow can be shot back again at Cao Cao's army to his great inconvenience."

"You are really superhuman," said Lu Su. "But how did you know there would be a thick fog today?"

"One cannot be a leader without knowing the workings of heaven and the ways of earth. One must understand the secret gates[2] and the interdependence of the elements[3], the mysteries of tactics and the value of forces. It is but an ordinary talent. I calculated three days ago that there would be a fog today, and so I set the limit at three days. Zhou Yu would give me ten days, but neither artificers nor materials, so that he might find occasion to

put me to death as I knew. But my fate lies with the Supreme, and how could Zhou Yu harm me?"

Lu Su could not but agree. When the boats arrived, five hundred soldiers were in readiness on the bank to carry away the arrows. Zhuge Liang bade them go on board the boats, collect them and bear them to the tent of the Commander-in-Chief. Lu Su went to report that the arrows had been obtained and told Zhou Yu by what means.

Zhou Yu was amazed and sighed sadly, saying, "He is better than I. His methods are more than human. "

Thick lies the fog on the river,

Nature is shrouded in white,

Distant and near are confounded,

Banks are no longer in sight.

Fast fly the pattering arrows,

Stick in the boats of the fleet.

Now can full tale be delivered,

Zhuge Liang is victor complete.

When, shortly after his return, Zhuge Liang went to the tent of the Commander-in-Chief, he was welcomed by Zhou Yu, who came forward to greet him, saying, "Your superhuman predictions compel one's esteem. "

"There is nothing remarkable in that trifling trick," replied he.

Zhou Yu led him within and wine was brought.

Then Zhou Yu said, "My lord sent yesterday to urge me to advance, but I have no master plan ready. I wish you would assist me, Master. "

"But where should I, a man of poor everyday ability, find such a plan as you desire?"

"I saw the enemy's naval camp just lately, and it looked very complete and well organized. It is not an ordinary place to attack. I have thought of a plan, but I am not sure it will answer. I should be happy if you would decide for me. "

"General," replied Zhuge Liang, "do not say what your plan is, but each of us will write in the palm of his hand and see whether our opinions agree. "

So brush and ink were sent for, and Zhou Yu first wrote on his own palm, and then passed the pen to Zhuge Liang who also wrote. Then getting close together on the same bench, each showed his hand to the other, and both burst out laughing, for both had written the same word, "Fire. "

"Since we are of the same opinion," said Zhou Yu, "there is no longer any doubt. But our intentions must be kept secret. "

"Both of us are public servants, and what would be the sense of telling our plans? I do not think Cao Cao will be on his guard against this, although he has had two experiences. You may put your scheme into force. "

They finished their wine and separated. Not an officer knew a word of the general's plans.

英译注释

1. secretaries：军政司，即管理军中事务的官员，此处译者简译为"秘书，干事"。

2. the secret gates：奇门，最早源于黄帝战蚩尤的《奇门遁甲》，是古人认识客观世界的一种比较完整的时、空、象、数、理模型。太乙、奇门、六壬，并称"三式"，是中国术数三大绝学。奇门以地元为主，测集体事。邓罗以secret gates 来传译"奇门"虽隐省了其文化内涵，但 secret 一词能体现诸葛亮的过人之学。

3. the interdependence of the elements：阴阳。现在"阴阳"多直接翻译成汉语拼音 yin yang。阴阳相生相克，是古代圣贤将自然界中各种对立又相联的现象抽象归纳出的概念。邓罗的理解是很准确的，而 elements 和观天象借东风完美契合。

英译评述

　　《三国演义》的语言基本风格是"文不甚深，言不甚俗"，浅近文言和白话的有机结合使其既为文人雅士所钟情又受市井百姓所喜爱。其文"简洁精练、生动传神、晓畅自然、灵话多变、气势充沛"。《三国演义》上涉天文，下及地理，中表治国齐家、斗志设谋、风俗人情、伦理道德，内容极其庞杂。罗贯中还巧妙地引用大量诗词名篇，如开篇杨慎的《临江仙》、孔明的《隆中对》、前后《出师表》、曹操的《短歌行》、曹植的《铜雀台赋》等。可见，翻译此书对译者的学识和语言功力都是巨大的挑战。

　　邓罗的译文通畅易懂，其在英语读者中引起的轰动倒是很好地复制了原作在中国读者中所引起的热烈反响。邓罗在中国工作和生活了40年，他的中文造诣极高，对原著的理解很准确，再现了原著的语言，极力地保留了原著的语调及神韵。

　　邓罗的译本没有添加任何注解，有利于读者轻松地阅读。对于一些汉语文化特有的内容，他巧妙地运用了归化策略。如他用 Leviathan 来指"鲲"，Leviathan（利维坦）是《圣经》中最大的海洋生物；"二十余里"译为 seven miles。而在翻译"大禹""娄离之目"和"蓬莱"等内容时则采用语言补偿的手段，把它们在汉语中的内涵联想意义表达出来。"大禹"在音译的 Yu 前补充了表示身份的 King；"娄离之目"后补充了表现其特征的 keen；而"蓬莱"是中国人的仙岛，故此，邓罗在其前加了一个 fair 来修饰。而对于"冯夷"和"屏翳"这样的信息，他则简单地直接翻译为 sea and river gods。虽然省去了风神，但并不影响意义的表达，不影响读者的理解。这种不加任何注解的做法有利于读者的阅读，但是也不利于读者拓展知识，了解异语文化。

　　译文中也存在一些理解不当之处。如"两个移近坐榻"被译为 Then getting close together on the same bench。另外，由于力所不及，在全书的翻译中，邓罗删节了一些诗词部分的翻译，这也成为邓译本颇受指责之处。

Ⅰ. Translation Practice.

Directions：Translate the following sentences into English.

1. 天下大势，分久必合，合久必分。

2. 子治世之能臣，乱世之奸雄。

3. 万事俱备，只欠东风。

4. 赔了夫人又折兵。

5. 既生瑜何生亮？

Ⅱ. Translation Comparison.

Directions：Compare the following versions of translation of the opening poem of *Romance of the Three Kingdoms* in terms of interpretation, style, strategy, etc.

原文：滚滚长江东逝水，浪花淘尽英雄。是非成败转头空。青山依旧在，几度夕阳红。白发渔樵江渚上，惯看秋月春风。一壶浊酒喜相逢。古今多少事，都付笑谈中。

——杨慎《临江仙》

Moss Roberts' Translation：

On and on the Great River rolls, racing east.

Of proud and gallant heroes its white-tops leaves no trace,

As right and wrong, pride and fall turn all at once unreal.

Yet ever the green hills stay

To blaze in the west-waning day.

Fishers and woodsmen comb the river isles,

White-crowned, they've seen enough of spring and autumn tide

To make good company over the wine jar,

Where many a famed event

Provides their merriment.

C. H. Brewitt-Taylor's Translation：

O so vast, O so mighty,

The Great River rolls to sea,

Flowers do waves thrash,

Heroes do sands smash,

When all the dreams drain,

Same are loss and gain.

Green mountains remain,

Under pink sunsets,

Hoary fishers and woodcutters,

Along the banks, find calm water,

In autumn moon or in spring wind,

By the wine jars, fill porcelain.

Discuss talk and tale,

Only laugh and gale...

Ⅲ. **Oral Presentation**.

Directions: Identify the incorrect translations in Chapter 46, come up with your own translations and present them in class with the help of PPT.

第二节 《红楼梦》选译

曹雪芹 (1715—约1763),清代文学家,名沾,字梦阮,号雪芹;素性放达,涉猎广泛:金石、诗书、绘画、园林、中医、织补、工艺、饮食等,无不喜爱,且颇有造诣。他出身于一个"百年望族"的大官僚地主家庭,因家庭的衰败饱尝人世辛酸,后凭借坚韧不拔之毅力,历经多年艰辛,创作出极具思想性、艺术性的伟大作品《红楼梦》。

该书以宝黛钗的爱情为主线描写了贾、王、薛、史四大家族的兴衰史。《红楼梦》是一部中国封建社会末期的百科全书;小说以上层贵族社会为中心,极其真实、生动地描写了十八世纪上半叶中国末期封建社会的全部生活,是这段历史生活的缩影。《红楼梦》曾被评为中国最具文学成就的古典小说及章回体小说的巅峰之作，被认为是"中国四大名著"之首。在现代，还产生了一门以研究《红楼梦》为主题的学科"红学"，产生了评论派、考证派、索隐派、创作派等四大学派。

【中文原文】

西厢记妙词通戏语，牡丹亭艳曲警芳心❶（节选）

曹雪芹

　　闲言少叙。且说宝玉自进园来，心满意足，再无别项可生贪求之心，每日只和姊妹丫鬟们一处，或读书，或写字，或弹琴下棋，作画吟诗，以至描鸾刺凤，斗草簪花[1]，低吟悄唱，拆字猜枚，无所不至，倒也十分快意。他曾有几首四时即事诗，虽不算好，却是真情真景。

"春夜即事"云：

霞绡云幄任铺陈，隔巷蛙声听未真。

枕上轻寒窗外雨，眼前春色梦中人。

盈盈烛泪因谁泣，点点花愁为我嗔。

自是小鬟娇懒惯，拥衾不耐笑言频。

"夏夜即事"云：

倦绣佳人幽梦长，金笼鹦鹉唤茶汤。

窗明麝月开宫镜，室霭檀云品御香。

琥珀杯倾荷露滑，玻璃槛纳柳风凉。

水亭处处齐纨动，帘卷朱楼罢晚妆。

---

❶　曹雪芹，高鹗. 红楼梦［M］. 北京：中华书局，2005：163–165.

"秋夜即事"云：

绛芸轩里绝喧哗，桂魄流光浸茜纱。

苔锁石纹容睡鹤，井飘桐露湿栖鸦。

抱衾婢至舒金凤，倚槛人归落翠花。

静夜不眠因酒渴，沉烟重拨索烹茶。

"冬夜即事"云：

梅魂竹梦已三更，锦罽[2]鸺[3]衾睡未成。

松影一庭惟见鹤，梨花满地不闻莺。

女儿翠袖诗怀冷，公子金貂酒力轻。

却喜侍儿知试茗，扫将新雪及时烹。

不说宝玉闲吟，且说这几首诗，当时有一等势利人，见是荣国府十二三岁的公子做的，抄录出来，各处称颂；再有一等轻薄子弟，爱上那风流妖艳之句，也写在扇头壁上，不时吟哦赏赞。因此上竟有人来寻诗觅字，倩画求题的。宝玉一发得意，每日家做这些外务。

谁想静中生动，忽一日，不自在起来，这也不好，那也不好，出来进去，只是闷闷的。园中那些女孩子，正是混沌世界天真烂熳之时，坐卧不避，嘻笑无心，那里知宝玉此时的心事？那宝玉心内不自在，便懒在园内，只在外头鬼混，却又痴痴的。茗烟见他这样，因想与他开心，左思右想，皆是宝玉玩烦了的，只有这件，宝玉不曾见过。想毕，便走到书坊内，把那古今小说，并那飞燕、合德、武则天、杨贵妃的"外传"与那传奇角本，买了许多来引宝玉。宝玉一看，如得珍宝。茗烟又嘱咐道："不可拿进园去，若叫人知道了，我就'吃不了兜着走'呢。"宝玉那里肯不拿进去？踟蹰再四，单把那文理雅道些的，拣了几套进去，放在床顶上，无人时才看；那粗俗过露的，都藏于外面书房内。

那日正当三月中浣[4]，早饭后，宝玉携了一套《会真记》，走到沁芳闸桥那边桃花底下一块石上坐着，展开《会真记》，从头细看。正看到"落红成阵"，只见一阵风过，树上桃花吹下一大斗来，落得满身满书满地皆是花片。宝玉要抖将下来，恐怕脚步践踏了，只得兜了那花瓣，来至池边，抖在池内。那花瓣浮在水面，飘飘荡荡，竟流出沁芳闸去了。

回来只见地下还有许多花瓣，宝玉正踟蹰间，只听背后有人说道："你在这里做什么？"宝玉一回头，却是林黛玉来了：肩上担着花锄，花锄上挂着纱囊，手内拿着花帚。宝玉笑道："好，好，来把这个花扫起来，撂在那水里去罢。我才撂了好些在那里呢。"黛玉道："撂在水里不好，你看这里的水干净，只一流出去，有人家的地方什么没有？仍旧把花遭塌了。那畸角上我有一个花冢，如今把他扫了，装在这绢袋里，埋在那里，日久随土化了，岂不干净。"

宝玉听了，喜不自禁，笑道："待我放下书，帮你来收拾。"黛玉道："什么书？"宝玉见问，慌的藏之不迭，便说道："不过是《中庸》《大学》。"黛玉道："你又在我跟前弄鬼。趁早儿给我瞧瞧，好多着呢。"宝玉道："妹妹，要论你，我是不怕的。你看了，好歹别告诉别人。真正这是好文章！你若看了，连饭也不想吃呢。"一面说，一面递了过去。黛玉把花具放下，接书来瞧，从头看去，越看越爱。不顿饭时，将十六出俱已看完。但觉词句警人，余香满口。虽看完了，却只管出神，心内还默默记诵。宝玉笑道："妹妹，你说好不好？"林黛玉笑道："果然有趣。"宝玉笑道："我就是个'多愁多病的身'，你就是那'倾国倾城的貌'。"林黛玉听了，不觉带腮连耳通红，登时竖起两道似蹙非蹙的眉，瞪了两只似睁非睁的眼，桃腮带怒，薄面含嗔，指宝玉道："你这该死的胡说！好好的，把这淫词艳曲弄了来，说这些混账话来欺负我。我告诉舅舅、舅母去！"说到"欺负"二字，就把眼睛圈儿红了，转身就走。

宝玉着了忙，向前拦住道："好妹妹，千万饶我这一遭，原是我说错了。若有心欺负你，明儿我掉在池子里，叫个癞头鼋[5]吃了去，变个大忘八，等你明儿做了'一品夫人'病老归西的时候，我往你坟上替你驮一辈子碑去。"说的林黛玉"噗嗤"的一声笑了，一面揉着眼，一面笑道：

"一般唬的这么个调儿，还只管胡说。呸，原来也是个'银样蜡枪头'。"宝玉听了，笑道："你说说，你这个呢？我也告诉去。"林黛玉笑道："你说你会'过目成诵'，难道我就不能'一目十行'么？"宝玉一面收书，一面笑道："正经快把花埋了罢，别提那些个了。"二人便收拾落花。

正才掩埋妥协，只见袭人走来，说道："那里没找到？摸在这里来。那边大老爷身上不好，姑娘们都过去请安，老太太叫打发你去呢，快回去换衣服罢。"宝玉听了，忙拿了书，别了黛玉，同袭人回房换衣不提。

这里林黛玉见宝玉去了，听见众姊妹也不在房中，自己闷闷的。正欲回房，刚走到梨香院墙角外，只听见墙内笛韵悠扬，歌声婉转，林黛玉便知是那十二个女孩子演习戏文。虽未留心去听，偶然两句吹到耳内，明明白白一字不落道："原来姹紫嫣红开遍，似这般，都付与断井颓垣。"林黛玉听了，倒也十分感慨缠绵，便止步侧耳细听，又唱道是："良辰美景奈何天，赏心乐事谁家院？"听了这两句，不觉点头自叹，心下自思："原来戏上也有好文章，可惜世人只知看戏，未必能领略其中的趣味。"想毕，又后悔不该胡想，耽误了听曲子。再听时，恰唱到："只为你如花美眷，似水流年……"黛玉听了这两句，不觉心动神摇。又听道："你在幽闺自怜"等句，越发如醉如痴，站立不住，便一蹲身坐在一块山子石上，细嚼"如花美眷，似水流年"八个字的滋味。忽又想起前日见古人诗中有"水流花谢两无情"之句，再词中又有"流水落花春去也，天上人间"之句，又兼方才所见《西厢记》中"花落水流红，闲愁万种"之句，都一时想起来，凑聚在一处。仔细忖度，不觉心痛神驰，眼中落泪。正没个开交，忽觉背后有人击他一下，及回头看时，原来是个女子，未知是谁，下回分解。

中文注释

[1] 簪花（zān huā）：插花于冠。

[2] 锦屩（jì）：华美的地毯。

[3] 鹴（shuāng）：雁。

〔4〕中浣（huàn）：中旬。

〔5〕鼋（yuán）：动物名，亦称"绿团鱼"，俗称"癞头鼋"，爬行纲，鳖科。

Pao-yü and Tai-yü make use of some beautiful passages from the *Record of the Western Side-building* to bandy jokes. The excellent ballads sung in the *Peony Pavilion* touch the tender heart of Tai-yü.
By Cao Xueqin
Translated by H. Bencraft Joly

Ever since he shifted his quarters into the park, his heart was full of joy, and his mind of contentment, fostering none of those extraordinary ideas, whose tendency could be to give birth to longings and hankerings. Day after day, he simply indulged, in the company of his female cousins and the waiting-maids, in either reading his books, or writing characters, or in thrumming the lute, playing chess, drawing pictures and scanning verses[1], even in drawing patterns of argus pheasants[2], in embroidering phoenixes, contesting with them in searching for strange plants[3], and gathering flowers, in humming poetry with gentle tone, singing ballads with soft voice, dissecting characters[4], and in playing at mora[5], so that, being free to go everywhere and anywhere, he was of course completely happy. From his pen emanate four ballads on the times of the four seasons, which, although they could not be looked upon as first-rate, afford anyhow a correct idea of his sentiments, and a true account of the scenery.

The ballad on the spring night runs as follows:

The silken curtains, thin as russet silk, at random are spread out.

---

❶ 《红楼梦》已有 20 多种不同文字的译本，有摘译、节译、全译三种形式。本书译文摘选自英国人乔利（H. Bencraft Joly）1892 年出版的前五十六回节译本。本译文来自于 The Project Gutenberg EBook。

The croak of frogs from the adjoining lane but faintly strikes the ear.

The pillow a slight chill pervades, for rain outside the window falls.

The landscape, which now meets the eye, is like that seen in dreams by man.

In plenteous streams the candles' tears do drop, but for whom do they weep?

Each particle of grief felt by the flowers is due to anger against me.

It's all because the maids have by indulgence indolent been made.

The cover over me I'll pull, as I am loth to laugh and talk for long.

This is the description of the aspect of nature on a summer night：

The beauteous girl, weary of needlework, quiet is plunged in a long dream.

The parrot in the golden cage doth shout that it is time the tea to brew.

The lustrous windows with the musky moon like open palace-mirrors look;

The room abounds with fumes of sandalwood and all kinds of imperial scents.

From the cups made of amber is poured out the slippery dew from the lotus.

The banisters of glass, the cool zephyr enjoy flapped by the willow trees.

In the stream-spanning kiosk, the curtains everywhere all at one time do wave.

In the vermilion tower the blinds the maidens roll, for they have made the night's toilette.

The landscape of an autumnal evening is thus depicted：

In the interior of the Chiang Yün house are hushed all clamorous din and noise.

The sheen, which from Selene[6] flows, pervades the windows of carnation gauze.

The moss-locked, streaked rocks shelter afford to the cranes, plunged in sleep.

The dew, blown on the t'ung tree by the well, doth wet the roosting rooks.

Wrapped in a quilt, the maid comes the gold phoenix coverlet to spread.

The girl, who on the rails did lean, on her return drops the kingfisher flowers!

This quiet night his eyes in sleep he cannot close, as he doth long for wine.

The smoke is stifled, and the fire restirred, when tea is ordered to be brewed.

The picture of a winter night is in this strain：

The sleep of the plum trees, the dream of the bamboos the third watch have already reached.

Under the embroidered quilt and the kingfisher coverlet one can't sleep for the cold.

The shadow of fir trees pervades the court, but cranes are all that meet the eye.

Both far and wide the pear blossom covers the ground, but yet the hawk cannot be heard.

The wish, verses to write, fostered by the damsel with the green sleeves, has waxéd cold.

The master, with the gold sable pelisse, cannot endure much wine.

But yet he doth rejoice that his attendant knows the way to brew the tea.

The newly-fallen snow is swept what time for tea the water must be boiled.

But putting aside Pao-yü, as he leisurely was occupied in scanning some verses, we will now allude to all these ballads. There lived, at that time, a class of people, whose wont was to servilely court the influential and wealthy, and who, upon perceiving that the verses were composed by a young lad of the Jung Kuo Mansion, of only twelve or thirteen years of age, had copies made, and taking them outside sang their praise far and wide. There were besides another sort of light-headed young men, whose heart was so set upon licentious and seductive lines, that they even inscribed them on fans and screen-walls, and time and again kept on humming them and extolling them. And to the above reasons must therefore be ascribed the fact that persons came in search of stanzas and in quest of manuscripts, to apply for sketches and to beg for poetical compositions, to the increasing satisfaction of Pao-yü, who day after day, when at home, devoted his time and attention to these extraneous matters. But who would have anticipated that he could ever in his quiet seclusion have become a prey to a spirit of restlessness? Of a sudden, one day he began to feel discontent, finding fault with this and turning up his nose at that; and going in and coming out he was simply full of ennui. And as all the girls in the garden were just in the prime of youth, and at a time of life when, artless and unaffected, they sat and reclined without regard to retirement, and disported themselves and joked without heed, how

could they ever have come to read the secrets which at this time occupied a place in the heart of Pao-yü? But so unhappy was Pao-yü within himself that he soon felt loth to stay in the garden, and took to gadding about outside like an evil spirit; but he behaved also the while in an idiotic manner.

Ming Yen, upon seeing him go on in this way, felt prompted, with the idea of affording his mind some distraction, to think of this and to devise that expedient; but everything had been indulged in with surfeit by Pao-yü, and there was only this resource, (that suggested itself to him,) of which Pao-yü had not as yet had any experience. Bringing his reflections to a close, he forthwith came over to a bookshop, and selecting novels, both of old and of the present age, traditions intended for outside circulation on Fei Yen, Ho Te, Wu Tse-t'ien, and Yang Kuei-fei, as well as books of light literature consisting of strange legends, he purchased a good number of them with the express purpose of enticing Pao-yü to read them. As soon as Pao-yü caught sight of them, he felt as if he had obtained some gem or jewel. "But you mustn't," Ming Yen went on to enjoin him, "take them into the garden; for if any one were to come to know anything about them, I shall then suffer more than I can bear; and you should, when you go along, hide them in your clothes!"

But would Pao-yü agree to not introducing them into the garden? So after much wavering, he picked out only several volumes of those whose style was more refined, and took them in, and threw them over the top of his bed for him to peruse when no one was present; while those coarse and very indecent ones, he concealed in a bundle in the outer library.

On one day, which happened to be the middle decade of the third moon, Pao-yü, after breakfast, took a book, the "Hui Chen Chi," in his hand and walked as far as the bridge of the Hsin Fang Lock. Seating himself on a block of rock, that lay under the peach trees in that quarter, he opened the "Hui Chen Chi" and began to read it carefully from the beginning. But just as he came to the passage: "the falling red (flowers) have formed a heap," he felt a gust of wind blow through the trees, bringing down a whole bushel of peach blossoms; and, as they fell, his whole person, the entire surface of the book as well as a large extent of ground were simply bestrewn with petals of the blossoms. Pao-yü was bent upon shaking them down; but as he feared lest they should be trodden under foot, he felt constrained to carry the petals in his coat and walk to the bank of the pond and throw them into the stream. The petals floated on the surface of the water, and, after whirling and swaying here and there, they at length ran out by the Hsin Fang Lock. But, on his return under the tree, he found the ground again one mass of petals, and Pao-yü was just hesitating what to do, when he heard someone behind his back inquire, "What are you up to here?" and as soon as Pao-yü turned his head round, he discovered that it was Lin Tai-yü, who had come over carrying on her shoulder a hoe for raking flowers, that on this hoe was suspended a gauze-bag, and that in her hand she held a broom.

"That's right, well done!" Pao-yü remarked smiling; "Come and sweep these flowers, and throw them into the water yonder. I've just thrown a lot in there myself!"

"It isn't right," Lin Tai-yü rejoined, "to throw them into the water. The water, which you see, is clean enough here, but as soon as it finds its way out, where are situated other people's grounds, what isn't there in it? so that you would be misusing these flowers just as much as if you left them here! But in that corner, I have dug a hole for flowers, and I'll now sweep these and put them into this gauze-bag and bury them in there; and, in course of many days, they will also become converted into earth, and won't this be a clean way (of disposing of them)?"

Pao-yü, after listening to these words, felt inexpressibly delighted. "Wait!" he smiled, "until I put down my book, and I'll help you to clear them up!"

"What's the book?" Tai-yü inquired.

Pao-yü at this question was so taken aback that he had no time to conceal it. "It's," he replied hastily, "the *Chung Yung* and the *Ta Hsüeh*[7]!"

"Are you going again to play the fool with me? Be quick and give it to me to see; and this will be ever so much better a way!"

"Cousin," Pao-*yü* replied, "as far as you yourself are concerned I don't mind you, but after you've seen it, please don't tell anyone else. It's really written in beautiful style; and were you to once begin reading it, why even for your very rice you would't have a thought?"

As he spoke, he handed it to her; and Tai-*yü* deposited all the flowers on the ground, took over the book, and read it from the very first page; and the more she perused it, she got so much the more fascinated by it, that in no time she had finished reading sixteen whole chapters. But aroused as she was to a state of rapture by the diction, what remained even of the fascination was enough to overpower her senses; and though she had finished reading, she nevertheless continued in a state of abstraction, and still kept on gently recalling the text to mind, and humming it to herself.

"Cousin, tell me is it nice or not?" Pao-*yü* grinned.

"It is indeed full of zest!" Lin Tai-*yü* replied exultingly.

"I'm that very sad and very sickly person," Pao-*yü* explained laughing, "while you are that beauty who could subvert the empire and overthrow the city."

Lin Tai-*yü* became, at these words, unconsciously crimson all over her cheeks, even up to her very ears; and raising, at the same moment, her two eyebrows, which seemed to knit and yet not to knit, and opening wide those eyes, which seemed to stare and yet not to stare, while her peach-like cheeks bore an angry look and on her thin-skinned face lurked displeasure, she pointed at Pao-*yü* and exclaimed: "You do deserve death, for the rubbish you talk! Without any provocation you bring up these licentious expressions and wanton ballads to give vent to all this insolent rot, in order to insult me; but I'll go and tell uncle and aunt. ”

As soon as she pronounced the two words "insult me", her eyeballs at once were suffused with purple, and turning herself round she there and then walked away; which filled Pao-yü with so much distress that he jumped forward to impede her progress, as he pleaded: "My dear cousin, I earnestly entreat you to spare me this time! I've indeed said what I shouldn't; but if I had any intention to insult you, I'll throw myself tomorrow into the pond, and let the scabby-headed turtle eat me up, so that I become transformed into a large tortoise. And when you shall have by and by become the consort of an officer of the first degree, and you shall have fallen ill from old age and re-turned to the west[8], I'll come to your tomb and bear your stone tablet for ev-er on my back!"

As he uttered these words, Lin Tai-yü burst out laughing with a sound of "pu ch'ih", and rubbing her eyes, she sneeringly remarked: "I too can come out with this same tune; but will you now still go on talking nonsense? Pshaw! You're, in very truth, like a spear-head, (which looks) like silver, (but is really soft as) wax!"

"Go on, go on!" Pao-yü smiled after this remark, "and what you've said, I too will go and tell!"

"You maintain," Lin Tai-yü rejoined sarcastically, "that after glancing at anything you're able to recite it; and do you mean to say that I can't even do so much as take in ten lines with one gaze?"

Pao-yü smiled and put his book away, urging: "Let's do what's right and proper, and at once take the flowers and bury them; and don't let us allude to these things!"

Forthwith the two of them gathered the fallen blossoms; but no sooner had they interred them properly than they espied Hsi Jen coming, who went on to observe: "Where haven't I looked for you? What! Have you found your way as far as this! But our senior master, Mr. Chia She, over there isn't well;

and the young ladies have all gone over to pay their respects, and our old lady has asked that you should be sent over; so go back at once and change your clothes!"

When Pao-yü heard what she said, he hastily picked up his books, and saying good bye to Tai-yü, he came along with Hsi Jen, back into his room, where we will leave him to effect the necessary change in his costume. But during this while, Lin Tai-yü was, after having seen Pao-yü walk away, and heard that all her cousins were likewise not in their rooms, wending her way back alone, in a dull and dejected mood, towards her apartment. When upon reaching the outside corner of the wall of the Pear Fragrance Court, she caught, issuing from inside the walls, the harmonious strains of the fife and the melodious modulations of voices singing. Lin Tai-yü readily knew that it was the twelve singing-girls rehearsing a play; and though she did not give her mind to go and listen, yet a couple of lines were of a sudden blown into her ears, and with such clearness, that even one word did not escape. Their burden was this:

These troth are beauteous purple and fine carmine flowers,

which in this way all round do bloom,

And all together lie ensconced along the broken well,

and the dilapidated wall!

But the moment Lin Tai-yü heard these lines, she was, in fact, so intensely affected and agitated that she at once halted and lending an ear listened attentively to what they went on to sing, which ran thus:

A glorious day this is, and pretty scene, but sad I feel at heart!

Contentment and pleasure are to be found in whose family courts?

After overhearing these two lines, she unconsciously nodded her head, and sighed, and mused in her own mind. "Really," she thought, "there is fine diction even in plays! but unfortunately what men in this world simply know is to see a play, and they don't seem to be able to enjoy the beauties contained in them."

At the conclusion of this train of thought, she experienced again a sting of regret, (as she fancied) she should not have given way to such idle thoughts and missed attending to the ballads; but when she once more came to listen, the song, by some coincidence, went on thus:

It's all because thy loveliness is like a flower and like the comely spring,

That years roll swiftly by just like a running stream.

When this couplet struck Tai-yu's ear, her heart felt suddenly a prey to excitement and her soul to emotion; and upon further hearing the words:

Alone you sit in the secluded inner rooms to self-compassion giving way.

—and other such lines, she became still more as if inebriated, and like as if out of her head, and unable to stand on her feet, she speedily stooped her body, and, taking a seat on a block of stone, she minutely pondered over the rich beauty of the eight characters:

It's all because thy loveliness is like a flower and like the comely spring,

That years roll swiftly by just like a running stream.

Of a sudden, she likewise bethought herself of the line:

Water flows away and flowers decay, for both no feelings have.

—which she had read some days back in a poem of an ancient writer, and also of the passage:

When on the running stream the flowers do fall, spring then is past and gone;

—and of:

Heaven (differs from) the human race.

—which also appeared in that work; and besides these, the lines, which she had a short while back read in the Hsi Hiang Chi[3]:

The flowers, lo, and on their course the waters red do flow!

Petty misfortunes of ten thousand kinds (my heart assail!)

both simultaneously flashed through her memory; and, collating them all together, she meditated on them minutely, until suddenly her heart was stricken with pain and her soul fleeted away, while from her eyes trickled down drops of tears. But while nothing could dispel her present state of mind, she unexpectedly realised that someone from behind gave her a tap; and, turning her head round to look, she found that it was a young girl; but who it was, the next chapter will make known.

英译注释

1. scanning verses：吟诗。scan 指诗句合辙押韵。

2. argus pheasants：眼斑雉，一种大鸟（大眼斑雉）产于南亚和东印度群岛；尾巴长；羽毛色泽鲜艳；带有眼状斑纹。

3. contesting with them in searching for strange plants：斗草。斗草是古代流行于女孩子中的一种游戏，又称"斗百草"。"斗草"分"武斗"和"文斗"。所谓"文斗"，就是对花草名，女孩们采来百草，以对仗的形式互报草名，谁采的草种多、对仗的水平高、能坚持到最后，谁便赢。因此玩这种游戏没点植物知识和文学修养是不行的。

4. dissecting characters：拆字。拆字，又称"测字""破字""相字"等，是中国古代的一种推测吉凶的方式，主要做法是以汉字加减笔画，拆开偏旁，打乱字体结构进行推断。在现代社会中，拆字成为一种有趣的游戏，逐渐消除了迷信色彩。

5. playing at mora：猜枚，猜拳。

6. Selene：<希神> 月之女神，此处乔利用其来指"桂魄"。

7. *Chung Yung*：《中庸》，也被译为 *The Doctrine of the Mean*；*Ta Hsüeh*：《大学》，又译为 *The Great Learning*。

8. returned to the west：归西。英语中有两个与死相关的表达：go west：<口语>（人）死，上西天，完蛋；return to dust：归于尘土，去世。乔利把两者结合起来，因为 go west 虽然字面上与汉语的归西十分契合，但它的内涵意义不佳，不合适。

9. Hsi Hiang Chi：《西厢记》，即前文宝黛共读的《会真记》（*Hui Chen Chi*）。《会真记》又名《莺莺传》，是唐朝元稹所作，其故事后来被改编成很多版本，最有名的是王实甫的《西厢记》。乔利把回目名中的《西厢记》按意译译成了 *Record of the Western Side-building*。

英译评述

《红楼梦》是中国封建社会末期的一部百科全书，包罗万象，人物众多，关系盘根错节，加上大量的诗词歌赋，因此翻译《红楼梦》极具挑战。然而，作为世界文学史上的一部旷世杰作，它又吸引着来自不同语言文化的人勇敢地迎接这项挑战。《红楼梦》已有 20 多种文字的译本，有的语种还有多个译本。

本书所选的是 1892 年英国人乔利的译本，这是一个最早的较为完整的英译本。该译本虽只译了前 56 回，但译文流畅，忠实原著，保持了原文的文学性；吴宓先生评价其为"密合原文""无所删汰"。乔译本还有一大特点——没有增添文化脚注，主要采用了增益和归化的办法。如将"斗草"译为 contesting with them in searching for strange plants，就采用了增益的手法说明了斗草游戏的玩法；而"猜枚"则归化为来自意大利语的 playing at mora。

乔利的预期读者是潜在的汉语学习者，译文紧扣原文字面意义。为了句法准确，逻辑清晰，他把增加的连接成分，补充的语义内容放在括号中，以示与原文的区别。例如：you're, in very truth, like a spear-head, (which looks) like silver, (but is really soft as) wax!（是个银样蜡枪头）；又如：the falling red (flowers) have formed a heap（落红成阵）。

复杂的汉语姓氏称谓的翻译也大有学问。由于汉字姓氏多为单音节，颇有同音不同姓的现象存在，加之英译以后没有了音调的区分，且威妥码记音有缺陷，同音姓氏就更多了，极易造成混乱。如 23 回中前半部分有贾芹之母周氏和赵姨娘都被译为 Dame Chou。汉语亲戚关系划分细致，称谓丰富，与英文区别甚大，翻译时应仔细对待。本回中"舅舅舅母"就被归化为 uncle and aunt。而宝玉口中的"好妹妹"却不能直译为 sister，这会造成英语读者的误解，故乔利将之译为了 cousin，虽然失去了原文中的情愫，却不失为明智之举。

Ⅰ. **Research and Oral Presentation**.

Directions：Conduct a research on "How to Translate Kinship Terms", and present it in class with the help of PPT.

Ⅱ. **Writing**.

Directions：Cao Xueqin excelled at describing his characters in graphic detail. Study the English version of the appearance descriptions of the major characters in the novel, and then write a description of someone you know.

第三节　《聊斋志异》选译

　　蒲松龄（1640—1715），清代文学家，字留仙、剑臣，别号柳泉居士，山东淄川（今属淄博市）人。他出身于一个没落的地主家庭，一生刻苦好学，在科举场中却很不得意，满腹经纶，却屡试不第，到了 71 岁，才援例成为贡生。在艰难时世中，他逐渐认识到像他这样出身的人难有出头之日，于是把满腔愤懑和一生心血寄托在《聊斋志异》的创作中。

　　《聊斋志异》是一部文言短篇小说集，共有短篇小说498 篇。《聊斋志异》表面上是谈鬼说狐，其实是借花妖狐魅反映社会人生，其内容大致分为四部分。其一，揭露与嘲讽贪官污吏、恶霸豪绅贪婪狠毒的嘴脸，笔锋刺向封建政治制度，这类作品以《促织》《席方平》《商三官》《向杲》等篇最有代表性。其二，蒲松龄对腐朽的科举制度有切身的体会，通过《司文郎》《考弊司》《书痴》等篇，无情地揭开了科举制度的黑幕，勾画出考官们昏庸贪婪的面目，剖析了科举制度对知识分子灵魂的禁锢与腐蚀，谴责了考场中营私舞弊的风气。其三，对人间坚贞、纯洁的爱情及为了这种爱情而努力抗争的底层妇女、穷书生予以衷心的赞美，代表作品有《鸦头》《细侯》等。《聊斋志异》中还有相当多的狐鬼精灵与人相恋的故事，颇具浪漫情调。在这些故事里，塑造了很多容貌美丽、心灵纯洁的女性形象，如红玉、婴宁、香玉、青凤、娇娜、莲香等。其四，有些短篇是阐释伦理道德的寓意故事，具有教育意义，如《画皮》《崂山道士》等。

《聊斋志异》充满了浪漫主义精神和惊人的想象力，这主要表现在对正面人物的塑造上，特别是表现在由花妖狐魅变来的女性形象上。另外，作者善于运用梦境和上天入地、虚无变幻的手法营造情节，冲破现实的束缚，表现自己的理想和愿望。这部小说是中国文言短篇小说的巅峰之作。

画皮[1]

蒲松龄

太原王生，早行，遇一女郎，抱幞[1]独奔，甚艰于步。急走趁之，乃二八姝丽，心相爱乐。问："何夙夜踽踽独行？"女曰："行道之人，不能解愁忧，何劳相问。"生曰："卿何愁忧？或可效力，不辞也。"女黯然曰："父母贪赂，鬻[2]妾朱门。嫡[3]妒甚，朝詈[4]而夕楚辱之，所弗堪也，将远遁耳。"问："何之？"曰："在亡之人，乌有定所。"生言："敝庐不远，即烦枉顾。"女喜，从之。生代携幞物，导与同归。女顾室无人，问："君何无家口？"答云："斋耳。"女曰："此所良佳。如怜妾而活之，须秘密，勿泄。"生诺之。乃与寝合。使匿密室，过数日而人不知也。生微告妻。妻陈，疑为大家媵妾[5]，劝遣之。生不听。

偶适市，遇一道士，顾生而愕。问："何所遇？"答言："无之。"道士曰："君身邪气萦绕，何言无？"生又力白。道士乃去，曰："惑哉！世固

---

❶ 蒲松龄. 聊斋志异 ［M］. 北京：中华书局，2013：34-36.

有死将临而不悟者!"生以其言异,颇疑女。转思明明丽人,何至为妖,意道士借魇禳[6]以猎食者。无何,至斋门,门内杜,不得入。心疑所作,乃逾垝垣[7],则室门亦闭。蹑迹而窗窥之,见一狞鬼,面翠色,齿巉巉[8]如锯。铺人皮于榻上,执采笔而绘之。已而掷笔,举皮,如振衣状,披于身,遂化为女子。睹此状,大惧,兽伏而出。急追道士,不知所往。遍迹之,遇于野,长跪乞救,请遣除之。道士曰:"此物亦良苦,甫能觅代者,予亦不忍伤其生。"乃以蝇拂授生,令挂寝门。临别,约会于青帝庙。

生归,不敢入斋,乃寝内室,悬拂焉。一更许,闻门外戢戢[9]有声。自不敢窥也,使妻窥之。但见女子来,望拂子不敢进,立而切齿,良久乃去。少时,复来,骂曰:"道士吓我,终不然,宁入口而吐之耶!"取拂碎之,坏寝门而入,径登生床,裂生腹,掬生心而去。妻号。婢入烛之,生已死,腔血狼藉。陈骇涕不敢声。

明日,使弟二郎奔告道士。道士怒曰:"我固怜之,鬼子乃敢尔!"即从生弟来。女子已失所在。既而仰首四望,曰:"幸遁未远。"问:"南院谁家?"二郎曰:"小生所舍也。"道士曰:"现在君所。"二郎愕然,以为未有。道士问曰:"曾否有不识者一人来?"答曰:"仆早赴青帝庙,良不知,当归问之。"去,少顷而返,曰:"果有之。晨间一妪来,欲佣为仆家操作,室人止之,尚在也。"道士曰:"即是物矣。"遂与俱往。仗木剑,立庭心,呼曰:"孽魅!偿我拂子来!"妪在室,惶遽无色,出门欲遁。道士逐击之。妪仆,人皮划然而脱,化为厉鬼,卧嗥如猪。道士以木剑枭其首,身变作浓烟,匝地作堆。道士出一葫芦,拔其塞,置烟中,飗飗然[10]如口吸气,瞬息烟尽,道士塞口入囊。共视人皮,眉目手足,无不备具。道士卷之,如卷画轴声,亦囊之,乃别欲去。

陈氏拜迎于门,哭求回生之法。道士谢不能。陈益悲,伏地不起。道士沉思曰:"我术浅,诚不能起死。我指一人,或能之,往求必合有效。"问:"何人?"曰:"市上有疯者,时卧粪土中。试叩而哀之。倘狂辱夫人,夫人勿怒也。"二郎亦习知之,乃别道士,与嫂俱往。

见乞人颠歌道上,鼻涕三尺,秽不可近。陈膝行而前。乞人笑曰:

"佳人爱我乎?"陈告以故。又大笑曰:"人尽夫也,活之何为?"陈固哀之。乃曰:"异哉!人死而乞活于我,我阎罗耶?"怒以杖击陈,陈忍痛受之。市人渐集如堵。乞人咯痰唾盈把,举向陈吻曰:"食之!"陈红涨于面,有难色,既思道士之嘱,遂强啖焉。觉入喉中,硬如团絮,格格而下,停结胸间。乞人大笑曰:"佳人爱我哉!"遂起,行已不顾。尾之,入于庙中。迫而求之,不知所在,前后冥搜,殊无端兆,惭恨而归。

既悼夫亡之惨,又悔食唾之羞,俯仰哀啼,但愿即死。方欲展血敛尸,家人伫望,无敢近者。陈抱尸收肠,且理且哭。哭极声嘶,顿欲呕。觉鬲[11]中结物,突奔而出,不及回首,已落腔中。惊而视之,乃人心也,在腔中突突犹跃,热气腾蒸如烟然。大异之,急以两手合腔,极力抱挤。少懈,则气氤氲自缝中出,乃裂缯帛急束之。以手抚尸,渐温,覆以衾裯。中夜启视,有鼻息矣。天明,竟活。为言:"恍惚若梦,但觉腹隐痛耳。"视破处,痂结如钱,寻愈。

异史氏曰:"愚哉世人!明明妖也,而以为美。迷哉愚人!明明忠也,而以为妄。然爱人之色而渔之,妻亦将食人之唾而甘之矣。天道好还,但愚而迷者不寤耳。可哀也夫!"

中文注释

[1] 幞(fú):同"袱"。
[2] 鬻(yù):卖。
[3] 嫡(dí):正室。
[4] 詈(lì):骂。
[5] 媵(yìng)妾:陪嫁的人,侧室。
[6] 魇禳(yǎn ráng):镇压邪祟叫"魇",祛除灾变叫"禳",均属道教法术。
[7] 堁垣(guǐ yuán):倒塌的矮墙。
[8] 巉巉(chán):锋利尖锐。
[9] 戢戢(jí):象声词,形容细小之声。

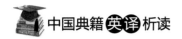

[10] 飐飐 (liú) 然：微风吹动的样子。

[11] 鬲：通 "膈"。

The Painted Skin[1]

By Pu Songlin

Translated by Herbert Allen Giles

At T'ai-yüan there lived a man named Wang. One morning he was out walking when he met a young lady carrying a bundle and hurrying along by herself. As she moved along with some difficulty①, Wang quickened his pace and caught her up, and found she was a pretty girl of about sixteen. Much smitten he inquired whither she was going so early, and no one with her. "A traveller like you," replied the girl, "cannot alleviate my distress; why trouble yourself to ask?" "What distress is it?" said Wang; "I'm sure I'll do anything I can for you." "My parents," answered she, "loved money, and they sold me as concubine into a rich family, where the wife was very jealous, and beat and abused me morning and night. It was more than I could stand, so I have run away." Wang asked her where she was going; to which she replied that a runaway had no fixed place of abode. "My house," said Wang, "is at no great distance; what do you say to coming there?" She joyfully acquiesced; and Wang, taking up her bundle, led the way to his house. Finding no one there, she asked Wang where his family were; to which he replied that that was only the library. "And a very nice place, too," said she; "but if you are kind enough to wish to save my life, you mustn't let it be known that I am here." Wang promised he would not divulge her secret, and so she remained

---

❶ 本书选用的是英国汉学家翟理思（Herbert Allen Giles，1845—1935，或译作翟理斯）的译本。译文出自 The Project Gutenburg EBook.

there for some days without anyone knowing anything about it. He then told his wife, and she, fearing the girl might belong to some influential family, advised him to send her away. This, however, he would not consent to do; when one day, going into the town, he met a Taoist priest, who looked at him in astonishment, and asked him what he had met. "I have met nothing," replied Wang. "Why," said the priest, "you are bewitched; what do you mean by not having met anything?" But Wang insisted that it was so, and the priest walked away, saying, "The fool! Some people don't seem to know when death is at hand." This startled Wang, who at first thought of the girl; but then he reflected that a pretty young thing as she was couldn't well be a witch, and began to suspect that the priest merely wanted to do a stroke of business. When he returned, the library door was shut, and he couldn't get in, which made him suspect that something was wrong; and so he climbed over the wall, where he found the door of the inner room shut too. Softly creeping up, he looked through the window and saw a hideous devil, with a green face and jagged teeth like a saw, spreading a human skin upon the bed and painting it with a paint-brush. The devil then threw aside the brush, and giving the skin a shake out, just as you would a coat, threw it over its shoulders, when, lo! it was the girl. Terrified at this, Wang hurried away with his head down in search of the priest who had gone he knew not whither; subsequently finding him in the fields, where he threw himself on his knees and begged the priest to save him.

"As to driving her away," said the priest, "the creature must be in great distress to be seeking a substitute for herself[2]; besides, I could hardly endure to injure a living thing."[3] However, he gave Wang a fly-brush, and bade him hang it at the door of the bedroom, agreeing to meet again at the Ch'ing-ti temple. Wang went home, but did not dare enter the library; so he hung up the brush at the bedroom door, and before long heard a sound of footsteps outside. Not daring to move, he made his wife peep out; and she saw the girl

standing looking at the brush, afraid to pass it. She then ground her teeth and went away; but in a little while came back, and began cursing, saying, "You priest, you won't frighten me. Do you think I am going to give up what is already in my grasp?" Thereupon, she tore the brush to pieces, and bursting open the door, walked straight up to the bed, where she ripped open Wang and tore out his heart, with which she went away. Wang's wife screamed out, and the servant came in with a light; but Wang was already dead and presented a most miserable spectacle. His wife, who was in an agony of fright, hardly dared cry for fear of making a noise; and next day she sent Wang's brother to see the priest. The latter got into a great rage, and cried out, "Was it for this that I had compassion on you, devil that you are?" proceeding at once with Wang's brother to the house, from which the girl had disappeared without anyone knowing whither she had gone. But the priest, raising his head, looked all round, and said, "Luckily she's not far off." He then asked who lived in the apartments on the south side, to which Wang's brother replied that he did; whereupon the priest declared that there she would be found. Wang's brother was horribly frightened and said he did not think so; and then the priest asked him if any stranger had been to the house. To this he answered that he had been out to the Ch'ing-ti temple and couldn't possibly say; but he went off to inquire, and in a little while came back and reported that an old woman had sought service with them as a maid-of-all-work, and had been engaged by his wife. "That is she," said the priest, as Wang's brother added she was still there; and they all set out to go to the house together. Then the priest took his wooden sword, and standing in the middle of the court-yard, shouted out, "Base-born fiend, give me back my fly-brush!" Meanwhile the new maid-of-all-work was in a great state of alarm, and tried to get away by the door; but the priest struck her and down she fell flat, the human skin dropped off, and she became a hideous devil. There she lay grunting like a pig, until the priest grasped his wooden sword and struck off her head. She then became a dense column of smoke curling up from the ground, when the priest took an uncorked gourd and threw it right into the midst of the smoke. A sucking noise was heard, and the whole column was drawn into the gourd; after which the priest corked it up closely and put it in his pouch.④ The skin, too, which was complete even to the eyebrows, eyes, hands, and feet, he also rolled up as if it had been a scroll, and was on the point of leaving with it, when Wang's wife stopped him, and with tears entreated him to bring her husband to life. The priest said he was unable to do that; but Wang's wife flung herself at his feet, and with loud lamentations implored his assistance. For some time he remained immersed in thought, and then replied, "My power is not equal to what you ask. I myself cannot raise the dead; but I will direct you to someone who can, and if you apply to him properly you will succeed." Wang's wife asked the priest who it was; to which he replied, "There is a maniac in the town who passes his time grovelling in the dirt. Go, prostrate yourself before him, and beg him to help you. If he insults you, shew no sign of anger." Wang's brother knew the man to whom he alluded, and accordingly bade the priest adieu, and proceeded thither with his sister-in-law.

They found the destitute creature raving away by the road side, so filthy that it was all they could do to go near him. Wang's wife approached him on her knees; at which the maniac leered at her, and cried out, "Do you love me, my beauty?" Wang's wife told him what she had come for, but he only laughed and said, "You can get plenty of other husbands. Why raise the dead one to life?" But Wang's wife entreated him to help her; whereupon he observed, "It's very strange: people apply to me to raise their dead as if I was king of the infernal regions[1]." He then gave Wang's wife a thrashing with his staff, which she bore without a murmur, and before a gradually increasing crowd of spectators. After this he produced a loathsome pill which he told her she must swallow, but here she broke down and was quite unable to do

so. However, she did manage it at last, and then the maniac crying out, "How you do love me!" got up and went away without taking any more notice of her. They followed him into a temple with loud supplications, but he had disappeared, and every effort to find him was unsuccessful. Overcome with rage and shame, Wang's wife went home, where she mourned bitterly over her dead husband, grievously repenting the steps she had taken, and wishing only to die. She then bethought herself of preparing the corpse, near which none of the servants would venture; and set to work to close up the frightful wound of which he died.

While thus employed, interrupted from time to time by her sobs, she felt a rising lump in her throat, which by-and-by came out with a pop and fell straight into the dead man's wound. Looking closely at it, she saw it was a human heart; and then it began as it were to throb, emitting a warm vapour like smoke. Much excited, she at once closed the flesh over it, and held the sides of the wound together with all her might. Very soon, however, she got tired, and finding the vapour escaping from the crevices, she tore up a piece of silk and bound it round, at the same time bringing back circulation by rubbing the body and covering it up with clothes. In the night, she removed the coverings, and found that breath was coming from the nose; and by next morning her husband was alive again, though disturbed in mind as if awaking from a dream and feeling a pain in his heart. Where he had been wounded, there was a cicatrix about as big as a cash[2], which soon after disappeared.

The Chronicler of the Strange remarks: "How foolish men are, to see nothing but beauty in what is clearly evil! And how benighted to dismiss as absurd what is clearly well-intended! It is folly such as this that obliges the lady Chen to steel herself to eat another man's phlegm, when her husband has fallen prey to lust. Heaven's Way has its justice, but some mortals remain foolish and never see the light!"

译文原注

① Impeded, of course, by her small feet. This practice is said to have o-riginated about A. D. 970, with Yao Niang, the concubine of the pretender Li Yü, who wished to make her feet like the "new moon". The Manchu or Tar-tar ladies have not adopted this custom, and therefore the empresses of modern times have feet of the natural size; neither is it in force among the Hakkas or hill—tribes of China and Formosa.

The practice was forbidden in 1664 by the Manchu Emperor, K'ang Hsi; but popular feeling was so strong on the subject that four years afterwards the prohibition was withdrawn. Protestant missionaries are now making a dead set at this shameful custom, but so far with very indifferent success; as parents who do not cramp the feet of their daughters would experience no small difficulty in finding husbands for them when they grow up. Besides, the gait of a young lady hobbling along, as we should say, seems to be much ad-mired by the other sex. The following seven reasons why this custom still keeps its hold upon the Chinese mind emanate from a native convert:

"1st. —If a girl's feet are not bound, people say she is not like a woman but like a man; they laugh at her, calling her names, and her parents are a-shamed of her.

"2nd. —Girls are like flowers, like the willow. It is very important that their feet should be bound short so that they can walk beautifully, with minc-ing steps, swaying gracefully, thus showing they are persons of respectability. People praise them. If not bound short, they say the mother has not trained her daughter carefully. She goes from house to house with noisy steps, and is called names. Therefore careful persons bind short.

"3rd. —One of a good family does not wish to marry a woman with long feet. She is commiserated because her feet are not perfect. If betrothed,

and the size of her feet is not discovered till after marriage, her husband and mother-in-law are displeased, her sisters-in-law laugh at her, and she herself is sad.

"4th. —The large footed has to do rough work, does not sit in a sedan when she goes out, walks in the streets barefooted, has no red clothes, does not eat the best food. She is wetted by the rain, tanned by the sun, blown upon by the wind. If unwilling to do all the rough work of the house she is called 'gormandizing and lazy.' Perhaps she decides to go out as a servant. She has no fame and honour. To escape all this her parents bind her feet.

"5th. —There are those with unbound feet who do no heavy work, wear gay clothing, ride in a sedan, call others to wait upon them. Although so fine they are low and mean. If a girl's feet are unbound, she cannot be distinguished from one of these.

"6th. —Girls are like gold, like gems. They ought to stay in their own house. If their feet are not bound they go here and go there with unfitting associates; they have no good name. They are like defective gems that are rejected.

"7th. —Parents are covetous. They think small feet are pleasing and will command a high price for a bride."

— On Foot – Binding, by Miss S. Woolston.

② The disembodied spirits of the Chinese Inferno are permitted, under certain conditions of time and good conduct, to appropriate to themselves the vitality of some human being, who, as it were, exchanges places with the so-called "devil." The devil does not, however, reappear as the mortal whose life it has become possessed of, but is merely born again into the world; the idea being that the amount of life on earth is a constant quantity, and cannot be increased or diminished, reminding one in a way of the great modern doctrine of the conservation of energy. This curious belief has an important bearing that will be brought out in a subsequent story.

③ Here again is a Taoist priest quoting the Buddhist commandment, "Thou shalt not take life." The Buddhist laity in China, who do not hesitate to take life for the purposes of food, salve their consciences from time to time by buying birds, fishes, etc. and letting them go, in the hope that such acts will be set down on the credit side of their record of good and evil.

④ This recalls the celebrated story of the fisherman in the *Arabian Nights*.

英译注释

1. infernal regions：地狱，阴间。
2. cash：可指纸钱也可指硬币。此处 cash 不如用 coin 准确易懂。

英译评述

《画皮》是《聊斋志异》中脍炙人口的篇章。蒲松龄继承了文言文的精炼、简洁、准确、生动及骈散结合等优良传统，又从口语中提炼出大量具有鲜明特点、清新、隽永、活泼、诙谐而又富有表现力的语言。他大量采用口语，但又不同于白话小说，通过文言虚字的运用，仍然保持文言的特征，创造了《聊斋志异》独具特色的语言艺术风格。

翟理思对原文的理解准确到位，其译文忠实而流畅。为了展示原著文言文写作的特点，他在翻译中也选用了 whither, thither, shew 等古英语和诗歌中常用的词汇，在遣词方面也更多地选用了英语中较文雅、正式的语汇，以表现原作者蒲松龄的文人笔法。不难看出，翟理思在忠实于原文的基础上为极力保持原作风姿所做的努力。

翟理思为帮助译入语读者更好地理解故事，加注了文化脚注。脚注②和③是对陌生的文化背景的介绍。脚注④引入英语读者熟悉的《一千零一夜》故事，以期帮助读者理解鬼魅化作浓烟被收入道士葫芦的画面。其中，有趣的是注脚①——介绍了古代中国女子裹足的现象及七大原因。脚注洋洋洒洒，

俨然独立成文。而实际上，原文中只有一句"甚艰于步"，将其译为 she moved along with some difficulty 已能表达原意了。这一注解在一定程度上是因译者个人喜好而加的。译者注释在很多时候是必不可少的，也有助于译入语读者对陌生文化的了解，但是，注解不宜过滥，否则会使读者兴趣索然。霍克斯在其翻译的《红楼梦》序言中就把阅读一部译注繁多的小说比作"戴着锁链打网球"。因此，译者在加脚注时一定要慎重。

Ⅰ. **Translation Practice.**

Directions：Translate the following into English.

王曰："弟子操作多日，师略授小技，此来为不负也。"道士问："何术之求。"王曰："每见师行处，墙壁所不能隔，但得此法足矣。"道士笑而允之。乃传以诀，令自咒毕，呼曰："入之!"王面墙，不敢入。又曰："试入之。"王果从容入，及墙而阻。道士曰："俯首骤入，勿逡巡!"王果去墙数步，奔而入；及墙，虚若无物；回视，果在墙外矣。大喜，入谢。道士曰："归宜洁持，否则不验。"遂助资斧，遣之归。抵家，自诩遇仙，坚壁所不能阻。妻不信。王效其作为，去墙数尺，奔而入，头触硬壁，蓦然而踣。妻扶视之，额上坟起，如巨卵焉。妻揶揄之。王惭忿，骂老道士之无良而已。（节选自《崂山道士》）

Ⅱ. **Research and Oral Presentation.**

Directions：Conduct a research on "Annotation in Translation", and present it in class with the help of PPT.

下篇

诗歌

第一章

先秦诗歌

导　读

　　《诗经》是中国最早的一部诗歌总集，先秦时期称《诗》，又称《诗三百》或《三百篇》，共汇集了自西周初年至春秋中叶大约五百多年的三百零五篇诗歌。西汉时被尊为儒家经典，始称《诗经》，并沿用至今。《诗经》分为"风""雅""颂"三个部分。《风》共十五国风，皆是地方民歌，其文学成就最高，主题包括对爱情、劳动等美好事物的吟唱，也包括怀故土、思征人及反压迫、反欺凌的怨叹与愤怒。《雅》分为《小雅》（七十四篇）和《大雅》（三十一篇），皆为宫廷乐歌，共一百零五篇。"雅"是正声雅乐，用于贵族享宴或诸侯朝会。《大雅》多为贵族所作，《小雅》多为个人抒怀。《颂》则为宗庙祭祀之诗歌，共四十首，内容多为贵族祭祀，祈丰年，颂祖德。《诗经》对后代诗歌发展产生了深远影响，是我国古典文学现实主义传统的源头。本章节选了《诗经》中《风》《雅》《颂》比较典型的几个篇章，并结合几位外国汉学家和国内译者的翻译，探讨《诗经》中先贤的爱情观、宗庙祭祀文化以及个人抒怀，学习如何从汉英对比角度对《诗经》中所展现的思想进行阐发译介。

第一节　《诗经》选译

周南·关雎

　　《关雎》居《诗经》之首，亦是《风》之始，通常被认为是一首描写男女恋爱的情歌。在艺术上此诗巧妙地采用了"兴"的表现手法。首章以雎鸟做比，叫声合鸣，相依相恋，兴起淑女陪君子的联想。余下各章，又以采荇菜兴起主人公对女子热情奔放的追求。全诗语言优美动听，运用叠韵、双声和叠词，增强了诗歌的音韵美、形式美以及拟声传情、写人状物的生动性。

周南·关雎❶

关关[1]雎鸠[2]，在河之洲[3]。窈窕[4]淑女，君子好逑[5]。

参差荇菜[6]，左右流之[7]。窈窕淑女，寤寐[8]求之。

求之不得，寤寐思服[9]。悠哉[10]悠哉，辗转反侧。

参差荇菜，左右采之。窈窕淑女，琴瑟友之[11]。

参差荇菜，左右芼[12]之。窈窕淑女，钟鼓乐之[13]。

中文注释

[1]关关：象声词，雌雄二鸟相互应和之声。

[2]雎鸠（jū jiū）：一种水鸟名，即王鴡。

[3]洲：水中的陆地。

[4]窈窕（yǎo tiǎo）淑女：贤良美好的女子。

[5]好逑（hǎo qiú）：好的配偶。逑："仇"的假借字，意为匹配。

[6]荇（xìng）菜：水草类植物。

[7]左右流之：时而向左、时而向右地择取荇菜。

[8]寤寐（wù mèi）：醒和睡，指日夜。

[9]思服：思念。服：想。

❶ 孔子. 诗经［M］. 程俊英，译注. 上海：上海古籍出版社，1985：3-4.

[10] 悠哉（yōu zāi）：悠悠思念，绵绵不断。

[11] 琴瑟友之：琴与瑟，皆是弦乐器。琴五或七弦，瑟二十五或五十弦。友：动词，亲近之意。此句意为弹琴鼓瑟以亲近她。

[12] 芼（mào）：选取，挑选。

[13] 钟鼓乐之：敲钟鼓乐让她开心。

The Odes of Chow and the South[①]❶

Song of Welcome to the Bride of King Wan[②]1

Trans. by William Jennings

Waterfowl[③] their mates are calling[④],

On the islets in the stream.

Chaste and modest maid! fit partner

For our lord (thyself we deem).

Waterlilies,[⑤] long or short ones, —

Seek[⑥] them left and seek them right.

'Twas this chaste and modest maiden

He hath[2] sought for, morn and night.

Seeking for her, yet not finding,

Night and morning he would yearn

Ah, so long, so long! — and restless

On his couch would toss and turn.

Waterlilies, long or short ones, —

---

❶　William Jennings. The Shi King, The Old "Poetic Classic" of The Chinese: A Close Metrical Translation with Annotations [M]. London: George Routledge and Sons, Limited, 1891: 35-36.

Gather⑥, right and left, their flowers.

Now the chaste and modest maiden

Lute and harp⑦ shall hail as ours.

Long or short the waterlilies,

Pluck⑥³ them left and pluck them right.

To the chaste and modest maiden

Bell and drum⑧ shall give delight.

译文原注

① "Chow" here means the Royal State, or crown-lands, as distinguished from the Feudal States around. It was the district in which the ancient Chow family had had their seat from B. C. 1325 to King Wǎn's time (B. C. 1231—B. C. 1135). It lay between the rivers Han and Wai (the latter a tributary of the Ho, or Yellow River). By "the South" we are to understand the States or country south of this Chow.

② The song is supposed to have been made by the inmates of the Palace, the ladies of the harem, who, it seems, were far from being jealous of her. Her retiring, gentle ways and chaste disposition made her a proper match as the principal wife of this virtuous prince. (For an account of Wan see the whole of Part III, Book I.; in Odes 2 and 4 of that book will also be found reference to his bride. Her name was T'ai−sze.)

③ There is a difference of opinion as to the name of the birds: some say they are ospreys or fish − hawks, some a species of duck, found always in pairs and inseparable.

④ Kwan, Kwan, onomatopoetic, like our "quack, quack"; but the Chinese commentators will have it that it is the harmonious call and response of the pairs of birds.

⑤ Strictly, an aquatic gentian, marsh −flower; sought for its beauty and purity.

⑥ I give the meaning of these perplexing verbs as found in the old Chinese Dictionary, the Urh - ya.

⑦ "Lute" is here given for an instrument with a single octave of strings; "harp" for a larger instrument of the same kind with several octaves.

⑧ Bells and drums were much used in old China as musical instruments.

英译注释

1. King Wan：即文王，姓姬，名昌，周王朝的缔造者。

2. hath：为古英语，意思和功能与 have、has 一样。

3. pluck：用作动词，意为摘、拔、扯。

英译评述

许渊冲在《英语世界》（2014 年第 8 期）中发表"英译诗词如何走向世界"一文，对辜正坤的《关雎》题名翻译颇不满意。辜将之译为 Osprey。雎鸠到底为何鸟？有人认为是王鴡，所选译文中，译者詹宁斯将其译为 waterfowl，水鸟之意，是笼统的称谓，但还是没有准确译出雎鸠之意；另外有人认为是鱼鹰，正如辜所译。许渊冲对辜取"鱼鹰"做出评论，认为其用词不当，因为如果把男女爱情比喻为鱼鹰与鱼，捕食者与猎物的意象会令人反感，同时暗含着一种不平等的社会地位，在西方读者看来这会显得奇怪甚至抵触。英国作家吉卜林曾断言："东方是东方，西方是西方，二者永不相遇。"如果按照吉卜林的观点，或许辜正坤的题译对于中国人来说尚可接受，然而，许渊冲从普世的角度去看待，从世界读者的欣赏审美与接受力出发，认为译成 Cooing and Wooing 比较好，既体现出男追女的画面，又呈现出雎鸠所发出的"关关"叫声，这正契合了原题目《关雎》的寓意：取第一句"关关雎鸠"的中间两字，既突出了鸟叫声，又突出了鸟的名称。而詹宁斯的题目英译为 Song of Welcome to the Bride of King Wan，从忠实角度来说，显得不对等；从音韵和形象来看，也难以看出原题目的寓意色彩。通过译者自己的脚注可以看出，他基本上将《关雎》理解为描写宫廷中男追女绵绵情谊之诗以及婚礼之诗，而非一般的爱情诗，更不是普通百姓的情歌。"君子"在《诗经》的时代是对贵族的泛称，而且这位"君子"家备琴瑟钟鼓之乐，说明其具有显赫的社会地位。如若仅仅把此诗解释为"民间情歌"，稍显不足，因为它所描绘的亦含有贵族阶层的生活之意。如果把《关雎》当作婚礼上的歌来看，从"窈窕淑女，君子好逑"，唱到"琴瑟友之""钟鼓乐之"，喜气洋洋，亦未尝不可。从此角度看，詹宁斯的译文在主题方面做得还算到位。如果从许渊冲的普世论角度看，或许题目的英译还缺乏音形上的美。

值得一提的是对于周文王的生卒年份历来众说纷纭，难以定论。译者在原注中明确指出周文王的生卒年份为公元前 1231 年至 1135 年，稍显不严谨。还有说法称周文王生于公元前 1152 年，卒于公元前 1056 年，其在位期间因礼贤下士、广罗人才、勤于政事、重视民生，被后世视为一代明君。

邶风·绿衣

《绿衣》乃一悼亡诗，表达了丈夫悼念亡妻的思念之情。诗人目睹亡妻遗物，倍感伤心，便浮想联翩，由绿衣联想到治丝，惋惜亡妻治家的能干及贤德。诗人描写细腻，情感丰富，构思巧妙，由外入里，层层递进。

邶风·绿衣❶

绿兮衣兮，绿衣黄裏。心之忧矣，曷[1]维其已！

绿兮衣兮，绿衣黄裳。心之忧矣，曷维其亡[2]？

绿兮丝兮，女所治兮。我思古人，俾[3]无訧[4]矣。

絺兮绤兮[5]，凄其以风。我思古人，实获我心。

---

❶ 孔子. 诗经 [M]. 程俊英，译注. 上海：上海古籍出版社，1985：45–46.

中文注释

[1]曷（hé）：通"何"。

[2]亡：通"忘"，或意为停止。

[3]俾（bǐ）：使（达到某种效果），比如俾众周知。

[4]訧（yóu）：同尤，意为罪过、过失。

[5]缔绤（chī xì）：缔绤葛布的统称。葛之细者曰缔，粗者曰绤。引申为葛服。

英文译本

Luhe①

Trans. by James Legge

Green is the upper robe,

Green with a yellow lining!

The sorrow of my heart, —

How can it cease

Green is the upper robe;

Green the upper, and yellow the lower garment!

The sorrow of my heart, —

How can it be forgotten

[Dyed] green has been the silk; —

It was you who did it.

[But] I think of the ancients,

That I may be kept from doing wrong.

---

① James Legge, The Chinese Classics（Vol. Ⅳ）: The She-King［M］. Taipei: SMC Publishing Inc., 1991: 41-42.

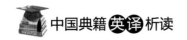

Linen[1], fine or coarse,[2]

Is cold when worn in the wind.

I think of the ancients,

And find what is in my heart.

英译注释

1. linen：adj. 亚麻的，亚麻布制的。
2. coarse：adj. 粗糙的；粗俗的；下等的。

英译评述

理雅各的译文基本直译于原文，也比较忠实地传达了原文的信息，属于无韵散文体翻译。原文"绿"字重复，译文也不断重复"绿"字，前三阕用倒装手法来突出衣服的颜色。最后一阕译者用 Linen，fine，coarse 三个形容词来指"絺绤""葛布"，实乃点睛之笔，直接体现"絺绤""葛布"的布料特点及其反映的穿着人群为普通人，让读者迅速领略到此种简陋、贫穷的生活与绿衣高贵生活的前后对比，更加烘托出对亡妻的思念。原文绿衣之意，一直有学者认为绿衣非普通人穿着之物，原因有二。其一"绿"可通为"禄"，所以"绿衣"便是"禄衣"。《礼记》中有禄衣之称："诸侯夫人祭服之下，鞠衣为上，展衣次之，禄衣次之。众妾亦以贵贱之等服之。鞠衣黄，展衣白，禄衣黑，皆以素纱为里"。其二，古代普通老百姓只能穿素衣，带颜色的衣服皆为有身份的贵族服饰。理雅各在翻译"绿衣"时，为了强调这种地位非凡的衣物，便巧妙地加了 upper 来修饰后面的 robe。并且在翻译"绿衣黄裳"时，有意地译为 Green the upper, and yellow the lower garment，意在突显出绿色与黄色衣物所反映的地位悬殊。因此，此诗反映的是一位有地位的男子对其爱妻的思念、悼念之诗。译者很好地把握住了该主题。

大雅·灵台

《大雅·灵台》是一首帝王园林游赏诗，讲述的是周文王因灵德高尚受百姓爱戴，百姓为之建造灵台及周文王游园，园中养兽，敲钟奏鼓瑟，庆欢愉。

大雅·灵台❶

经始灵台，经之营之。庶民攻之，不日成之。经始勿亟[1]，庶民子来。

王在灵囿[2]，麀鹿[3]攸伏。麀鹿濯濯[4]，白鸟翯翯[5]。王在灵沼[6]，于[7]牣[8]鱼跃。

虡[9]业[10]维枞[11]，贲[12]鼓维镛[13]。于论[14]鼓钟，于乐辟雍。

于论鼓钟，于乐辟雍[15]。鼍[16]鼓逢逢[17]。矇瞍[18]奏公[19]。

中文注释

[1]亟：通"急"。

[2]灵囿：园林名，用于古代君王畜养禽兽之用。

[3]麀（yōu）鹿：母鹿。

[4]濯濯（zhuó）：肥大强壮。

[5]翯翯（hè）：沽白亮丽。

[6]灵沼：池沼名。

[7]于（wū）：叹美声。

---

❶ 孔子. 诗经［M］. 程俊英，译注. 上海：上海古籍出版社，1985：516–517.

[8]牣（rèn）：满。

[9]虡（jù）：用来悬钟的木架。

[10]业：装在虡上的横板。

[11]枞（cōng）：虡上载钉，用以悬钟。

[12]贲（fén）：借为"鼖"，意为大鼓。

[13]镛（yōng）：大钟，古代的一种乐器。

[14]论：通"伦"，意为有次序。

[15]辟廱（bì yōng）：离宫名。

[16]鼍（tuó）：扬子鳄。

[17]逢逢（péng）：鼓声。

[18]矇瞍：古代用于称呼盲人。古代乐官、乐工常由盲人担任。

[19]公：读为"颂"，意为歌。或通"功"，意为奏功，成功。

英文译本

Delight of the People on Seeing the Magnificence with which King Wan Surrounded Himself❶

Trans. by William Jennings

The King designed his wondrous¹ tower:

'Twas his design, 'twas his device;

His people undertook the work,

And all was finished in a trice!

In planning it he urged no haste,

Yet all like children round him pressed.

Behold him in his wondrous park,

---

❶　William Jennings. The Shi King, The Old "Poetic Classic" of The Chinese: A Close Metrical Translation with Annotations [M]. London: George Routledge and Sons, Limited, 1891: 290.

Where stages and hinds lie down in herds,

His stags and hinds all sleek and fat; ——

Around him glinting snow-white birds.

Behold him on his wondrous lake,

Where crowding fish their frolic² take.

Like row of trees his music – stand!

Big drums, big bells thereon they pile. ——

O harmony of drum and bell!

Delightsome that pavilioned isle!

Delightsome that pavilion'd isle!①

With harmony of drum and bell!

Drums of iguana³ – hide resound.

Those blind ones② do their parts (right well).

译文原注

① A building surrounded by a moat, in which the young princes received instruction in various arts.

② The musicians of the Court were all blind.

英译注释

1. wondrous：adj. 奇妙的；令人惊奇的；非常的。

2. frolic：adj. 嬉戏的，欢乐的。

3. iguana：n. 鬣蜥蜴。

英译评述

上海豫园的三穗堂悬挂着一块匾额，上面书写着"灵台经始"。此四字便来自《大雅·灵台》中的开头诗句。"灵台"是古台名，遗址位于今陕西西安西北部。灵台乃百姓为周文王所建，用以歌颂其灵德高尚，使百姓归附。灵

台有何用途？是用于祭奠、祭祀还是用来观鸟、察气象？郑玄笺云："天子有灵台者所以观祲象，察气之妖祥也。"而陈子展在《诗经直解》亦说道："据孔疏，此灵台似是以观天文之雏型天文台，非以观四时施化之时台（气象台），亦非以观鸟兽鱼鳖之囿台（囿中看台）也。"译者译成 wondrous tower，只是简单地传达出这是一座令人惊奇的塔，难以窥见其文化内涵，用 wondrous 来指灵，亦不能传达周文王那种因灵德之美而受百姓爱戴之意。原文"麀鹿攸伏"指的是雌鹿悠然地躺伏在树荫下，而译者仅用 hinds 来指雌鹿，并没译出雌鹿那种生活在皇家灵园中悠然自在，与百姓、君王同乐的内涵。"鼍"意为扬子鳄，而译文却译成 iguana，鬣蜥蜴。译者把由扬子鳄皮制成的鼓，译成是用蜥蜴皮制成的鼓，这种误译彰显出了中西文化的不对等。

商颂·玄鸟

《玄鸟》是一首宋国君王祭祀歌颂祖先的乐歌，讲述了宋国诸侯祭祀殷商高宗武丁的情形，追述了殷商民族的始祖玄鸟以及开国君主成汤的功绩，高度赞颂了殷商高宗武丁复兴殷商，使得国泰民安、四方来朝的功绩，同时表达了庄重的祭祀氛围和虔诚的祝愿。该诗笔墨简练，寥寥数笔勾勒出了殷商史事，却又带有神话色彩，塑造了一个人、神合一的武丁形象。

商颂·玄鸟❶[1]

天命玄鸟，降而生商[2]，宅[3]殷土芒芒[4]。古帝命武汤[5]，正[6]域彼四方。

---

❶ 孔子. 诗经［M］. 程俊英，译注. 上海：上海古籍出版社，1985：678.

方命[7]厥[8]后[9]，奄有九有[10]。商之先后，受命不殆[11]，在武丁孙子。

武丁孙子，武王靡不胜[12]。龙旂[13]十乘，大糦[14]是承。

邦畿[15]千里，维民所止，肇域彼四海。

四海来假[16]，来假祁祁[17]。景[18]员[19]维河，殷受命咸[20]宜，百禄是何[21]。

［1］玄鸟：黑色、神秘的燕子。

［2］商：指商的始祖契。有传说认为娀（sōng）氏之女简狄误吞燕卵而生契，契建国于商（今河南商丘）。

［3］宅：居。

［4］芒芒：同"茫茫"，形容疆域宽广。

［5］武汤：成汤字号武王。

［6］正：通"征"，治。

［7］方命：遍告。

［8］厥：其。

［9］后：君主，诸侯。

［10］九有：九州。

［11］殆：通"怠"，懈怠。

［12］胜：任。

［13］龙旂（qí）：古时一种旗帜，上画龙形，竿头系铜铃。

［14］大糦（chì）：黍稷。

［15］畿（jī）：疆。

［16］假：至。

［17］祁祁：众多。

［18］景：山名，商所都。

［19］员：周围。

［20］咸：皆。

［21］何：同"荷"，担负。

中国典籍**英译**析读

英文译本

At a Royal Sacrifice ❶

Trans. by William Jennings

At Heaven's behest¹ the dusky bird① flew down,

And was the parent of the House of Shang, ——

Which dwelt in Yin², and greatly multiplied.

And long ago God charged the warlike T'ang

To fix their boundaries on every side.

Then had the princes their commission given.

Anon³ they held the territories nine; ②

And he, the first in Shang to be the king,

The appointment held unthreatened with decline, ——

Now vested in a scion⁴ of Wu-ting⁵. ③

And Wu-ting's scion is a warrior-king,

And ne'er a task for him is too severe.

Ten chariots with his dragon-banners④ bring

Large store of sacrificial millet⁶ here.

His royal lands extend a thousand li, ⑤

And there his people's settled dwellings be, ——

And thence his landmarks stretch to every sea.

From every sea⑥ men come, all hither bound;

They come, and here in multitudes are found,

---

❶ William Jennings. The Shi King, The Old "Poetic Classic" of The Chinese: A Close Metrical Translation with Annotations [M]. London: George Routledge and Sons, Limited, 1891: 378–379.

Where flows the Ho (the hill of) King around.

Most meet it was that Yin received the Call,

Now bearing its great honours one and all.

译文原注

①The swallow. The legend is told in various ways. Chu-Hi says that Ki-an-ti, the ancestress of the House of Shang, prayed at a sacrifice for a son, and thereupon came a swallow and left an egg, which Kian-ti swallowed, after which she gave birth to Sie, who became the Prince of Shang.

②The division of the kingdom into nine provinces was made in the time of the Emperor Yu (2205B. C. —2197 B. C.). Afterwards the number was doubled.

③Wu-ting reigned 1324B. C. —1265. B. C. Hence the Ode may be dated sometime during the thirteenth century B. C.

④This is said to refer to the arrival of the princes to assist at the royal sacrifice.

⑤ A li is about one-third of an English mile.

⑥Lit . , the four seas, the supposed four boundaries of the earth.

英译注释

1. behest：n. 命令；邀请；请求。

2. Yin：殷，指商地。

3. anon：adv. 不久；立刻；另一次。

4. scion：n. （农学）接穗；子孙。

5. Wu-ting：武丁（约前 1250—前 1192 在位），中国商朝第 23 位国王，在位 59 年，庙号高宗；商王盘庚的侄子，著名军事统帅。在位时期，武丁曾攻打鬼方，并任用贤臣傅说为相，妻子妇好为将，使商朝经济、文化、政治、军事得到空前发展，史称"武丁中兴"或"武丁盛世"。

6. millet：n. 小米；粟；稷。

英译评述

玄鸟，古代神话中的一种神鸟。关于玄鸟的特征，《山海经》记载之：四

翅鸟类，羽毛呈淡黄色，喜食鹰肉，性暴戾，居于平顶山。此外，还有一个传说，讲述的是商的祖先是玄鸟，因为据《史记·殷本纪》记载，商契的母亲简狄有次在郊外，因为误吞玄鸟之卵而怀孕，之后便生下商契。《郑笺》也同样记载过："降，下也。天使燕下而生商者，谓燕遗卵，娀（松）氏之女简狄吞之而生契。"此首诗也证实了这个传说："天命玄鸟，降而生商。"译者詹宁斯用 dusky bird 来指玄鸟，恐怕不是很恰当，因为 dusky 意思是暗淡的、微暗的，虽然可以一定程度上透露出玄鸟阴暗的暴戾特征，但是这种贬低负面的信息传达胜过于正面的信息，尽管译者对此鸟和商朝的关系传说做了注解。此外，虽然"玄"的意思有黑色、暗淡之意，但是其意思还含有深奥、神秘的色彩。而原文所传达的玄鸟之意更侧重于这种神秘感，这种神秘感在詹宁斯的注解中也是可以得到印证的，但令人遗憾的是詹宁斯在诗行英译玄鸟时并没有突出这种神秘性。所以，倘若改为 occult bird 或许更加恰当些，因 occult 有神秘、超自然、难以理解之意，正好突出了玄鸟的神秘性。就诗歌形式而言，原诗是四言偶有五言韵体诗，共五阕，每阕押韵不一，有些阕有转韵现象。译者在形式上，也用韵体诗的形式来翻译，每阕押韵多样化，使译文在音韵上更加具有美感和动感。

Ⅰ. Translation Practice.

Directions：Please translate the following lines into English.

1. 采采芣苢，薄言采之。(《国风·周南·芣苢》)

2. 喓喓草虫，趯趯阜螽。(《国风·召南·草虫》)

3. 硕鼠硕鼠，无食我黍！(《国风·魏风·硕鼠》)

4. 视民不恌，君子是则是效。(《小雅·鹿鸣之什·鹿鸣》)

5. 周虽旧邦，其命维新。(《大雅·文王之什·文王》)

Ⅱ. Writing Practice.

Directions：Write an essay of about 200 words, stating your understanding of the outlooks of love and marriage revealed in *Shi Jing*：*The Book of Songs*

第二节　《楚辞》选译

导读

　　继《诗经》之后，对中国文学最具有深远影响的一部诗歌总集便是《楚辞》。《楚辞》被认为是骚体类文章的总集，同时还是中国第一部浪漫主义诗歌总集。"楚辞"的名称由来已久，源自西汉初期，经历了由战国楚人屈原始创、屈后仿作、汉初搜集、刘向编辑成集几个阶段，成书于公元前26年至公元前6年间。《楚辞》原收屈原、宋玉及汉代淮南小山、王褒、东方朔、刘向等人辞赋共十六篇，后王逸增加《九思》，成十七篇。全书以屈原的作品为主，其余各篇亦承袭屈赋的形式。之所以叫《楚辞》，因其运用了楚地（即今湖北、湖南、安徽西部一带）的文学样式、风土物产和方言声韵等，带有浓厚的楚地地方色彩。《楚辞》对整个中国文化系统有着非同寻常的意义，尤其是文学方面，创作出了"楚辞体"、骚体，开创了中国浪漫主义文学的诗篇。在国际汉学界，《楚辞》一直是热门研究。本章节选了《楚辞》中《九歌》的部分章节，并结合外国汉学家和国内译者的翻译，学习如何从汉英角度对《楚辞》中所展现的思想进行阐发译介。

九歌·国殇（节选）

　　《九歌》是一组祭歌，共11篇，是屈原据民间祭神乐歌的再创作。《九歌·国殇》是一首挽诗，放逐中的诗人追悼秦楚战争中为楚国战死疆场的爱国将士，同情他们暴尸荒野、无人替之操办丧礼祭祀的凄凉景况，歌颂和礼赞了楚国将士的英雄气概和爱国精神，对雪洗国耻寄予殷切希望，抒发了诗人的爱国热情。

中文原文

九歌·国殇❶（节选）

屈原

操吴戈兮被[1]犀甲[2]，车错毂[3]兮短兵接。旌[4]蔽日兮敌若云，矢[5]交坠兮士争先。

凌[6]余阵兮躐[7]余行，左骖[8]殪[9]兮右刃伤。霾[10]两轮兮絷[11]四马，援玉枹[12]兮击鸣鼓。

天时怼[13]兮威灵怒，严杀尽兮弃原野。出不入兮往不反[14]，平原忽[15]兮路超远。

带长剑兮挟秦弓[16]，首身离兮心不惩[17]。诚既勇兮又以武，终刚强兮不可凌。

身既死兮神以灵[18]，魂魄毅兮为鬼雄。

中文注释

[1] 被（pī）：通"披"，穿着。

[2] 犀甲：犀牛皮制作的铠甲，特别坚硬。

[3] 毂（gǔ）：车轮的中心部分，有圆孔，可以插轴，这里泛指战车的轮轴。

[4] 旌：旌旗。

[5] 矢：箭。

[6] 凌：侵犯。

---

❶ 黄学森选注. 楚辞［M］. 珠海：珠海出版社，2002：68.

[7] 躐（liè）：践踏。

[8] 骖（cān）：骖马。

[9] 殪（yì）：死。

[10] 霾（mái）：通"埋"。

[11] 絷（zhí）：缚，绑住。古代作战，在激战将败时，埋轮缚马，表示坚守不退。

[12] 枹（fú）：鼓槌。

[13] 怼（duì）：怨恨。

[14] 反：通"返"。

[15] 忽：渺茫。

[16] 秦弓：指良弓。战国时，秦地木材质地坚实，所造弓射程远。

[17] 惩：悔恨。

[18] 神以灵：指死而有知，英灵不泯。神：指精神。

Battle[1]

By Qu Yuan

Trans. by Arthur Waley

"We grasp our battle – spears: we don[1] our breast – plates of hide.

The axles of our chariots[2] touch: our short swords meet

Standards obscure[3] the sun: the foe roll up like clouds.

Arrows fall thick: the warriors press forward.

They menace our ranks: they break our line.

The left-hand trace-horse is dead: the one on the right is smitten[4].

---

[1] Arthur Waley. Tr. A Hundred and Seventy Chinese Poems [M]. London: Constable and Company Ltd, 1918: 23−24.

The fallen horses block our wheels: they impede⁵ the yoke – horses!"

They grasp their jade drum–sticks: they beat the sounding drums.

Heaven decrees⁶ their fall: the dread Powers are angry.

The warriors are all dead: they lie on the moor – field.

They issued but shall not enter: they went but shall not return.

The plains are flat and wide; the way home is long.

Their swords lie beside them: their black bows, in their hand.

Though their limbs were torn, their hearts could not be repressed.

They were more than brave: they were inspired with the spirit of "Wu"^①.

Steadfast⁷ to the end, they could not be daunted⁸.

Their bodies were stricken, but their souls have taken Immortality—

Captains among the ghosts, heroes among the dead.

译文原注

① military genius.

英译注释

1. don：v. 穿上。

2. chariot：n. 二轮战车；v. 驾驭。

3. obscure：adj. 昏暗的；晦涩的；隐蔽的；无名的。

4. smite：v. 打击，摧毁（过去分词 smitten）。

5. impede：v. 阻碍；妨碍；阻止。

6. decree：v. 命令；颁布；n. 法令；判决。

7. steadfast：adj. 坚定的；不变的。

8. daunted：v. 使气馁，使畏缩；威吓。

英译评述

　　国殇，指为国捐躯的人。"殇"指未成年之死，亦指死难之人。古代将尚未成年（不足二十岁）而夭折者称为殇。按古代葬礼，在战场上"无勇而死"者，照例不能敛以棺枢，不能葬入墓地，亦被称为"殇"的无主之鬼。韦理将题目"国殇"译成Battle，只是传达了该诗的主题是关于战争，未能真正传达屈原对那些为楚国牺牲疆场的将士们的同情与哀悼之意。此外，译者把"吴戈"仅译成battle-spears，并没指出此戈之属性和特征，要知道当时吴国的冶铁技术较先进，吴戈因锋利而闻名，诗人用"吴戈"意在说明当时楚国将士所使用的武器并不落后。还有在英译骚体特征词"兮"时，韦理不像许渊冲那样译成oh，而是直接用冒号"："来指代。这也是一种译法，但是在语流方面和情感抒发方面，符号不如使用oh直接和爽快。此外，冒号的作用在于为前词、前句进行引入、说明、例证；而"兮"是助词，相当于现代汉语里的"啊""哦""哎"等，用以表达丰富的情感。因此，用冒号来对等"兮"不是特别的恰当。

第二章

唐 诗

导 读

　　唐代（618—907）是中国古典诗歌发展的全盛时期，唐诗是世界文学宝库中一颗璀璨的明珠。大部分唐诗收录于《全唐诗》中，有 42863 首。唐诗选本层出不穷，流传最广的当属清朝学人蘅塘退士编选的《唐诗三百首》。唐诗的创作按照时间分为四个阶段：初唐、盛唐、中唐、晚唐。唐代盛产诗人，李白、杜甫、白居易、王维等更被誉为世界闻名的伟大诗人。唐诗按主题可以分为山水田园诗、边塞诗、赠别诗、闺怨诗等。唐诗题材广泛多样，涉及政治动态、社会风俗、自然现象、劳动生活、个人感受等，比如有的描绘祖国山河壮丽多娇；有的歌颂正义战争，抒发爱国思想；有的抒写个人抱负和遭遇；有的表达儿女爱慕之情，诉说朋友交情、人生悲欢；从侧面反映了当时社会的阶级矛盾和阶级状况，揭露了封建社会的黑暗。唐诗创作方法分现实主义和浪漫主义两大流派，大多数的伟大作品结合了这两种创作方法，成为我国古典诗歌的优秀典范。

第一节　初唐诗选译

春江花月夜

　　张若虚（约660—720），初唐诗人，扬州人，在唐中宗神龙年间（705—707），以文词俊秀驰名京都，与贺知章、张旭、包融并称为"吴中四士"。张若虚的诗仅存两首于《全唐诗》中：一首是《代答闺梦还》，另一首是《春江花月夜》。

《春江花月夜》是一篇脍炙人口的名作，千古绝唱，有"以孤篇压倒全唐"之誉，被闻一多先生誉为"诗中的诗，顶峰上的顶峰"。张若虚也因这一首诗"孤篇横绝，竟为大家"。诗题令人心驰神往——春、江、花、月、夜，这五种事物集中体现了人生最感人的良辰美景，构成了奇妙的艺术境界。以富有生活气息的清丽之笔，创造性地再现了江南春夜的景色，如同月光照耀下的万里长江画卷，意境空明，缠绵悱恻，抒发了游子思归的真挚情感、离愁别绪及富有哲理意味的人生感慨，表达了对生命永恒之渴望，其韵律优美、宛转悠扬，词清语丽，洗净了六朝宫体诗的浓脂艳粉，给人以澄澈空明、清丽自然的感觉。

春江花月夜❶

张若虚

春江潮水连海平，海上明月共潮生。滟滟[1]随波千万里，何处春江无月明。

江流宛转绕芳甸[2]，月照花林皆似霰[3]。空里流霜不觉飞，汀[4]上白沙看不见。

江天一色无纤尘，皎皎空中孤月轮。江畔何人初见月，江月何年初照人。

人生代代无穷已，江月年年望相似。不知江月照何人，但见长江送流水。

白云一片去悠悠，青枫浦上不胜愁。谁家今夜扁舟子，何处相思明月楼。

可怜楼上月徘徊，应照离人妆镜台。玉户帘中卷不去，捣衣砧[5]上拂还来。

此时相望不相闻，愿逐月华流照君。鸿雁长飞光不度，鱼龙潜跃水成文。

昨夜闲潭梦落花，可怜春半不还家。江水流春去欲尽，江潭落月复西斜[6]。

斜月沉沉藏海雾，碣石[7]潇湘[8]无限路。不知乘月几人归，落月摇情满江树。

---

❶ 萧涤非. 唐诗鉴赏辞典 [M]. 上海：上海辞书出版社，1983：51-52.

中文注释

[1] 滟 (yàn) 滟：波光荡漾的样子。

[2] 芳甸 (diàn)：芳草丰茂的原野。

[3] 霰 (xiàn)：空中落下白色不透明的小冰粒，形容月光下春花洁白晶莹剔透。

[4] 汀 (tīng)：沙滩。

[5] 捣衣砧 (zhēn)：捶布石、捣衣石。

[6] 复西斜 (xiá)：洛阳方言乃当时标准国语，"斜"在洛阳方言中读作 xiá。

[7] 碣 (jié) 石：北方之地，与后面的潇湘正好一南一北，暗指路途遥远，相聚无望。

[8] 潇湘：湘江与潇水，皆流经湖南。

英文译本

Moon Thoughts[1]

By Chang Jo-hsü

Trans. by W. J. B. Fletcher

Over a river by the ocean floating

That flows not for the tide

The moon uprises on the waters' motion

With equal kingdom wide.

The Ocean's face is radiant with her glory,

Perfumed through flowery banks the river flows,

And serpents[1] with a winding desultory[2]

By flowering woods that gleam as purest snows.

---

[1] W. J. B. Fletcher. Gems of Chinese Verse [M]. Shanghai: Commercial Press, 1919: 169–170.

So white that ivory no outline shows,

Nor seen the white sand on the shore thereby.

The fleckless[3] sky meets with the stainless sea:

And wheel-large floats in vast eternity

The moon, upon the flawless crystal sky.

Who by this river first beheld her face,

Whom by this river did the moon first see.

Ah, many generations of his race

Have come, and past into infinity

While she rode lightly in immensity.

I do not know for whom her beams alway

Shine—but the river waters flow away!

And one white fleck of cloud them follows too,

Tracing their windings with its pearly hue.

Tonight who floats upon the tiny skiff

From what high tower yearns out upon the night

The dear beloved in the pale moonlight,

Alone, so lonely with the lonely moon?

In the deep chamber where her hair she braids, —

And where the moon oft kissed our arms entwined—

Where, oh, we parted—lo, she rolls the blind

And inward steps the moon with silent pace:

Or noiseless gazes on her thoughtful face

When busied in the working of her maids.

To each unknown our thoughts go forth to meet.

How would I ride the moonbeams to thy feet!

The wild swans and the geese go sailing by

But rob not any brightness from the sky;

And fishes ripples on the water pleat.

Last night, when dreaming, ah, I seemed to see

That many flowers had fallen by this stream.

And low I moaned, "Already spring will flee

And I can barely see thee in a dream."

The waters bear away the spring; and now

But scattered stars remain upon the bough.

The moon is sinking to her western hall,

Darkened and drooping in the sea mists' pall.

From thee to me I cannot tell how far!

How many with the moon home wandered are

I cannot tell—But as the shadowy trees

Stir on the stream with sighings sad and lone,

So sighs my soul to thee, my own, my own!

英译注释

1. serpent: n. 蛇（尤指大蛇），此处译者将之动词化，来对应"江流宛转绕芳甸"。

2. desultory: adj. 断断续续的；散漫的。

3. fleckless: adj. 无斑点的，完美的；用来修饰原诗中的"江天"，表达"无纤尘"。

英译评述

原诗共 36 句，每四句一换韵，译文共 50 句，以诗韵体对应原诗，每阕押韵富于变化，节奏轻缓，在音韵上把思乡表现得淋漓尽致。

原诗标题很有特色，融春、江、花、月、夜五个意象为一体，勾勒出美好的景象，有人认为此诗着重点在江上，亦有人认为在夜上，还有人认为在月亮上。原诗除了标题之外，在诗文中共出现 4 次春，11 次江，2 次花，15 次月，2 次夜。在数量上也可以看出作者突出了月亮的重要性。译者英译题目为简单的 Moon Thoughts，虽然在标题中未能一下子把原诗五种意象一下子忠实地传递给译入语的读者，但是译者却把握了原诗重点突出月下江边游子思乡、借月抒情的主题。译者为了突出月的重要性，在译文中仅出现 2 次春，9 次江（包括 river，waters，stream），3 次花（flowery，flowering，flowers），15 次月（包括代词及转喻词，如，her face，her glory，white ivory，wheel-large 等），2 次夜。译者比较忠实地传达了原诗的意象美和突出点，虽在译文中弱化了其他意象，但是并不代表没有体现这些意象。

原诗开篇便就题生发，描绘出江潮连海，月共潮生的春江月夜气势及宏伟的壮丽画面。"生"字把月亮的静与潮水的动巧妙地结合在一起，赋予了明月与潮水活泼的生命。译文在处理这两句诗时突出月亮，把它作为主语，其他作为定状补成份倒装放在句首，译出了月亮"犹抱琵琶半遮面"的感觉，之后一个动词 uprise，鲜活地让月亮的静与海水的动响应在一起。

译者处理"江畔""人生"这四句富有人生感悟的诗句时，非常直率简练地直译出了诗人的情怀：皓月当空，感叹人生短暂即逝，却未陷入古人悲悯、颓废、绝望、自寻烦恼的窠臼，而是别具一格，对人类代代无穷尽抱以美好的祝福和愿望。

译者对"白云"两句，采取的是意译。"白云"两句描写了春江花月夜游子漂泊他乡、思念家乡亲人之情。白云飘忽不定，象征"扁舟子"的行踪不定，译者很好地把这种漂泊感体现了出来。但是"青枫浦"未被很好地译出来，甚至还存在误译。"青枫浦"乃地名，位于湖南浏阳县境内。然"枫""浦"通常在诗中用来表示离别的景物和处所，与诗行前面"谁家""何处"设问二句互文见义。诗人正因游泊他乡，想到不止一家、一处有离愁别恨，故用"青枫浦"来转达一种相思，牵出月下的他与他想念的亲人。一往一复，突出乡愁。译者直接把这句误译成白云 Tracing their windings with its pearly hue，未能忠实传达原诗含义。

译者在英译闺中思妇对游子思念那几句，在诗意传达月光照思妇方面颇到位。原诗用"月"来烘托她的思念之情，把"月"拟人化，怀着对思妇的怜悯之情，让其"徘徊"于思妇闺房，不忍离去，让柔和的月光清辉为游子

吻在妆镜台上、玉户帘上、捣衣砧上，并和思妇做伴，为她解愁。译者没有译出"徘徊"，但用拟人的词 kiss 来描绘月光亲吻他们的手臂，以游子的角度试想此刻江上的月光亦照在远方亲人的手臂上，表达出了这种月伴思妇的意境。译者在处理"妆镜台""捣衣砧"时，不是直译成对应的名词，而是将之译成思妇的梳妆动作和侍女服侍的动作。第一个译法尚可接受，第二个就有点误译之嫌，因为诗人通过"玉户帘""捣衣砧"展示思妇触景生情，反而思念尤甚，想赶走恼人的月色，可是月色"卷不去""拂还来"，却旋照着怨妇，烦恼倍增。而译者在"卷"和"拂"两个痴情的动作上，却没法生动地表现出思妇内心的那种愁怅和迷惘。

译者在英译"鸿雁""鱼龙"两句上也是直译。原诗句表达了游子想到自己和亲人共望月光却无法相知相见，只好依托鸿雁和池鱼来遥寄相思的心情。然而，望月空，鸿雁远飞，却飞不出月华，飞而无用；望江面，鱼跃水面，只泛起阵阵波纹，跃而徒劳。对熟悉古人用鸿雁传信、池鱼传尺素寓意的中国人来说，这种直译是非常可取的，但是对于不懂这背后含义的译入语读者来说，或许意译或尾注把传信为任的鱼雁、池鱼传达出来会更好些。

在传达"碣石""潇湘"上，译者虽然没有直译此两地名，仅仅用"你""我"来体现两地相隔，亲人天各一方，具有异曲同工之妙。

总之，译者在英译此诗上，采用直译与意译相结合的方法，比较忠实地传达了原诗的诗意、诗歌形式和韵律美。

滕王阁诗

王勃（约650—约676），初唐诗人，汉族，字子安，古绛州龙门（今山西河津）人，出身儒学世家，与杨炯、卢照邻、骆宾王并称为"初唐四杰"，并为四杰之首。其擅长五律和五绝，代表作品有《送杜少府之任蜀州》；亦擅长骈文，所作皆是上乘之作，代表作品有《滕王阁序》等。

唐高宗上元三年（676年），诗人远道去交趾（今越南）探父，途经洪州（今江西南昌），参与阎都督宴会，即席作《滕王阁序》。《滕王阁序》全文运思谋篇，先叙述了洪都雄伟地势、游赏时间、珍异物产、杰出人才及尊贵宾客，接着展示了一幅流光溢彩、壮美秀丽的滕王阁秋景图，近观远眺，浓墨重彩，接着描写宴会情形，转而引出人生的感慨，最后自叙遭际，写下了四韵八句。所节选部分正是序末所附的这首含蓄、凝练诗作，概括了序的内容。此四韵八句，是王勃为感谢朋友摆设宴席，宴别之际又遇知音知己，故赋诗作文，以此留念。该诗由地及景，由景及人，由景及情，反映了诗人对滕王阁美景的赞美，抒发了诗人对物是人非、时光易逝的感慨。

滕王阁[1]诗❶

王勃

滕王高阁临江渚，佩玉鸣鸾罢歌舞。

画栋朝飞南浦[2]云，珠帘暮卷西山[3]雨。

闲云潭影日悠悠，物换星移几度秋。

阁中帝子[4]今何在？槛外长江空自流。

中文注释

[1] 滕王阁：江南三大名楼之一，故址在今江西南昌赣江滨，从此处俯视远望，视野均极开阔，盛传为唐太宗李世民的弟弟滕王李元婴所建，其骄奢淫逸，品行不端，但精通歌舞，善画蝴蝶，颇有艺术才情，修建此阁为供其歌舞享乐之需。

[2] 南浦：地名，南昌西南。浦：水边或河流入海的地方（多用于地名）。

[3] 西山：南昌名胜，一名南昌山、洪崖山、厌原山。

❶ 萧涤非. 唐诗鉴赏辞典 ［M］. 上海：上海辞书出版社，1983：18-19.

[4] 帝子：指滕王李元婴。

Ichabod❶

By Wang Po

Trans. by Herbert A. Giles

Near these islands¹ a palace was built by a prince,

But its music and song have departed long since;

The hill-mists of morning sweep down on the halls,

At night the red curtains lie furled on the walls.

The clouds o'er the water their shadows still cast,

Things change like the stars²: how few autumns have passed

And yet where is that prince? Where is he? —No reply,

Save the plash of the stream rolling ceaselessly by.

英译注释

1. these islands：指赣江江中小洲。

2. Things change like the stars：物换星移，形容时代的变迁、万物的更替。

英译评述

翟里斯的译文采用意译手法将原诗大概意思译出，虽不是逐字地把每行主要意象译出，却把握了王勃对物是人非、时光飞逝感慨的主题，尤其体现在标题的英译上。Ichabod，作为叹词，表示呜呼，唉之意，作为名词有其典故，指基督教《圣经·撒母耳记上》中男孩的名字，非尼哈的一个儿子，据《圣经》中所说，如此命名是为纪念非利士人夺去约柜，暗指荣耀已离去。译者用在此处可能暗指李渊幼子滕王李元婴曾经辉煌，如今物是人非，歌舞不

---

❶ Herbert A. Giles. Chinese Poetry in English Verse [M]. London：Bernard Quaritch，1898：42.

再，荣耀不再。译者未将原诗行中几处意象译出，如"佩玉鸣鸾"指滕王阁中舞女身上佩戴的玉饰、响铃，而是直接点出歌舞已不再；"日悠悠"可以指每日无拘无束地游荡，亦可指骄阳游荡晴空，译文中虽未体现此意象，但是译者把骄阳意象融入潭水上空白云投下的影子，自然而然令人联想到晴空骄阳。原诗的韵律为前四句押一韵，之后转韵，后四句押一韵。译文采用 aab-bccdd 的形式来对应，使译文在韵律上更富节奏感，仿佛将时间如流水、物换星移的节奏很好地表现了出来。

第二节　盛唐诗选译

早发白帝城

唐肃宗乾元二年（759）春，诗人因永王璘案流放夜郎，取道四川赴贬地，行至白帝遇赦，惊喜交加，随即乘舟东下江陵时而作此诗。此诗意在描摹自白帝至江陵一段长江水急流速、舟行若飞的情况，抒发了诗人当时喜悦、畅快的心情。

早发白帝城[1]

李白

朝辞白帝彩云间，千里江陵一日还。

两岸猿声啼不住，轻舟已过万重山。

---

[1] 萧涤非. 唐诗鉴赏辞典［M］. 上海：上海辞书出版社，1983：304.

Quitting Poti① at Dawn❶

By Li Po

Trans. by W. J. B. Fletcher

Poti amid its rainbow clouds we quitted with the dawn,

A thousand li in one day's space to Kiang−ling¹ are borne.

Ere² yet the gibbon's② howling along the banks was still,

All through the cragged Gorge our skiff had fleeted with the morn.

☐译文原注☐

① Poti is a town in Szechuen. The poet celebrates the swift current of the Yangtze down the Gorges of Szechuen.

② The constant reference to the gibbon in the Tang poems would seem to imply that at that time China was much more wooded than at present. So far as I know monkeys are not common along the Yangtze nowadays; but they may still be seen on the higher reaches of the West River.

☐英译注释☐

1. Kiang-ling：江陵，今湖北省江宁县。
2. Ere：常用于诗歌中，同 before。

☐英译评述☐

该诗意象奇异，风格清新，以画入诗，描写了白帝城地势之高，锋棱之挺拔，去江陵路之遥远，赞美了长江三峡两岸的锦绣河山，由于诗人刚被释放，心情畅快之极，故以山影猿声烘托行舟飞进，轻如无物，水势如泻，亦

---

❶ W. J. B. Fletcher. Gems of Chinese Verse [M]. Shanghai：Commercial Press, 1919：26.

是快船快意，令人神往。译者忠实地英译原诗标题，在形式和内容上保持与原标题的表层结构大致对应。

原诗七言绝句，押韵押一二四，译文非常忠实地体现了原诗形态，以七步抑扬格韵体诗对应，押韵为 aaba 型。译者因自己独特的审美情趣以求形似意似，故用音译直译方法把原诗的地名译出，保留了英译时的"科学性"；此外为了让西方读者了解地名含义，在译文后还做了注释。这样的处理，不仅能让西方读者产生独特的审美联想和效果，知道白帝城与李白在中国文化文学中的地位，还会让其向往中国，产生来该地旅游的愿望，很好地起到了中西文化交流的作用。此外，译者在英译"白帝城"时，只留 Poti，而把"城"的概念放在注释中，一方面译者可能顾虑到诗行中韵律节奏的问题，不加 city or town 以免影响全诗意境美，能更好地把李白的飘逸之感表现出来；另一方面也避免了西方读者对"城"（city）的误解。因为 city 在西方读者的印象中是人口密集，建筑、商店聚集之地，而汉语中的"城"有城墙、城堡、城郭、城市等意思，更加强调城墙以内的区域。鉴于李白所处的年代，白帝城应该是一个小城镇，故译者选取 town，而不用 city。

春望

杜甫（712—770），生于河南巩县，祖籍湖北襄阳，字子美，自号少陵野老，世称杜少陵，心系苍生，胸怀国事，被誉为唐代伟大的现实主义诗人，与李白合称"李杜"。由于其诗风独特，影响深远，被后人称为"诗圣"，其诗因显示了唐代由盛转衰的历史过程而被称为"诗史"。其善于运用各种诗歌形式，尤长于律诗，他的大约 1500 首诗歌被保留了下来，收集于《杜工部集》，含《春望》《北征》《三吏》《三别》等名作。其诗语言精炼，内容深刻，风格以沉郁为主，内容多深切同情穷苦人民，大胆揭露当时的社会矛盾，希望君主能奉行儒家的仁政思想，实现"致君尧舜上，再使风俗淳"的宏伟抱负。

《春望》是一首五言律诗，先写春日长安悲惨、凄凉的破败之景象，感叹

中国典籍英译析读

兴衰，接着写诗人思念亲人、心系国事之情怀，充满着凄苦哀思。此诗对仗精巧，格律严整，声情悲壮，抒发了诗人的爱国情操。该诗写于天宝十五年（757）三月，此前两年正值安禄山起兵叛乱，社会动荡不安，人民流离失所，诗人投奔唐肃宗途中被叛军俘获，解送至长安，不久被放，诗人站在长安城上，目睹一片萧条、凄零的景象，百感交集，便写下此诗。

春望❶

杜甫

国破山河在，城春草木深。

感时花溅泪，恨别鸟惊心。

烽火连三月，家书抵万金。

白头搔更短，浑欲不胜簪。

The Hope of Spring❷

By Tu Fu

Trans. by W. J. B. Fletcher

A nation[1], though fallen, the land yet remains.

When Spring fills the City, its foliage is dense.

In grief for the times, a tear the flower stains.

---

❶ 蘅塘退士. 唐诗三百首全解 [M]. 赵昌平解. 上海：复旦大学出版社，2006：141.
❷ W. J. B. Fletcher. More Gems of Chinese Poetry [M]. Shanghai：Commercial Press, 1919：96.

In woe for such parting, the birds fly from thence.

For three months² unceasing the bale fires³ now flare.

A letter from home costs a fortune to bring.

These worries scratch off my last falling grey hair.

My own foolish wishes my pen cannot wing.

英译注释

1. nation：此处译者将之对应原文中的"国"，有待商榷，因为原文中的"国"是指国都长安（今陕西西安）。

2. three months：这里的三月指正月、二月、三月。

3. bale fires：烽火。古时边防报警的烟火，此处指安史之乱的战火。

英译评述

在诗歌对仗方面，原诗前三联对仗工整，译者意识到这点，故译文也尽量保持这种对仗形式。原诗押韵一韵到底，译文采用工整的隔行交互押韵 ab-abcdcd 押韵格式，重轻音交错出现，读来朗朗上口，回转悠扬，音律优美，再现原诗凄凉、悲惨之基调。诗人最后一句想要表达的是心怀祖国山河，同情百姓离苦，而头发日渐稀少，无法用束发簪子横插住以免散开。译者由于未能理解"簪"之深意，将之误译成了 pen。此外，译者将本是副词动词结构的"浑欲"理解成形容词名词结构的"浑欲"，认为诗人因为年老，头发日渐稀疏，笔将难以再言其愚蠢的愿望。关于"三月"的理解，向来有争议，有人认为是指三月份，而有学者认为是指连续三个月。而译者的理解是指烽火连续烧了三个月之意。从安禄山叛乱的时间 [玄宗天宝十四载（755）冬安禄山起兵叛变，唐肃宗至德元载（756）六月安禄山率叛军攻下长安，诗人写诗的时间是天宝十六年（757）三月] 来看，烽火烧了应该不止三个月，故此处烽火连接的应该是 756 年的三月和 757 年的三月，此外题目的《春望》也预示着此诗写于春季，而三月正是春季之首月，所以译成 March 会更加准些。

石壕吏

　　《石壕吏》是杜甫著名的组诗"三吏三别"之一。此诗作于公元759年（乾元二年），当时正值安史之乱，朝廷派郭子仪等节度使平息，率兵20万围攻安庆绪（安禄山的儿子）所占的邺郡（今河南安阳），本胜利在望，却由于策略失误，加上又有内部矛盾，导致唐军败退，退守河阳（今河南孟州），又由于兵力不足，便四处抽丁补充兵力。杜甫被贬为华州司功参军，因此离开洛阳，途径新安、石壕、潼关，夜宿晓行，赶往华州任所。途中诗人见到哀鸿遍野、民不聊生，引发了内心强烈的情感波动。在途经新安县往西行并投宿石壕村时，遇到吏卒深夜捉人，便记录所见所闻，完成此不朽诗篇。此诗精炼，句句叙事，无抒情语，亦无议论语，却融抒情、议论于叙事中，场面细节自然真实，爱憎分明，展现了由"安史之乱"引起的战争给广大劳动人民带来的深重灾难，揭露了当时封建统治者的残酷，表达了诗人对穷苦人民的深切同情。

石壕吏❶

杜甫

暮投石壕村[1]，有吏夜捉人。老翁逾[2]墙走，老妇出门看。

吏呼一何怒！妇啼一何苦！听妇前致词："三男邺城[3]戍[4]。

一男附书至，二男新战死。存者且偷生，死者长已矣。

室中更无人，惟有乳下孙。有孙母未去，出入无完裙。

---

❶ 萧涤非. 唐诗鉴赏辞典［M］. 上海：上海辞书出版社，1983：435.

老妪力虽衰，请从吏夜归。急应河阳^[5]役，犹得备晨炊"。

夜久语声绝，如闻泣幽咽。天明登前途，独与老翁别。

中文注释

[1] 石壕村：现为干壕村，位于今河南陕县东七十里。

[2] 逾（yú）：翻越。

[3] 邺（yè）城：即相州，在今河南安阳。

[4] 戍（shù）：防守，此处指服役。

[5] 河阳：今河南孟州，当时安禄山叛军与郭子仪等官兵在此对峙。

The Pressgang❶

By Tu Fu

Trans. by Herbert A. Giles

There, where at eve I sought a bed,

    A pressgang¹ came, recruits to hunt;

Over the wall the goodman sped,

    And left his wife to bear the brunt².

Ah me! The cruel serjeant's³ rage!

    Ah me! How sadly she anon⁴

Told all her story's mournful page, —

    How three sons to the war had gone;

How one had sent a line to say

❶ Herbert A. Giles. Chinese Poetry in English Verse [M]. London：Bernard Quaritch, 1898：90-91.

That two had been in battle slain:

He, from the fight had run away,

But they could ne'er come back again.

She swore 'twas[5] all the family—

Except a grandson at the breast;

His mother too was there, but she

Was all in rags and tatters drest.

The crone[6] with age was troubled sore,

But for herself she'd not think twice

To journey to the seat of war

And help to cook the soldiers' rice.

The night wore on and stopped her talk;

Then sobs upon my hearing fell...

At dawn when I set forth to walk,

Only the goodman cried Farewell!

英译注释

1. pressgang：n. （强迫他人服役的）抓壮丁队。

2. brunt：n. 冲击；主要冲力；此处译者指代抓人官吏。

3. serjeant：n. 陆战队士官之通称。

4. anon：adv. 不久；立刻；另一次。

5. 'twas：it was。

6. crone：指老妪。

英译评述

原诗是五言诗，每四句一换韵，押一、二、四句，译文采用工整的隔行交互押韵 abab 对应。翟里斯为方便译入语国家的读者阅读欣赏，便采用意译方式英译原诗，并删除原诗中所有的地名。对于石壕吏，诗人采用虚化处理，直接用副词 there，where 对应。此外，在译动词"投"时，诗人采用了动宾词组 sought a bed 进行补足，方便读者理解。译者在处理原诗的感叹词"呼""啼"时，采用了呼语 Ah me 对应，突出了老妪面对官吏询问时的悲苦。在处理"无完裙"时，译者不直接译成 broken dresses，而是用更形象的 rags and tatters 代替，展现百姓的穷苦生活。译者同时也非常具有鲜明的政治倾向性，通过把抓壮丁的官吏译成 pressgang，"老翁"译成 the goodman（goodman 表示丈夫，主人之意，good man 则表示好人），似乎旨在强调对比，官吏之坏、百姓之善跃然纸上，同时淋漓尽致地表现出杜甫对欺压穷苦百姓的凶恶官吏的憎恨。

第三节 中唐诗选译

草

　　白居易（772—846），字乐天，号香山居士，河南郑州新郑人，唐代伟大的现实主义诗人，后世称之为"诗魔"和"诗王"。他的诗歌题材广泛，形式多样，语言平易通俗；官至翰林学士、左赞善大夫。著有《白氏长庆集》，代表诗作如《草》《卖炭翁》《琵琶行》《长恨歌》等。

　　《草》原题为《赋得古原草送别》，为贞元三年（787）诗人十六岁应考时而作，是一首借物抒情诗。诗人通过描写草原萋萋芳草生命力顽强，野火再烈，大地春回，草将再生，历经轮回来衬托送别朋友依依惜别之心境，以草写离情，巧妙妥贴。

草❶

白居易

离离原上草，一岁一枯荣。

野火烧不尽，春风吹又生。

远芳侵古道，晴翠接荒城。

又送王孙去，萋萋满别情。

The Grass❷

By Po Chü – i

Trans. by W. J. B. Fletcher

How densely thick the grass upon the plain!
Decay and splendor one year to it brings.

The corpse – fires¹ burn it down—but all in vain—
With each new breath of Spring it lives again.

Its fragrance creeps across the Ancient Ways².
Its sun-lit verdure o'er the ruin strays.

Its growth speeds Nature's lover on his ways.
With wild farewells its long luxuriance³ rings.

---

❶ 蘅塘退士. 唐诗三百首全解 [M]. 赵昌平解. 上海：复旦大学出版社，2006：187.

❷ W. J. B. Fletcher. Gems of Chinese Verse [M]. Shanghai：Commercial Press, 1919：142.

英译注释

1. corpse-fires：译者用鬼火指原诗中的"野火"。
2. Ancient Ways：古道，古老的驿道。
3. luxuriance：n. 萋萋，茂盛的样子。

英译评述

译者前四句英译采取直译手法，后四句主要采用意译手法。前四句押韵格式为 abaa，后四句为 aaab。译者通过形式上的押韵使野草的枯荣轮回得到了很好的体现。此外，原诗"野火烧不尽，春风吹又生"表达了草之顽强生命力和韧劲，成了千古绝唱。译者在译这两句时通过破折号、but 和 all 的结合，把草的顽强生命力巧妙地体现了出来。此外，译者不将"春风"译成 Spring wind 或 Spring gale，而是转译成 breath of Spring，把"风"比作春天的气息，更加鲜活地体现了春天的魅力和魄力——春天一来，枯草返青。"王孙"本指贵族后代，诗人用来指游子、远方的友人。或许是受西方浪漫派影响，译者将之译为 Nature's lover，着重强调春风一到，古道上芳草依依，必将给予游子大自然的馈赠，淡化原诗游子的伤感，让其心中充满对自然和生命的热爱。译者的创造性使译文更富有诗意，也使译入语国家的读者更易于接受这种歌颂大自然之歌，悟大自然之道。

江雪

柳宗元（773—819），字子厚，唐宋八大家之一，唐代文学家、哲学家、散文家和思想家，因居住河东（现山西芮城、运城一带），世称"柳河东"或"河东先生"。因官终柳州刺史，又称"柳柳州"。其诗文留存达 600 余篇，骈文近百篇，成就大于诗。柳宗元写景状物，笔锋犀利，讽刺辛辣，论说性强。著有《河东先生集》，代表作有《江雪》《溪居》《渔翁》《小石潭记》等。

《江雪》是一首山水诗，描绘了一幅山中鸟绝、人踪湮没、渔翁独钓的远景孤冷、意境幽僻、情调凄寂的寒江雪景图。全诗意象清晰明朗、精雕细琢。首句入韵，重声韵，每句首字合辙押韵，使韵味十足，回味无穷。诗人因参加以王叔文为首的政治革新运动失败而被贬柳州，便通过写山水诗，自喻隐居山水间的渔翁，寄托自己孤傲、清高之性情，抒发政治失意之苦闷。

江雪❶

柳宗元

千山鸟飞绝，万径人踪灭。

孤舟蓑笠翁，独钓寒江雪。

River Snow❷

By Liu Zongyuan

Trans. by Gary Snyder

These thousand peaks[1] cut off the flight of birds.

On all the trails, human tracks are gone.

A single boat—coat[2]—hat[3]—an old man!

Alone fishing chill river snow.

英译注释

1. thousand peaks：译者采用转喻方式以局部"千顶峰"来指整体"千山"。

2. coat：蓑（suō），蓑衣，由蓑草或棕榈皮编成，古代用来防雨的衣服。

3. hat：笠（lì），斗笠，由竹篾编成，古代用来防雨的帽子。

---

❶ 蘅塘退士. 唐诗三百首全解［M］. 赵昌平解. 上海：复旦大学出版社，2006：276.

❷ Gary Snyder. Translations［J］. The Literary Review. 32, 3（1989）：445.

英译评述

　　译者斯奈德本身也是诗人，其诗风受儒道和禅宗思想影响而明显内敛。因其诗歌题材多关注自然风光、环境问题以及人在自然中的位置，斯奈德成为六七十年代美国环境保护运动的诗歌代言人。斯奈德喜欢在体察自然世界时进行冥思、启悟灵魂。其诗歌语言明朗、精练、朴实。柳宗元这首诗的英译风格明显受到其诗歌创作的影响，原诗中典型的东方型"天人合一"的寂静神秘感得到了准确传达。英译用词简单，语言简练，不追求复杂的语法结构，重在凸出诗中意象。通过动词词组 cut off 把"千山"拒"飞鸟"而不见鸟踪迹的神秘感突显出来。此外，通过 trail 和 track 押头韵，译者对比"径"与"人迹"，传神地突出了柳宗元诗行传达的悲凉感。最后两句中，诗人用更为简单的句式结构勾勒出了渔翁独自垂钓寒江上的孤寂画面。当然，译者用 coat、hat 来对应"蓑笠"似乎显得有点苍白，如果能对其进行注释，把这种中国农耕渔作时的服饰传达给英语读者，那么读者便能更好体会原诗所传达的渔翁带蓑笠御雪独钓寒江的"天人合一"的艺术效果。

Ⅰ. **Translation Theory**.

Directions：Please analyze Giles' rendering from the perspective of Lawrence Venutti's theory of domestication and foreignization.

夜雨寄北❶

李商隐

君问归期未有期，巴山夜雨涨秋池。

何当共剪西窗烛，却话巴山夜雨时。

---

❶ 蘅塘退士. 唐诗三百首全解［M］. 赵昌平解. 上海：复旦大学出版社，2006：311.

英文译本

Souvenirs[1]

By Li Shangyin

Trans. by Herbert A. Giles

You ask when I'm coming: alas, not just yet...

How the rain filled the pools on that night when we met!

Ah, when shall we ever snuff candles again,

And recall the glad hours of that evening of rain?

Ⅱ. **Translation Practice.**

Directions：Please translate the following poem by Bai Juyi into English.

长恨歌[2]（节选）

惟将旧物表深情，钿（*diàn*）合金钗寄将去。钗留一股合一扇，钗擘黄金合分钿。

但教心似金钿坚，天上人间会相见。临别殷勤重寄词，词中有誓两心知。

七月七日长生殿，夜半无人私语时。在天愿作比翼鸟，在地愿为连理枝。

天长地久有时尽，此恨绵绵无绝期。

Ⅲ. **Writing Practice.**

Directions：Write an essay of about 200 words, stating your understanding of the basic characteristics of Li Bai's poetry.

[1] Herbert A. Giles. Chinese Poetry in English Verse［M］. London：Bernard Quaritch, 1898：134.

[2] 蘅塘退士. 唐诗三百首全解［M］. 赵昌平解. 上海：复旦大学出版社, 2006：90.

第三章

宋 词

导 读

词，始于唐，成型于五代，盛于宋，是中国古代文学皇冠上光辉夺目的明珠。宋词是继唐诗后的又一种文学体裁，与唐诗并称双绝，都代表一代文学之盛，它兼有文学与音乐两方面的特点。词大致可分小令（58 字以内）、中调（59~90 字）和长调（91 字以上，最长达 240 字）。宋词主要分为婉约派和豪放派两大类。婉约派代表人物有李煜、欧阳修、晏殊、晏几道、李清照、柳永、秦观等。婉约派侧重儿女风情，语言圆润，音律谐婉，清新绮丽，结构缜密深细，具有柔婉美。豪放派代表人物有苏轼、王安石、辛弃疾、陆游等。豪放派的特点体现在内容视野广阔，气象雄放恢弘，喜用诗文手法，语词宏博，用典较多，不拘格律，或悲壮或慷慨高亢。宋词在西渐传播中的译介不如唐诗广泛和受重视，起步较晚，专著性的译本较少。20 世纪 40 年代开始海内外对宋词的研究关注加强，20 世纪的后 30 年代对宋词的研究繁荣，译著逐渐增多，大为可观。

第一节　婉约派词选译

相见欢·无言独上西楼

　　李煜（937—978），南唐最后一位国君，字重光，号钟隐、莲峰居士，史称李后主，与其父李璟并称"南唐二主"，皆为五代时期的著名词人。975

年，宋军攻陷南唐都城金陵（今江苏南京），李煜降宋，被俘囚禁待罪于汴京，因曾守城相拒，被宋太祖赵匡胤封为"违命侯"。之后因作感怀故国之词《虞美人》被宋太宗赵光义毒死。李煜虽不精于政治，但其艺术才华非凡：音律、绘画、书法、诗文均有一定造诣，尤以词的成就最高，被誉为"千古词帝"。其词内容大体分为两类：一为降宋之前的前期作品，主要描写宫廷生活和男女情爱，题材较窄；二为降宋后的后期作品，成就超过前期，主要反映失国之痛和去国之思，对往事无限眷恋，哀婉凄凉，代表作有《相见欢·无言独上西楼》《虞美人·春花秋月何时了》等。

《相见欢·无言独上西楼》是李煜后期词作品中极具代表性的一篇，被誉为宋初婉约派词的开山之作，反映了其被俘后对故国的思念以及忧愁。词牌名为《相见欢》，咏的却是离别愁。该词上阕选取典型的景物为下阕抒发感情作铺垫，下阕通过形象的比喻委婉、含蓄地抒发真挚的离愁别绪，反映了离乡去国的锥心怆痛。

相见欢·无言独上西楼❶

李煜

无言独上西楼，月如钩。寂寞梧桐深院锁清秋。

剪不断，理还乱，是离愁，别是一般滋味在心头。

---

❶ 许渊冲. 最爱唐宋词［M］，北京：中国对外翻译出版公司，2006：34.

Tune："Joy at Meeting[1]" ❶

By Li Yü

Trans. by Xu Yuanchong

Silent, I climb the Western Tower alone

And see the hook-like moon.

Parasol-trees[2] lonesome and drear

Lock in the courtyard autumn clear.

Cut, it won't sever;

Be ruled, 'twill never.

What sorrow 'tis to part!

It's an unspeakable taste in the heart.

英译注释

1. Joy at Meeting：相见欢，词牌名，原为唐朝教坊曲，又名"秋夜月""乌夜啼""上西楼"等。关于词牌名的英译，一般分为几种：音译，直接用汉语拼音对应；直译，直接按字面译出其意；意译，采用间接或相近的词表达原语的意思；还有一种是结合音译直译或音译意译，同时在英译时加上 Tune、To the tune of、To the Melody of 等。许译采用 Tune，直译牌名，这样的译法简洁明朗，能使英语国家的读者快速捕捉到原语信息以及该曲调所反映的主题和传达的情感。

2. Parasol-trees：梧桐，parasol 本意为遮阳伞或伞状阔叶。或许因中国的梧桐树叶大如伞，英语国家的字典编撰者用 the Chinese parasol tree 一词来指梧桐树。许译简化成 parasol tree，不仅考虑到诗歌的节奏韵律，同时也使译入语读者产生与中国读者近似的关于梧桐树的联想。

---

❶ 许渊冲. 最爱唐宋词 [M]，北京：中国对外翻译出版公司，2006：34.

英译评述

许译此诗在内容上忠实传神地传达了李煜的去国之离伤，思国之愁味。译者意识到词人通过首句"无言独上西楼"逐渐将人物引入画面的意图，因此为了功能对等将 silent 放句首意在突出李煜作为囚徒而"无言"的愁苦神态，并添加主语 I 勾勒出词人孤身登楼的身影。译者该句的翻译很好地传达了李煜的神态与动作，有助于英语国家的读者把握、感受词人内心深处的孤寂与悲凄。

接着，译者以词人作为观景主体，从其视角出发，描写出站在楼上所见之物，先是仰视 the hooked moon，之后俯望着寂静的院子，看着梧桐，寂寞油然而生，自身处境犹如这清秋梧桐一般锁在高墙深院中。译者为了突出这种人与景的交融，通过押韵 alone 与 moon、drear 与 clear 传神地传达出词人身陷凄惨秋景的境遇。译者意识到"锁"字的传神，故将本应该用作被动语态的 locked in 译成静态的不及物动词短语 lock in，并将之放在句首，旨在通过这种看似"主动"的状态反衬出李煜作为落魄亡国之君如同"清秋""梧桐"一般的无奈、孤寂之心，亡国之恨、思乡之情都被囚禁在深院中。

随着词人从外在景物描写转而抒发内心的愁绪，译者意识到词人新颖别致的暗喻，用丝喻愁，传神地英译出"剪不断，理还乱，是离愁"之悲愁。译者通过简短句式、省略句，运用 sorrow 一词种的 s 音形象地传达"丝""思"之意，功能对等地传达出已是亡国奴、阶下囚且历经世态炎凉、人间冷暖、痛苦折磨的李煜对故国家园、荣华富贵的追忆思念，以及对故国家园不堪回首、帝王江山毁于自己手中的悔恨。故译者在英译最后一句"别是一般滋味在心头"时，通过 unspeakable 一词，忠实地传达出李煜难以言语的忧愁（因为李煜作为昔日唯我独尊的天子，如今却成为阶下囚徒，不能像普通人一样把心头淤积的思、愁、苦、恨、悔号啕倾诉，而只能将其埋在心底，故难以言状，难以言说。）

在音美方面，译文富有韵律美。译者意识到原诗通过平仄押韵，做到声情合一，把仄声韵"断""乱"置于平韵"楼""钩""秋"（那时估计发 qou）、"愁""头"，形成抑扬顿挫的韵律，如愁思似断似续，故译者在英译时采用 aabb 的押韵形式，循环反复地展现词人离愁悲痛之情。

蝶恋花·越女采莲秋水畔

　　欧阳修（1007—1072），字永叔，号醉翁、六一居士，北宋政治家、文学家，是"唐宋散文八大家"之一。其文学成就体现在散文与词方面，著有《欧阳文忠公集》。欧阳修的散文抒情委婉，说理畅达；词婉约丽秀，承袭南唐余风，题材广泛，有咏史、述怀，也有民情风俗。欧阳修主导的北宋古文运动对词的革新体现在两方面：一、延续并扩大李煜所创立的词的抒情功能，抒发个人的人生感受；二、改变词的审美趣味，使其往通俗化方面发展。

　　《蝶恋花·越女采莲秋水畔》先是描写了越女结伴乘船去采莲所穿戴的服饰、莲池环境以及采莲时的动人情景，接着夜色渐临，风起雾降，池波涌动，来时伙伴难以寻见，烟雾中却隐约听见船桨声，似近似远，离愁泛起，境界惝恍迷离，让人遐想。该词语言通俗、形象鲜明、节奏明快、曲折深婉、曲终味永。

蝶恋花●

欧阳修

　　越女采莲秋水畔。窄袖轻罗，暗露双金钏[1]。照影摘花花似面。芳心只共丝争乱。

　　鸂鶒[2]滩头风浪晚。雾重烟轻，不见来时伴。隐隐歌声归棹远。离愁

　　● 唐圭璋．全宋词．北京：中华书局，1999：161.

引著江南岸。

中文注释

[1] 钏 (chuàn)：多用金、银、玉石等制成的镯子，束于臂腕间。

[2] 鸂鶒 (xī chì)：一种水鸟，似鸳鸯，色多紫，性喜水，多偶游，故称紫鸳鸯。

To the Tune 'Butterfly Loves Flowers[1]' ●

By Ouyang Xiu

Trans. by Ronald C. Egan

A Yüeh girl picks lotus on the autumn stream.

Her tight sleeve of thin silk

Dimly reveals a pair of golden bracelets.

Her reflection as she picks—flowers lovely as her face.

Her young heart is as tangled as the lotus threads.

On Mallard Bank[2] there are waves towards evening,

The haze is heavy, the mist light.

The companions she came with are nowhere in sight.

Faint singing can be heard from the distant returning boats.

Parting sorrow stretches along the southern bank.

英译注释

1. Butterfly Loves Flowers：译者直译原词牌"蝶恋花"。蝶恋花，源自唐

● Ronald C. Egan. The Literary Works of Ou-yang Hsiu (1007–1072) [M]. Cambridge: Cambridge University Press, 1984：184.

朝教坊曲，上下两阕，共六十字，多用来填写缠绵悱恻、多愁善感之内容。

2. Mallard Bank：译者用来指原词中的"鸂鶒滩头"。其实，原词中"鸂鶒滩头"是两种意象，而译者将其译成地名，也算是一种解读。"鸂鶒"是类似鸳鸯的水鸟，而译者译成了 mallard 意指野鸭，使原词的意象审美趣味荡然无存，原词旨在使成双成对的似鸳鸯的水鸟与越女难以找到来时之伴形成鲜明对比，以突出一种离愁。

英译评述

伊根采用直译的方法总体上忠实地传达了原词的意思。第一句中，欧阳修交代了人物（越女）、事件（采莲）、时间（秋）、地点（水畔），伊根直译出了这一秋景采莲图。"越"泛指浙江一带，译者通过音译将其译出，非常忠实原词，如果能对它的地理位置加以注释就更好了。tight sleeve of thin silk 中的 tight、thin 很好地突出了采莲女着装"窄""轻"的特点，展现出越女的绰约丰姿。此外，在英译"暗露"越女手腕上时隐时露的"金钏"时，译者意识到"双"的重要性，故用 bracelet 的复数形式，不仅突出了越女之美，还为后面与伙伴失散形成对比做铺垫。在英译越女采莲的神情时，译者用 lovely 一词，非常传神地把越女的容貌与花巧妙地结合在一起，展现给读者一种"天人合一"美感。接着译者将"芳心"译成 young heart 来指情窦初开的少女之心，对欧阳修运用的借喻理解得很到位。tangled 一词巧妙地把少女情窦初开之心与藕丝结合起来，突出了越女内心涌动、相思纷乱的情感。译者对下阕把握得也非常好，尤其是 waves towards evening 创造性地把原词"风浪晚"由静态转变为动态，用 towards 代替了原词中的 wind，译文虽没风，却胜有风。译文的最后一句也算一绝，parting sorrow 指代"离愁"，突出了越女与伙伴失散后的相思之忧，而这种"离愁"一直 stretches along（延伸），愁绪顺着轻舟一直延伸至南岸，突出愁绪的时间长，传达出原词句中展示到底伙伴找与没找到的言尽而意无穷之审美效果。在形式方面，译文以自由体诗的形式对应原词（原词押韵押仄声韵 an）。

第二节　豪放派词选译

水调歌头

苏轼（1037—1101），字子瞻，又字和仲，号东坡居士，宋代著名的书法家、文学家。其词题材广阔，语言清新豪健，善用夸张比喻，独具风格。继柳永之后，他全面改革词体，开豪放一派，突破词为"艳科"的传统格局，提高了词的文学地位，让词从附属于音乐的地位转变成一种独立的抒情诗体，根本上改变了词史的演变方向。著有《东坡易传》《东坡七集》《东坡乐府》等。代表作有《水调歌头·明月几时有》《江城子·十年生死两茫茫》《念奴娇·赤壁怀古》等。

《水调歌头·明月几时有》是苏轼于1076年（宋神宗熙宁九年）中秋在密州任太守时所作。当时与其弟苏辙七年未见，正值中秋明月之夜，词人怀念苏辙的同时展开了丰富想象和深度思考，融人世间悲欢离合之情于宇宙人生的哲理探寻之中，展现了词人复杂矛盾的思想感情，反映了词人积极向上、热爱生活的乐观态度。该词上阕描写了天上月宫景象，下阕描写地上人间的悲欢离合，落笔潇洒、铿锵有力、挥洒自如、情景交融、思想深邃、哲理韵味强。

水调歌头●

苏轼

丙辰中秋，欢饮达旦，大醉，作此篇，兼怀子由。

● 上疆邨民. 宋词三百首全解 [M]. 蔡义江解. 上海：复旦大学出版社，2007：76.

明月几时有，把酒问青天。不知天上宫阙^[1]，今夕是何年。我欲乘风归去，惟恐琼楼玉宇^[2]，高处不胜^[3]寒。起舞弄清影，何似在人间。

转朱阁，低绮户^[4]，照无眠。不应有恨，何事长向别时圆？人有悲欢离合，月有阴晴圆缺，此事古难全。但愿人长久，千里共婵娟^[5]。

中文注释

[1] 阙（què）：城门、宫门两侧的高台。

[2] 琼（qióng）楼玉宇：神话中月宫里的亭台楼阁。

[3] 胜（shèng，旧读 shēng）：承担、承受。

[4] 绮（qǐ）户：彩绘雕花的门户。

[5] 婵（chán）娟（juān）：指月中嫦娥，此处代指明月。

英文译本

Mid–Autumn Festival[1]❶

To the Tune of Shuitiaoket'ou[2]

By Su Shi

Trans. by Lin Yutang

How rare the moon, so round and clear!

With cup in hand, I ask of the blue sky,

"I do not know in the celestial sphere

What name this festive night goes by?"

I want to fly home, riding the air,

But fear the ethereal cold up there.

The jade and crystal mansions are so high!

Dancing to my shadow,

I feel no longer the mortal tie.

❶　林语堂. 东坡诗文选［M］. 天津：百花文艺出版社，2002：119，121.

She rounds the vermilion tower,

Stoops to silk-pad doors,

Shines on those who sleepless lie.

Why does she, bearing us no grudge,

Shine upon our parting, reunion deny?

But rare is perfect happiness—

The moon does wax, the moon does wane,

And so men meet and say goodbye.

I only pray our life be long,

And our souls together heavenward fly!

英译注释

1. Mid-Autumn Festival：原词只有词调，没有题目，之后有一个小序点明词作时间和缘由。译者的译文截取并英译小序中的"中秋"二字作为译文标题，虽道出该词主题与中秋有关和作词的大概时间，却未能忠实、详细地译出具体作词时间和因何而作，亦未能传达词人通过小序所想要表达对胞弟子由的思念和离别之情，一定程度上降低了读者的审美效果。

2. To the Tune of Shuitiaoket'ou：水调歌头，词牌名，源于隋唐，由隋炀帝所创，后入宋词，又名《水调歌》《台城游》《凯歌》《元会曲》。双调，九十五字，上阕九句、下阕十句，通常各押四平韵。译者采取音译方法，虽保留词牌原滋原味的特色，但因未作注释，一定程度上使译入语读者在信息捕捉和理解上受阻。

英译评述

林语堂的译文总体上忠实地传达了原词的意思，译文简练达意，通俗与典雅相结合，地道流畅。第一句译者使用感叹句，展现了月下独饮的词人对月亮的陡然发问，功能对等地保持了原词句的模糊意境，让读者发挥想象。原词中第一人称的使用比较少，译文用第一人称 I 比较多，除了中英语言结构上的差异原因之外，译者意在突出苏轼的孤独心境和离别之情。译文中用 She 拟人化原文中的"月光"，不仅符合译入语的表达习惯，同时美化了"月光"，凸显其形象感。对于"朱阁"，译者找到一个忠实的词 tower 来对应"阁"，古代"阁"指高大宏伟的建筑，tower 除了指塔之外，亦表示宏伟的建筑物。而译者在处理"绮户"时用具体形象的下义词 doors 来对应，因原文中的"户"与"阁"相对应，皆指代一个建筑物的整体，所以译文显得单薄些。"起舞弄清影，何似在人间"，意思是月光下，词人醉酒，身影跟着摆出各种舞姿，反问自己是否还在人间？译文反义语气不如原词强烈，正所谓只译出词意，未译出词魂。"不应有恨，何事长向别时圆"，译文将 why 提前至句首，中间插入 bearing us no grudge 的独立主格结构做条件假设，在结构处理上比较忠实地传达了原文的质疑反问语气，保持了审美趣味。在"千里共婵娟"的英译中，译者很好地把握了词人苏轼渴望与相隔千里的亲人团聚的愿望，希望能一起欣赏这美好的月光，不直接译出"婵娟"（指月光），而译出月光下人的 souls 朝"婵娟"飞去，强调词人殷切的愿望，虽没"婵娟"却感觉"婵娟"无处不在，深层次地理解并译出了词人的心境。在押韵上，译者多采用双元音的尾韵/iə/ /eə/ /ai/，和押头韵 /f/ /s/ /w/，音韵缓慢深沉，使词人离别之情循环往复，/ai / 对应第一人称 I，突出作为主体的词人月下对人生哲理的思考与感悟。

Translation Practice.

Directions：Please translate the following poem by Li Yu into English.

虞美人·春花秋月何时了

李煜

春花秋月何时了，往事知多少。小楼昨夜又东风，故国不堪回首月明中。雕阑玉砌应犹在，只是朱颜改。问君能有几多愁，恰似一江春水向东流。

第四章

元 曲

导 读

　　元曲又称词余、乐府，是唐诗、宋词之后的又一文学盛况，继承了诗词的清丽婉转，亦有其独特的魅力。元曲分为杂剧和散曲。杂剧是由套曲、间杂以及宾白和科范组成，专为舞台上演出的戏曲形式，如关汉卿的《窦娥冤》、王实甫的《西厢记》等。本章所选皆是散曲。散曲是用作清唱的歌词，包括小令和散套。小令，体制短小，通常是一支独立的曲子（少数有二三支）。散套由多支曲子组成，始终只用一韵。散曲曲牌跟宋词词牌一样，多种多样，不过名称比词牌更加俚俗，更接近民歌，如《人月圆》《山坡羊》《叨叨令》《红绣鞋》《喜春来》等。形式上，散曲与词非常相近；语言上，词含蓄典雅，散曲活泼通俗；格律上，词严格，散曲相对自由。总体上，元曲作品形式活泼、语言通俗、描绘生动、手法多变、风格清新、题材广泛，深刻揭露现实，锋芒直指社会弊端，直斥政治专权、社会黑暗，比历代诗词描写爱情更加大胆、泼辣，在中国古典文学史上放射出璀璨夺目的光芒。

第一节　人生理想

人月圆·卜居外家东园

　　元好问（1190—1257），汉族，金末元初是最有成就的文学家，文坛盟主，金元之际颇负厚望，在文学上起承前启后的桥梁作用。工文、词、曲，以诗作成就最高，其词可与宋朝名家媲美，为金代一朝之冠；其元散曲仅 6 首，虽传世不多，但影响很大，有倡导之功。曲风时而清新隽永，时而沉郁婉丽，语言用俗为雅，推陈出新。代表作有《人月圆·卜居外家东园》《喜春来·春宴》等。

《人月圆·卜居外家东园》是一首小令，上阕写卜居的原因和理想的卜居场所，下阕写移居后的新生活，展现了元好问的晚年理想生活。整首小令借景抒情，情藏景中，看似是元好问对山间田野悠然自得生活的向往，但细细品读，能看出曲人的无奈和悲愤。

人月圆·卜居外家东园❶

元好问

重冈已隔红尘断，村落更年丰。移居要就，窗中远岫，舍后长松。
十年种木，一年种谷，都付儿童。老夫惟有，醒来明月，醉后清风。

Tune：Man and Moon[1]

Moving to My Mother's East Garden[2]❷

By Yuan Haowen

Trans. by Xu Yuanchong

Hill on hill keeps apart the vanity fair[3]
From this village of bumper year.

❶ 许渊冲. 元曲三百首：汉英对照 [M]. 北京：中国对外翻译出版公司，2009：2.
❷ 许渊冲. 元曲三百首：汉英对照 [M]. 北京：中国对外翻译出版公司，2009：2.

I move house to come near

The window-enframed distant hill

And the pine-trees behind the windowsill.

I'll leave the woods and fields to the care

Of my children dear

So that I may do what I will.

Awake, I'll enjoy the moon so bright;

Drunk, the refreshing breeze so light.

英译注释

1. Man and Moon：人月圆，黄钟调曲牌名。译者采取直译方法，译出"人"与"月"两个意象，对于形容词"圆"却没有译出。"圆"是对人与月的修饰，元好问通过选取此曲牌，并对"圆"的状态进行描述，传达其放下世俗之念、追求人与自然和谐共生的思想，而曲牌英译缺乏这层面的意思。也许译者认为没有必要，因为正文的译文已经或多或少地透露出这一思想。

2. My Mother's East Garden：外家东园，此处的"外家"指其母亲张氏娘家的东园。此曲作于蒙古太宗十一年（1239 年），当时作者历尽磨难，颠沛流离多年后回到故乡秀容，居住在母亲张氏娘家东园中，见家乡安定太平、五谷丰登，如释重负，便作此曲。

3. vanity fair：红尘。许渊冲熟知英国著名小说家萨克雷的作品《名利场》，vanity fair 指虚荣浮华的世界，隐射各种社会丑恶现象，用它来对应红尘，不仅在文化内涵上具有功能对等，同时也非常有效地反映出了元好问对元朝暴政的不满以及对山水田野的向往。

英译评述

许式译文向来追求意美、形美、音美。这首元曲的英译也遵循这一原则。在意美上，译者除传达原曲意思外，通过使用动词和动词短语把原曲中一些意象之间的关系凸显出来。比如第一句，原句是一个因果关系句，因为重重的山岗阻断了世俗繁华的世界，所以这个村子就显得更加丰饶。译者不用 as 等原因状语从句，而是通过 keep apart from 的动词短语来体现前后句的因果关系，同时也暗示了后半句中的比较式。"十年种木，一年种谷，都付儿童"中的数量词皆属于虚数量词，故不译出，使得这两句的意思和整曲的主题更加契合。结构上，译者忠实原曲结构，原曲四大句，译文采用两句简单句和两句复合句来对应。此外，在音韵上，译文竭尽全力地保持原曲音韵，比如元曲中有韵脚/iu/（"就""岫""有"），译者相应地找到英语中相似的音/ill/（hill、windowsill、will）来对应。通过上下阕押同样的韵和格式，使上下阕在音韵节奏上更加紧凑，通过行内押韵同一元韵 /iː/ /ai/，并使用联韵（bright、light）结尾，传神地表达了元好问归居山林、与月同辉的愿望。

第二节　乡愁秋思

叨叨令·悲秋

周文质（？—1334），元代文学家，字仲彬，学问渊博，性尚豪侠，善绘画，能歌舞，攻曲调，谐音律，文笔新奇。其杂剧现仅存《苏武还乡》残曲；散曲现存四十三首小令、五套套数，主题多描写男女相思；代表作有《叨叨令·悲秋》《落梅风》等。

《叨叨令·悲秋》是一首散曲小令，作者通过各种双声叠字来描绘秋物，通过拟声词传秋声来营造愁杀人之悲秋气氛。该曲构思奇巧，独具匠心，纵笔铺叙，语言俚俗，音韵传神，音意交迸迭起，曲终奏雅，情景高度交融。

叨叨令·悲秋●

周文质

叮叮当当铁马儿乞留定琅^[1]闹，啾啾唧唧促织儿依柔依然^[2]叫。滴滴点点细雨儿淅零淅留^[3]哨^[4]，潇潇洒洒梧叶儿失留疏刺落。睡不着也么哥，睡不着也么哥。孤孤零零单枕上迷飚模登^[5]靠。

中文注释

[1] 乞留定琅〔dīng láng〕：象声词，铁马摇动的响声。

[2] 依柔依然：象声词，促织的叫声。

[3] 淅零淅留：状滴滴点点的细雨之声。

[4] 哨〔shào〕：雨经风而斜扫。

[5] 迷飚〔diū〕模登：形容迷惘困倦之神态。

An Autumn Night^{1●}

Zhou Wenzhi

Trans. by Wang Hongyin

The iron bells² under the eave ring pell—mell;

The cricket³ chirps in soft sobs, making me chill;

Drizzling rain drips and drops but never stops;

● 解玉峰. 元曲三百首［M］. 北京：中华书局，2009：78-79.

❷ 王宏印. 英译元曲百首［M］. 上海：上海外语教育出版社，2014：119.

Phoenix leaves fall and fall, withered and dead.

Sleepless, sleepless, this night!

Sleepless, sleepless, this night!

And I lean on the pillow, slipping into a dream.

英译注释

1. An Autumn Night：原曲题目是"悲秋"，表达的是作者对秋天的态度，而译文译成"秋夜"，虽展示了原曲景物发生的时间季节，却没有直接点出"悲"，或许译者认为文章处处是"悲"，无须点题，读者或许更能体会到诗意。不过译者未能译出曲牌名"叨叨令"。Wayne Schlepp 和许渊冲将之译为 Tune：Chattering Song。从曲牌的"叨叨"便可直观地感受到文中的各种双声叠字拟声词，相互辉映。

2. The iron bells：铁马，又叫檐马，指屋檐下的风铃。

3. cricket：促织，蟋蟀的别称，夏末秋初最盛。其鸣声报凉秋已至，因催促妇女速织布以制寒衣，故称"促织"。

英译评述

王宏印的译文总体上通顺流畅，忠实达意，音美形美。他对叠词、拟声词进行了有选择的翻译，认为拟声词不一定个个都英译出来，否则会"造成滑稽的感觉"。不过他和许渊冲都认为可以通过英语诗歌中独特的修辞、韵律来传达原曲双声叠字象声词的艺术特点。为了展示原曲双声叠字的艺术手法，王的译文首先采用押头韵和重复，比如 criket chirps, chill; soft sobs; Drizzling, drips, drops; fall and fall; Sleepless, sleepless。其次运用行内押韵，比如 bells, pell-mell; drips, drops, stops。译者采用相似的拟声词来传达原曲的拟声效果，用 pell-mell 混乱之音来传达原曲屋檐下铃声"留定琅闹"，用 chirps 加 soft sobs 传达"啾啾唧唧"的蟋蟀给主人公"依柔依然"的感觉。当然，此处的 chirp 有待商榷，因为通常指鸟鸣声，而非蟋蟀声。Wayne Schlepp 的译文用 chipping-chirring 拟声词似乎更加准确传神些。形容雨声"滴滴点点"，王用 drizzling 和 drips，准确忠实地拟声出细雨之声。对于梧桐叶的"潇

潇洒洒"，王仅用 fall and fall，相比 Schlepp 的 Rustling-rustling，拟声效果稍微差了些，不过落叶的画面感却很强。对比"失流疏刺"，指树叶片片落地之音，译者采用白描手法用静态的形容词 withered and dead，虽不如 Schlepp 的 lisping-whispering，却强调了梧桐的萧条状态，亦切合原曲悲秋主题。此外，译者用白描手法传达了原曲中的"迷飚模登"拟声词，slipping into a dream 译出了不知不觉陷入梦幻的意境，比 Schlepp 的 lying on the solitary pillow in silence 传神多了，使悲入梦，意境隽永。

Ⅰ. Translation Practice.

Directions：Please translate the following poem by Guan Hanqing into English.

一枝花·不伏老

关汉卿

我是个蒸不烂、煮不熟、

捶不匾、炒不爆、响珰珰一粒铜豌豆，

恁子弟每谁教你钻入他锄不断、斫不下、解不开、顿不脱、慢腾腾千层锦套头？

我玩的是梁园月，饮的是东京酒，赏的是洛阳花，攀的是章台柳。

Ⅱ. Writing Practice.

Directions：Write an essay of about **300** words, stating your understanding of the love in the following Chinese poem by Guan Hanqing, and elaborating on how the rendering conveys the love expressed in the original poem to English-speaking readers.

Chinese Poem：

白鹤令❶

关汉卿

香焚金鸭鼎，闲傍小红楼。

月在柳梢头，人约黄昏后。

English Rendering：

Tune：Song of White Crane❷

By Guan Hanqing

Trans. by Xu Yuanchong

Incense in golden censer burned,

I stand in red bower unconcerned.

The moon atop the willow tree,

At dusk my lover trysts with me.

---

❶ 许渊冲. 元曲三百首汉英对照 [M]. 北京：中国对外翻译出版公司，2009：36.

❷ 许渊冲. 元曲三百首汉英对照 [M]. 北京：中国对外翻译出版公司，2009：36.

参考文献

［1］曹雪芹, 高鹗．红楼梦［M］．北京：中华书局, 2005.

［2］蘅塘退士．唐诗三百首全解［M/OL］．赵昌平, 解．上海：复旦大学出版社, 2006.

［3］解玉峰．元曲三百首［M］．北京：中华书局, 2009.

［4］孔子．诗经［M］．程俊英, 译注．上海：上海古籍出版社, 1985.

［5］老子, 庄子．老子·庄子［M］．傅云龙, 陆钦, 注释．北京：华夏出版社, 2000.

［6］林语堂．东坡诗文选［M］．天津：百花文艺出版社, 2002.

［7］罗贯中．三国演义［M］．北京：中华书局, 2005.

［8］蒲松龄．聊斋志异［M］．北京：中华书局, 2013.

［9］屈原．楚辞［M］．黄学森, 选注．珠海：珠海出版社, 2002.

［10］上疆邨民．宋词三百首全解［M］．蔡义江, 解．上海：复旦大学出版社, 2007.

［11］史有为．《史记·七十列传·汲郑列传第六十》译注［EB/OL］．［2015-09-28］. http：//www. ziyexing. com/ files-5/shiji/Shiji_120. htm.

［12］司马迁．史记［M］．北京：中华书局, 1959.

［13］唐圭璋．全宋词［M］．北京：中华书局, 1999.

［14］王宏印．英译元曲百首［M］．上海：上海外语教育出版社, 2014.

［15］萧涤非．唐诗鉴赏辞典［M］．上海：上海辞书出版社, 1983.

［16］许渊冲．最爱唐宋词［M］．北京：中国对外翻译出版公司, 2006.

［17］许渊冲．宋词三百首：中英文对照［M］．北京：中国对外翻译出版公司, 2007.

［18］许渊冲．元曲三百首：汉英对照［M］．北京：中国对外翻译出版公司, 2009.

［19］杨宪益, 戴乃迭．宋词：汉英对照［M］．北京：外文出版社, 2001.

［20］元稹，等．唐宋传奇［M］．北京：华夏出版社，2015．

［21］周方珠．英译元曲 200 首［M］．合肥：安徽大学出版社，2009．

［22］朱熹．四书章句集注［M］．北京：中华书局，2011．

［23］CAO X. Hong Lou Meng or The Dream of the Red Chamber, Book I［EB/OL］. trans. JOLY H B. （2011–11–23）［2015–10–15］http：//www. gutenberg. org/cache/epub/9603/pg9603–images. html

［24］EGAN R C. The Literary Works of Ou-yang Hsiu（1007–1072）［M］. Cambridge：Cambridge University Press，1984.

［25］FLETCHER W J B. Gems of Chinese Verse［M］. Shanghai：Commercial Press，1919.

［26］FLETCHER W J B. More gems of Chinese Poetry［M］. Shanghai：Commercial Press，1919.

［27］GILES H. A. Chinese Poetry in English Verse［M］. London：Bernard Quaritch，1898.

［28］HUGHES E R. Chinese Philosophy in Classical Times［M］. London：J. M. Dent & Sons Ltd. ，1942.

［29］JENNINGS W. The Shi King, The Old "Poetic Classic" of The Chinese：A Close Metrical Translation with Annotations［M］. London：George Routledge and Sons，Ltd. ，1891.

［30］KISHLANSKY M A. Sources of World History, Volume I［M］. New York：HarperCollins College Publishers，1995.

［31］KU H. The Universal Order or Conduct of Life［M］. Shanghai：Shanghai Mercury，1906.

［32］LEGGE J. The Texts of Taoism［M］. New York：Dover Publications，Inc. ，1962.

［33］LEGGE J. The Chinese Classics［M］. Taipei：SMC Publishing INC. ，1991.

［34］LUO G. Romance of the Three Kingdoms［EB/OL］. Trans. BREWITT–TAYLOR C H. （2007–03–03）［2015–9–24］. http：//www. threekingdoms. com/046. htm.

［35］ MULLER A C. Great Learning ［EB/OL］. (2013-07-04) ［2015-08-26］. http：//www. acmuller. net/con – dao/greatlearning. html.

［36］ OWEN S. The Great Age of Chinese Poetry：The High T'ang ［M］. New Haven and London：Yale University Press, 1981.

［37］ POUND E. The Confucian Odes ［M］. New York：New Directions Paperbook, 1959.

［38］ POUND E. Cathay ［M］. London：Elkin Mathews, 1915.

［39］ PU S. Strange Stories from a Chinese Studio ［EB/OL］. trans. GILES H A. (2013-09-03) ［2015-10-26］. http：//www. gutenberg. org/files/43627/43627-h/43627-h. htm.

［40］ REXROTH K, CHUNG L. Li Ching-Chao：Complete Poems ［M］. New York：New Directions, 1979.

［41］ SCHLEPP W. San-chü：Its Technique and Imagery ［M］. Madison：The University of Wisconsin Press, 1970.

［42］ SNYDER G. Translations ［J］. The Literary Review. 1989, 32 (3)：443-446.

［43］ SSUMA C. Records of the Grand Historian of China, Vol II ［M］. Trans. Burton Watson. New York：Columbia University Press, 1961.

［44］ WALEY A. A Hundred and Seventy Chinese Poems ［M］. London：Constable and Company Ltd. , 1918.

［45］ WALEY A. More Translations from the Chinese ［M］. New York：Alfred A. Knopf, 1919.

［46］ XU Y. Elegies of the South ［M］. Beijing：China Intercontinental Press, 2012.

附录　英文译本译者简介

中国译者

1. 辜鸿铭（Ku Hung-ming, 1857—1928），清末民初著名学者。祖籍原福建省同安县（今厦门同安区），生于南洋英属马来西亚槟榔屿。10 岁时赴英国学习，在爱丁堡大学师从卡莱尔，获文学硕士学位。后在德国莱比锡大学攻读博士学位，精通英语、法语、德语、拉丁语、希腊语、马来语等 9 种语言，获 13 个博士学位，是清朝精通西洋科学、语言兼及东方华学的中国第一人，回国后曾在北京大学任教。他是文化保守主义者，清朝灭亡之后他还留着发辫，与胡适等革新派论战。他翻译了中国"四书"中的三部——《论语》《中庸》和《大学》，并著有《中国的牛津运动》（*The Story of a Chinese Oxford Movement*，1910）和《中国人的精神》（*The Spirit of Chinese People*，1915）等英文书，积极向西方人宣传东方文化和儒家精神，在西方影响巨大。

2. 林语堂（1895—1976），中国文学家、发明家。福建省漳州龙溪人，生于漳州市平和县坂仔镇，名玉堂，后改为语堂，圣约翰大学英文学士、美国哈佛大学比较文学硕士、德国莱比锡大学语言学博士，曾任北京大学英文系教授、厦门大学文学院院长、联合国教科文组织美术与文学主任、国际笔会副会长等职，1940 年和 1950 年两度获得诺贝尔文学奖的提名。中英文俱佳，是中国现当代首屈一指的跨文化作家，用英文撰写了大量介绍中国文化的作品，对中国思想文化在西方的传播做出了卓越的贡献。曾创办《论语》《人间世》《宇宙风》等刊物，作品包括英文小说 *Moment in Peking*（《京华烟云》）、英文传记《苏东坡传》、中英文散文和杂文文集《吾国与吾民》《人生的盛宴》《生活的艺术》以及译著《东坡诗文选》《浮生六记》等。1966 年定居台湾，1967 年受聘为香港中文大学研究教授，主持编撰《林语堂当代汉英词典》。1976 年在香港逝世，享年 80 岁。

3. 王宏印（1953— ），陕西华阴人。南开大学外国语学院教授，博士生

导师，中国典籍翻译研究会会长。主要从事中外文化典籍翻译与研究，兼及人文社科类比较研究和文学创作。已出版论、译著各类书籍 60 余部，发表学术论文 50 余篇，代表著作有《中国文化典籍英译》《中国古今民歌选译》《文学翻译批评论稿》《世界文化典籍汉译》《诗与翻译：双向互动与多维阐释》等。2014 年由上海外语教育出版社出版了其译作《英译元曲百首》。

4. 许渊冲（1921— ），1921 年生于江西南昌。先后毕业于西南联大、巴黎大学。北京大学文学翻译教授。英文著作有《中诗英韵探胜》《逝水年华》。译作方面，除了由英国企鹅出版公司出版的汉译英《不朽之歌》外，还有《诗经》《楚辞》《唐诗三百首》《宋词三百首》《李白诗选》《苏东坡诗词选》《西厢记》和《毛泽东诗词选》等英译或法译作品。外译汉方面则有福楼拜的《包法利夫人》等世界文学名著译作多种。2010 年，荣获中国翻译文化终身成就奖，2014 年获国际译界最高奖项之一——"北极光"杰出文学翻译奖。

西方译者

1. Brewitt-Taylor, Charles Henry（查尔斯·亨利·布鲁威特–泰勒，1857—1938），英国著名的汉学家，中文名为邓罗。他曾在福州船政学堂教书 10 载，此后 30 年里，他辗转于福州、北京、汕头、上海、沈阳、重庆等地，就职于中国海关。1925 年，他将《三国演义》（*Romance of Three Kingdoms*）翻译成英文出版，成为最早译介中国古代经典名著的先行者之一，大约 30 年后其他三部古典名著的欧美语言译本才陆续发行。邓罗采用了符合英语习惯的地道英语，不添加任何注解，使读者如读英文著作般轻松自如。其译本一经出版便几度售罄，深受文人学者褒誉，为广大读者所喜爱。直至今日，其译本仍继续发行。

2. Egan, Ronald C.（罗纳德·C·伊根，1948— ），中文名为艾朗诺，美国加州大学圣巴巴拉分校（UCSB）东亚系主任、名誉教授，哈佛大学博士，同时也是斯坦福大学东亚语言文化学院汉学家、教授。其有专著《欧阳修的文学作品》（*The Literary Works of Ou-yang Hsui*, 1984）、《词、意象、成就：苏轼传》（*Word, Image, and Deed in the Life of Su Shi*, 1994）、《美之问题：北宋美学思考与追求》 （*The Problem of Beauty: Aesthetic Thought and Pursuits in*

Northern Song Dynasty China，2006）、《女性才华之忧：李清照的一生》（*The Burden of Female Talent：The Poet Li Qingzhao and Her History in China*，2014）等。

3. Fletcher，William John Bainbrigge（威廉·约翰·拜恩布瑞各·弗莱彻，1879—1933），英国汉学家，曾任英国驻华领事馆翻译，1908 年起任福州、琼州、海口等地副领事、领事，退休后任广州中山大学英语教授，逝世于广州。1918 年出版了《英译唐诗选》（*Gems of Chinese Verse*），译唐诗 181 首。1919 年出版了《英译唐诗选续集》（*More Gems of Chinese Poetry*），译唐诗 105 首，并加以详细注解。两书共译唐诗 286 首，共收入诗人 92 位。

4. Hughes，Ernest Richard（欧内斯特·理查德·修斯，1883—1956），中文名为修中诚，英国伦敦会教士，曾就读于牛津大学。1911 年来华，在福建传教 18 年。1929—1932 年在上海中华基督教青年会全国协会任职。1933 年回英，任牛津大学中国宗教和哲学教师。1948—1952 年在美国加利福尼亚大学任教。曾翻译《大学》《庄子》等中国古典哲学著作。

5. Jennings，William（威廉姆·詹宁斯，生卒不详），英国汉学家，1891 年为英国伯克郡庞登教区的牧师，在此之前担任中国香港的圣约翰天主教堂殖民地的牧师。曾英译《论语》《诗经》等中国典籍。

6. Joly，Henry Bencraft（亨利·本克莱夫特·乔利，生卒不详），英国外交官。19 世纪末曾任英国驻澳门文化参赞，曾在北京求学，因痴迷《红楼梦》，便立志将其翻译成英文，然而，遗憾的是他未译完便去世了。其译本于 1892—1893 年出版，共 56 章。

7. Giles，Herbert A.（赫伯特·A. 翟理斯，1845—1935），英国汉学家。1884 年，曾任英国驻中国领事，后又任剑桥大学中文教授，1898 年出版《古今诗选》，1900 年又出版学术专著《中国文学中》。译著包括《古文选珍》《中诗英韵》《嶣山笔记：中国文学选》和司空图的《二十四诗品》。1923 年译著《古文选珍》再版，其中英译了白居易的《长恨歌》《琵琶行》等唐诗。

8. Legge，James（詹姆斯·理雅各，1815—1897），英国苏格兰汉学家，曾在香港主持英华书院。1861—1872 年相继出版了《中国经书》（*The Chinese Classics*）5 卷一共 7 本包括《论语》《大学》《中庸》《孟子》《书经》《诗

经》及《春秋左传》。1862 年更是获得王韬的协助，翻译中国经典。1867 年理雅各离开香港回苏格兰家乡克拉克曼南郡的杜拉村。王韬随后也前往苏格兰杜拉村，继续协助理雅各翻译《十三经》。1873 年访问中国，后又访问日本、美国，之后返回英国。1876—1897 年担任牛津大学第一任汉学教授。1879—1891 年相继出版《中国经典》（*The Sacred Books of China*）七卷包括《书经》《诗经（与宗教有关的部分)》《孝经》《易经》《礼记》《道德经》《庄子》。1897 年在牛津逝世。

9. Muller, A. Charles（A. 查尔斯·穆勒，1953— ），美国汉学家，先后在纽约州立大学、东京大学任教，主攻佛教研究和东亚文化。他翻译了中国的六部典籍："四书"和《道德经》《庄子》。他是数字化研究资源的积极推动者，译文与研究资料在网上公开，以此推动东方文化研究的发展。具体详见网址：http://www.acmuller.net。

10. Snyder, Gary（加里·斯奈德，1930— ），美国汉学家，生于旧金山，长于俄勒冈和华盛顿。1951 年毕业于里德学院，获农学学士学位，后入加州大学主攻东方语言文学。1956 年远赴日本，旅居 10 余年，并曾出家 3 年，醉心禅宗。回国后，定居加州北部山区。1985 年成为加州大学戴维斯分校的教授，讲授文学和"荒野思想"，2003 年当选为美国诗人学院院长。主要诗集有《砌石与寒山诗》（1959）、《神话与文本》（1960）、《僻野》（1968）、《观浪》（1970）、《龟岛》（1974）、《斧柄》（1983）、《非自然：新诗选》（1993）、《山水无边》（1997）等。其译著译有白居易、杜牧、王维、寒山、孟浩然、柳宗元等人的诗歌。

11. Waley, Arthur（亚瑟·威利，1889—1966），英国著名文学翻译家、汉学家。1907 年，威利从拉格比公学毕业后进入剑桥国王学院学习，主修古典文学专业。1913 年在大英博物馆担任东方出版物和手稿管理员助理，期间威利自学了中国古典文学、日本古典文学，以便更好地帮忙把馆内收藏的画册编入目录。1929 年，他辞去图书馆的工作，潜心研究东方文学和文化，同时还继续在伦敦东方和非洲研究学校做讲座。他一生撰著和译著 200 余种，其中大部分都与中国文化有关。译作包括《中国古诗 170 首》（*A Hundred and Seventy Chinese Poems*，1918）、《中国古诗选续集》（*More Translations from the*

Chinese，1919）、《道德经研究及其中国思想地位》（*The Way and its Power：A Study of the Tao Te Ching and its Place in Chinese Thought*，1934）、《诗经》（*The Book of Songs* ，1937）、《论语》（*The Analects of Confucius*，1938）、《中国古代三大思哲》（*Three Ways of Thought in Ancient China*，1939）、《美猴王》（*Monkey*，1942，《西游记》简写本）、《九歌：中国古代祭祀研究》（*The Nine Songs：A Study of Shamanism in Ancient China*，1955）、《袁枚：18 世纪中国诗人》（*Yuan Mei：Eighteenth Century Chinese Poet*，1956）等，并著有《中国画赏析导读》（*Introduction to the Study of Chinese Painting*，1923）、《白居易传》（*The Life and Times of Po Chü-i*，1949）、《鸦片战争之中国人所见》（*The Opium War through Chinese Eyes*，1958）、《李白生平及诗作》（*The Poetry and Career of Li Po*，1959）、《敦煌民谣与趣闻》（*Ballads and Stories from Tun-Huang*，1960）等作品。虽然他从没学过如何说汉语和日语，从没来过中国，威利一生为传播中国文学文化所做出的巨大贡献，已为世界学者所公认。1945 年威利被选为剑桥国王学院的荣誉成员，1952 年成为英国最高级巴斯爵士，1953 年因诗歌获得女王勋章，1956 年成为荣誉勋爵。1966 年威利与世长辞，葬于英国海格特墓地。

12. Watson，Burton（伯顿·华兹生，1925— ），美国汉学家、翻译家。1925 年生于纽约，1956 年完成了关于司马迁研究的博士论文，获得了哥伦比亚大学博士学位。1961 年，他翻译的《史记》英文版 *Records of the Grand Historian* 正式出版，使得他成为西方汉学届研究司马迁的首席译者和学术权威。他精通中文、日文，曾翻译《后汉书》《诗经》及李白、白居易、陆游的诗作。他曾以福特基金会海外学人的身份在日本京都大学从事研究，并先后在京都大学、哥伦比亚大学及斯坦福大学教授中文和日文。1979 年，荣获哥伦比亚大学翻译中心金牌奖章；分别于 1981 年、1995 年两次荣获美国笔会（PEN）的翻译奖项，且长期旅居日本。